To Richard
Paul & Mi.....
from
Geoffrey & Marjorie Lovejoy

C000065294

15-4·96

THE CALL IN THE CELLAR

There is a divinity that shapes our ends,
    Rough-hew them how we will.

(Hamlet V.ii)

To that Divinity, revealed by Jesus Christ as Love,
    this story of my life is gratefully dedicated.

That they may know you, the only true God,
    and Jesus Christ whom you have sent.

(John 17:3)

———————

THE CALL
IN THE CELLAR

The Memoirs of
Reverend G.W. Lovejoy

'A Nobody Used by God'

The Book Guild Ltd.
Sussex, England

The Book Guild Ltd.
25 High Street,
Lewes, Sussex

First published 1996
© Geoffrey Lovejoy 1996

Set in Times

Typesetting by Wordset
Hassocks, West Sussex

Printed in Great Britain by
Antony Rowe Ltd.
Chippenham, Wiltshire.

A catalogue record for this book is
available from the British Library

ISBN 1 85776 059 X

CONTENTS

Part III – Autumn Flowering

LIST OF ILLUSTRATIONS

FOREWORD

BY THE BISHOP OF WORCESTER
(The Rt. Revd Philip Goodrich)

I strongly recommend the reading of Geoffrey Lovejoy's memoirs. Here is a man who, when the surnames were given out, received exactly the right one! His life has been a life of joyful service in response to God's goodness and love. It is the story of a joyful pilgrimage and through all the changing scenes of life Geoffrey has shown a self-forgetting zest which has given him the energy of three. In it all Marjorie has been his devoted partner in ministry and joy. There was never a shred of self-pity in either of them.

I recommend the reading of this book because it is a cordial for drooping spirits. The Press would give the impression that the Church of England is about to disappear down the drain. It would be bad for them if it did. They would be short of quite a lot of copy! However, here is a priest who took all the opportunities that the Church of England and the Anglican Communion can offer. He just took them with both hands. One parish had been vacant six years when Geoffrey took it on and he did not fail. 'O taste and see how gracious the Lord is!' Read on. It will fascinate you. What a memory Geoffrey has!

PREFACE

Israel also came into Egypt: and Jacob was a stranger in the land of Ham. And he increased his people exceedingly: and made them stronger than their enemies; Whose heart turned so, that they hated his people: and dealt untruly with his servants. Then sent he Moses his servant: and Aaron whom he had chosen. And these shewed his tokens among them: and wonders in the land of Ham . . . . For why, he remembered his holy promise: and Abraham his servant.

Psalm 105: 23-27; 41

In his 'Bible Notes' in *Daylight* for January–April 1993, Dr Cleverley Ford writes: 'The Psalms are lyrical, they were composed to be sung, some with massed choirs and orchestras in the Temple. . . . This is history to sing about. It is a special kind of history. It is salvation history, the history of what God has done for his people. You have a salvation history and so have I.'

These memories are my 'salvation history'. I have tried to show how in his surprising and wonderful way God has fashioned me from birth, and how I have grown step by step in knowledge and in love. To this end, in Chapter 25 I have retyped five sermons and two retreat addresses, and in Chapter 26, 'In the Departure Lounge', I bring my story to its conclusion.

All my experiences have helped to shape me and I am what I am because of them. 'No man is an island.' So wrote John Donne, one-time absentee rector of St Nicholas, Sevenoaks. We are all inheritors of the past and fashioned by circumstance, and I cannot be grateful enough to God for the friends he has given me, for the fellow-priests who have inspired me, for the scriptures he has caused to be

xi

written, and for the writers of the books which have nourished me. I would acknowledge particularly the following:

The Postulates of a Christian Philosophy by Maurice
    Relton (1925)
The Unutterable Beauty by G A Studdert Kennedy (1927)
God Was Made Man by Leonard Hodgson (1928)
God in Christian Thought and Experience by
    W R Matthews (1930)
Le Milieu Divin by Pierre de Chardin (1957)
The Go-Between God by John Taylor (1972)
and the writings of Carlo Carretto

However, I read as slowly as I write and nowadays read very little. Moreover, as my concluding chapter explains, in these last few months I have grown very feeble. Nonetheless, I hope that many will enjoy reading these memoirs, and that friends remembered will write to me.

Finally, where a name on its first appearance in the text is printed in inverted commas, it is either to conceal the identity of the person concerned or, more frequently, because I am uncertain of its accuracy, having only a fallible memory to help me.

Geoffrey Lovejoy

61 Old Mill Close
Eynsford, Kent
DA4 0BN

PART I

UNCERTAIN SPRING

1

Earliest Memories

> My heart is inditing of a good matter. I speak of the things
> which I have made unto the king. My tongue is the
> pen of a ready writer.

So wrote the psalmist. His heart burned within him. So fired was
he with enthusiasm for his subject, he had to write.

I too find myself called to put down in order what God
has done for me but, alas, I am not and never have been a
fluent writer. Never? I remember the time when I was a child
when I liked writing letters, but that was long ago. Now it is
'pain and grief', hard work groping for the word I want. I must
just do my best to put on paper, as people have asked me to do,
things that have happened, people I have met, in a long and
varied ministry which in some ways reads almost like a fairy
tale.

I was born on July 2nd 1908, the second son of Frederick
James and Florence Edith Lovejoy, and my mother brought me up
to the best of her ability in a godly and Christian way. This meant
going with her and Jim, my elder brother, to Holy Trinity Church,
Hounslow, at 11 a.m. each Sunday. My father never went with us
and I remember my mother once upbraiding him for it: 'Why,
Jim, do you never come to church with me now? I wish you
would. You always used to come with me before we were
married.'

'Yes,' my father replied, 'yes, and all the time what was I
saying to myself under my breath? " All right, all right, but it's
only till the wedding day." '

This was a little surprising, for it was a great churchgoing age and churchgoing, as distinct from chapel-going, was a great status-symbol among the middle classes; and other things as well. Many years later, in my first parish, I recall remarking to a dapper little man who sold umbrellas how good it was to see him in his pew each Sunday.

'Yes, Mr Lovejoy,' he answered, 'I like going. It's good for trade!'

'Judge not and you shall not be judged.' Even today, when churchgoing is no more the 'done' thing and to go to church is a public act of witness, it still remains true that people go to church for a great variety of reasons. 'You should support the church.' 'It's good to meet people.' 'It helps you.' 'I like the singing.' 'I like a good sermon.' And so forth.

> Were there not ten cleansed, but where are the nine? There has not returned to give glory to God save this stranger.
>
> *Luke 17:18*

Maybe only one churchperson in ten, if asked, would reply, 'I like to say thank you.' No matter. Jesus came, he tells us, not to call the righteous but sinners. Sin? At this stage it never worried me. In the nineteen twenties we still heard occasional 'Hell-fire' sermons from the pulpit but they left me cold. I was, I told myself, going to be very good and I looked forward to a great reward in heaven.

There was one short period when I was also sent to Sunday school in the afternoon. The Vicar had appealed for more Sunday school children and my mother had responded. I was growing up, however, and I resented going. I wanted to be out playing, and one Sunday I rebelled.

'I'm not going.'

'But why?' asked my mother.

'I don't like the teacher. She's not nice.'

Poor girl. She was perhaps a little dull but she was perfectly nice. My mother, however, stupidly and to my great surprise, surrendered.. 'All right,' she replied. 'You can just come to church with me.' And so I did, and after that, every time I went to the local cinema and bought my ticket from my erstwhile teacher, I felt guilty.

At the turn of the century, my grandfather, originally a painter and decorator in Plumstead, bought an old-established corn business at 112–14, High Street, Hounslow. He was widowed and my father, still single, moved with him and they lived together over the shop. Then in 1904 my father married, and in due course both my brother and I were born.

We had a happy childhood and loved exploring in the large yard behind the shop. There was so much to see, so much going on. There was the granary, to which sacks of grain were pulled up by a hoist; there was the bakehouse, where Billy Williams and his mate Harry Hoare could be watched kneading dough; there was the mill, where we could watch two large millstones grinding up barley and oats; there was the hay-loft complete with a chaff-cutter – dust, noise and a whirling steel blade; and there was the engine-room, in which we watched, fascinated, the flashing pistons and the huge revolving flywheels of the Ruston Oil Engine driving by means of leather belts the grindstones in the mill and the chaff-cutter in the hay-loft. But most of all I loved the carts and horses. I liked all the horses but a horse which drew one of the cottle vans (forerunners of mobile shops) was a special favourite. I would stroke his nose or feed him with windfall apples picked up from the garden until he lathered at the mouth.

One day I heard that there had been an accident. A motor car had run into my beloved horse, his leg had been broken and he had had to be destroyed. I cried a lot when I went to bed. I prayed hard, 'Please God, grant he didn't suffer much.' What my prayer could do I rather wondered. It was, I felt, rather late. 'But you, God, you can do anything!' Today I am prepared to believe my prayer could have helped. 'The eternal God is thy refuge and underneath are the everlasting arms.' God is the ever-present One, outside of space and time. All that happens is eternally present to him, and my childish prayer and my favourite horse dying are as present with him today as they were then. 'O Lord,'

5

says the psalmist, 'thou has searched me out and known me . . . thou understandest my thoughts long before.' *Psalm 139:1.*

But could I, as a child, have grasped any such conception? Of course I could not. As a child, I spoke like a child, I thought like a child: Heaven was above the bright blue sky; God was a man up in the sky; truth was a matter of fact; right was right and wrong was wrong. Of course, one was told that God was everywhere but it meant little. The visual image of a man, albeit a superman, up in the sky prevailed and only, I believe, by stepping down to his level can we communicate with the child and lead him ultimately to something deeper. Trying to communicate deep philosophic conceptions to him before he is ready can prove disastrous.

An infant teacher once tried to teach a class of seven-year-olds that God is greater than anything we can imagine, that God has no human body. 'And what, dear,' asked one mother on her child's return, 'did you learn today at Sunday school?'

'We learned about God, Mummy. God is very strange, Mummy. He hasn't got a body. No, his neck and legs are joined straight together!'

My first real encounter with God was when I was about eight years old. In 1914, following a new and growing fashion, my grandfather bought a motor car, a BSA Silent Knight tourer. It was 12.9 horsepower and so solidly built it must have weighed over a ton. I remember especially the accelerator lever connecting with the carburettor, which was one and a half inches thick! The clutch was so fierce that brute strength was needed to push it out and hot water in the radiator was needed to start the engine in the morning. Oil-lamps supplied lighting at night. At this stage it was only used at weekends or Sunday trips, generally to Newlands Corner, Hindhead or Frensham Ponds. Once a year, however, we had a 60-mile day-trip to the sea – a tremendous occasion for which the car had to be specially serviced.

One year our destination was Southsea and, alas, the weather was dismal. As we passed the Punch Bowl at Hindhead

6

dark clouds gathered and rain seemed imminent. 'O God,' I prayed from the back seat of the car, 'please give us a fine day. Make the clouds disappear.' I looked up and instantly – miraculously, it seemed to me – the clouds began to disperse; you could see them melting away. Little bits of blue sky appeared, then more and more, and finally out came the sun.

'My!' was all I could exclaim. Awe overcame me. I had no doubt whatever but that it was my prayer which had done all this and I was overwhelmed, frightened even. What a terrific power this was with which God had entrusted us! How careful we must be in using it!

And so from childhood to adolescence. In 1920 I joined my brother at the Latymer Upper School, Hammersmith. Previously I had attended St John's House School, a small preparatory school newly established in Lampton Road, Hounslow, by a Miss Elsey. Miss Elsey we adored. She was young and full of enterprise. On different occasions she had taken us to the AFC aerodrome on Hounslow Heath to wave off a squadron of Sopwith Camels leaving for France; she had hired a Mr Pybus's lorry to let us see the crowds celebrating on the streets of London on November 11th, 1918; she had even taken the whole senior school, 14 in all, to Samuelson's Film Studios in nearby Isleworth in 1920, and we all featured in one of the earliest movies filmed in England: *David and Jonathan.*

But of religion we learned little because Miss Elsey was High Church and religious knowledge consisted almost exclusively of learning the Church Calendar, the seasons of the Church's year, the correct liturgical colours and so forth. However, each year on May 6th, the feast of St John ante Portam Latinam, when St John reputedly was boiled in oil unharmed, we went to Holy Trinity Church for an annual service and for it we had to learn the 23rd psalm. For this I have always been thankful.

Religious knowledge at the Latymer Upper School was more traditional, but taught with little imagination. Based on the scriptures, it largely consisted of reading round the class, and as we grew older, this seemed always to be the missionary journeys of St Paul. How tired I grew of them! However, the school had been founded in Tudor times on Ascension Day. Accordingly Ascension Day was the school's Foundation Day and, as such, a whole-day holiday. Thus the importance of Ascension Day was brought home to me.

There were in those days four streams in the top classes of the Latymer Upper School, A, B, C and D, to which you were allocated according to ability. All four streams, about 140 boys in all, took part in joint examinations in the summer. My brother Jim, two years my senior and later in life ordained, was a brain in the A stream and three years out of four came top of the 'joint'. On the other occasion he came second. My father, I remember, took him to task – he must keep trying! Later he became a double first at Cambridge.

I plodded along in the third stream and in 1923 found myself in 5C in the company of a group of hulking boys who led our form master, one Bill Clewly, a dreadful life. At the end of the school year, unaccountably, contrition filled them: 'Poor old Bill. He's not a bad sort really. Let's give him a parting present!' A walking-stick was decided upon and the next question was: What should they write?

I know,' said one of the instigators, 'let's write, "For all the help you have given us." He'll like that.'

On the last day of term the stick, with its accompanying note, was laid on his table and we duly awaited his arrival. I shall never forget what followed. Bill picked up the stick, puzzled, then read the note and, horror of horrors, burst into tears.

'It's the words,' he said, 'it's the words. I never thought I had helped any of you.'

We felt absolute worms.

I was duly confirmed with my brother and cousin in Holy Trinity Church, Hounslow. It made absolutely no impression on me. I had now reached the age of thinking for myself. I still said prayers at night but I questioned everything. The preparation classes were held in the Lady Chapel and based, as always in those days, on the Catechism. We were each provided with a Bible and the Vicar, the Revd Reginald French, regularly referred us to it. Having established a fact, he would say: 'Now let's be sure it's what the Bible says. Turn to page so-and-so.' So what? was my mental reaction. Because it's in the Bible it doesn't mean it's true. Nevertheless, I was duly confirmed and went thereafter to Holy Communion at 8 a.m. on the first Sunday in the month as instructed.

'What did you think of it?' asked my brother and cousin after our first Communion. I had no intention of unbaring my soul to them. 'Not bad,' I replied. 'It isn't 9 a.m. and we are finished with church for the day.'

2

Apprentice to The Corn Trade

In the summer of 1924, I was due to sit General Schools examinations, which, if passed with sufficient credits, were equivalent to matriculation. The sitting of General Schools was a parting of the ways for the candidates. Those academically minded could stay on at their secondary school for a further two years, take Higher Schools and sit for a university scholarship. Those not academically minded started work.

I was not academically minded. My grandfather was dead and it was decided that I should join my father in the family business. To this end in January 1925 I was apprenticed for two years to J & T Trower Ltd, wholesale and retail corn merchants in Colchester.

Their wholesale business was conducted from their granary on the River Colne at Colchester Hythe, and from their stalls in Braintree and Colchester Corn Exchanges. On Wednesday mornings I was with Mr Brame, the Managing Director, at their stall in Braintree Exchange and on Saturday mornings at their stall in Colchester. On the other mornings I was in the granary at the Hythe, watching sailing barges from the London docks discharging their cargoes, and writing out delivery notes for Harvey's van men. (Surprisingly, Trower's had no delivery vans of their own. Harvey's did all their work.)

In the granary I learnt the art of mixing meals and also the accepted practices i.e. tricks of the trade, for example the remedying of the dryness of the Canadian summers. Canadian oats arrived dry and dusty. As, then, the grains

10

passed from the elevators into the top-floor bins, a worker stood by watering them – with a watering-can, no less! – thus improving the appearance of the oats and the margin of profit. (You were selling water at the price of oats.) Skill was needed, however, to ensure that the water was completely absorbed before delivery to the customers. Over-watering could be fatal. As wholesalers, we supplied many small country millers in the Braintree district. In such cases oats would be sold free on rail (FOR) at the London docks and we never saw them. On one occasion the customer watered too lavishly and the oats were ruined. He complained bitterly that we had already treated them, and an acrimonious correspondence followed, but in this case our hands were clean.

We bought hay and straw from local growers and would supply customers as far afield as Newcastle but competition was fierce with, would you believe it? exporters in Canada. In those days such was the difference in sea and rail freight that it cost less to send hay by sea from Canada than by rail from Colchester.

One incident in the granary made a considerable impression on me. One of the granary hands was a simple soul easily influenced and one morning his mates decided to play a practical joke on him – to tell him he wasn't looking well.

'Eh, Albert,' one said to him on arrival, 'are you all right? You're looking pretty dicky to me.'

'Now, now,' said another to him a little later. 'Are you sure you're all right? You take it easy. I don't like the look of you this morning.'

And so the game continued. When the time for the morning break arrived – biscuits and cold tea – Albert had disappeared. To his mates' dismay, he had been taken really ill and had gone home sick.

As retailers, Trower's main shop was in the high street beneath their registered office, and I spent a good deal of time in it. While serving there one Saturday evening, I had the most vivid experience of God I have ever had, and it proved a turning-point in my life. It came completely out of the blue and was of a most pedestrian, even laughable, nature; and it all occurred because a customer asked for seven pounds of Clark's Melox Marvels. It was before the days of prepackaging, and ten or so hundredweight sacks of various dog biscuits were lined along the wall of the shop, opposite the counter. For large orders, however, we did not disturb the sacks on display but got the biscuits from supplies in the cellar. Mine was a large order and so, paper bag and scoop in hand, I started down the steps to the cellar. As I descended the last few steps I suddenly sensed something queer was happening and an overwhelming conviction filled me: God wants me! I knelt down. 'O God,' I said, 'this is most inconvenient. The lady is waiting for her Melox Marvels! But if you want me, make it clear later.' Then I shovelled the Melox Marvels into my bag. How God made it clear to me that he wanted me, I tell in the next chapter; but for the first time in my life my religion was becoming real.

This was partly through Bible reading. I was lodging with a Mrs Wray, a widow related to Mr Cunningham, the cashier in Trowers' office. He was a wizened little man who tried to be pleasant, but Miss Ford and Miss Green, the office typists, and myself went in fear of offending him. Mrs Wray had Babs, a timid girl of about 25, entirely dominated by her mother; two sons, John and Russell; and three lodgers, including myself. Russell was about my own age. I shared a bedroom with him and was, like him, provided with a bible and quarterly Scripture Union notes for use at bedtime. I used them conscientiously and valued them.

On Sundays I made my Communion once a month at my parish church St Mary's-by-the-Wall, and after breakfast cycled out to nearby country churches for Matins at 11 a.m.

My cycle was my greatest friend. All shops closed in Colchester on Wednesdays, and in fine weather, as soon as I had scrambled down some lunch, I would cycle out to such places as Clacton, Frinton, Brightlingsea and Mersea Island. I never took a companion. I always wanted to be alone, and alone, overlooking the sea, I read such books as *Tess of the D'Urbervilles*, *Jane Eyre* and Mrs Gaskell's *Cranford*, loving the solitude. In winter months when darkness fell early, I would find a café with a fire, order some tea and continue reading there until I was due to return. I read and dreamed dreams and felt that God was near.

One wet Sunday evening when I went to St Mary's-by-the-Wall for Evensong, the preacher was a Canon Andrews, Secretary of the Fellowship of the Maple Leaf. The Fellowship was a London-based organisation for sending Christian teachers to isolated schools on the Canadian prairies, and in his sermon Canon Andrews appealed for teachers. Foreign lands and stories of them had always fascinated me, and at one stage, before opting for the corn trade, I had toyed with the idea of going to Western Australia under the Fairbridge Farm Scheme.

Well, the immediate future planned for me was in my father's corn business, but I had offered myself to God, should he want me, in Trower's cellar, and as I listened to Canon Andrews I said to myself, If later the way opens for me, I would like to explore further this work of the Maple Leaf Fellowship. The prairies of Canada! Gee!

3

1927, Year of Crisis

In December 1926 I completed my apprenticeship and returned to Hounslow. W F Lovejoy & Sons Ltd was, I knew, in a parlous state. My father had none of my grandfather's drive and initiative and was unable to change with the times. The fields and market gardens around Hounslow were being built over and everywhere petrol lorries were replacing horses. Lovejoy's was basically a corn and forage business and my father could not adapt. In addition, no proper records were kept and it was impossible to tell where losses were being made. My father just carried on, harassed financially on every side, by income tax inspectors demanding returns they never got, by creditors clamouring for payment, and by empty shelves and bins. 'No, we have no wheat today. We can let you have oats or barley. Wheat will be coming in on Monday.'

In desperation in 1925 my father had pulled out of Hounslow High Street, and had sold the extensive property with its outbuildings, yard and garden to the United Dairies. This had enabled him to pay off the clamouring creditors, but with the sale went many childhood memories.

I have already told of how my brother and I loved exploring in the yard, romping in the hay-loft, and watching the chaff-cutter rattling away. There was also the garden – huge to our young eyes, and containing some thirty fruit trees which, when we were older, we climbed and picked; as we also picked for our parents, strawberries, raspberries and currants in their season. Also in the garden were chicken runs housing

14

some 200 white leghorns whose eggs were sold in the shop. *New-laid eggs from our own hens* ran the placard; but in off-seasons (and at other times) they were eggs from the local market.

Selling the High Street property was probably wise. Not so wise was my father's decision to move such business as he could to buildings at the back of 52 Hanworth Road, which my mother had inherited from an uncle and to which we had moved some ten years earlier. Hanworth Road was immediately behind the High Street. Nevertheless, with the move, the retail trade which my father hoped to retain plummeted and the losses continued.

By this time financial worries had reduced my mother to a bundle of nerves, and when I returned from Colchester having completed my apprenticeship I faced a choice. Should I make my father's or my mother's needs my first priority? I decided it must be the business, reasoning that while our financial straits remained, my mother's mental anxieties would never mend. She would continue worrying.

I chose wrongly. On April 12th 1927 my mother took her life and my father went to pieces. He had lost interest, he said, in the business. He would hand it over to me. I could do what I liked: I could run it or I could close it down. I chose to close it down, and largely through the good offices of Uncle Charlie, who ran a small corn-chandler's shop in Slough, we were able, eventually, to pay off all our creditors in full. Lidstone's Ltd, large corn merchants in Slough, supplied my uncle with corn and forage and he persuaded them to buy up all our remaining stock, whatever its condition – and some was very bad – at market prices. I would pay tribute here to their generosity.

So what? A door had opened. 'God indeed works in a mysterious way his wonders to perform.' I remembered my prayer on the steps of the cellar in Colchester: 'If you want me, show me'; and I remembered Canon Andrews' sermon in St Mary's-by-the-Wall.

One morning I drove the family car, the same solid BSA

15

four-seater of my childhood days, up to the London office of the Fellowship of the Maple Leaf and told my story to its Secretary. Canon Andrews listened attentively but said at the end, 'If you really wish to go as a teacher, we'll help you, but the majority of those we send out are already trained young women wanting adventure. May I say that the prairies need clergymen even more than teachers? Have you ever considered ordination?' I confessed that I hadn't but that, perhaps, was what God really wanted of me. He then phoned the Colonial and Continental Church Society – 'Col. and Con.,' as it was called – and told me that they would be interested to see me. He gave me their address and how I could get there and I drove round to see them. They would let me know, they said.

Next morning, very nervously, I went round to the Vicarage. The Revd Reginald French was digging in his front garden. He invited me in and greeted my news cautiously. He was not sure that I would be happy with the Col. and Con. They were, he informed me, a very Low Church society. He thought that I would be happier with SPG (the Society for the Propagation of the Gospel; now USPG), which Holy Trinity Church supported.

More phone calls; more interviews. If accepted, I was told, the Society would be prepared to pay for my training on three conditions. If trained by them and ordained, I must be prepared:

(i) After two years in an English parish to go wherever overseas they wished to send me.

(ii) To serve for five years overseas unmarried.

(iii) To work overseas as long as health and strength permitted.

I wanted to serve God and I wanted to travel and, after all, I reflected, even banks demanded that their clerks should remain single until, at about 28, they had risen to a position in which they were able to support a wife. I do not think that ordinands today, with all their demands – they must have this; they must have that – know that they are born!

In due course I appeared before the SPG Selection Committee. I was in a rather difficult position. As I explain in Chapter 25 in my Diamond Jubilee sermon, my faith at the time was all at sixes and sevens. I did not even know whether I believed in God, and I was quite unable to give the Committee Chairman an assurance he asked for.

Nonetheless, some ten days later I heard that I had been accepted and that in January 1929 I was to go to Dorchester Missionary College near Oxford to start my training.

4

College Days

In 1927 Dorchester Missionary College consisted of a block of two-storeyed buildings flanking the pavement of the old A423 as it wended its way through the small historic village of Dorchester-on-Thame, nine miles south of Oxford. The second floors of these buildings were small study-bedrooms for the up to 24 students of the college. Conditions were late-Victorian. Apart from electric light, mod cons were non-existent. True, hot-water pipes took the chill off the rooms in winter, but a china jug and basin provided the only supply of water and one or other of the three houseboys 'slopped out' the chamber-pots each morning. Earth closets and showers in an outbuilding known as the 'topos' served our daytime needs. The ground floors were the public rooms: kitchen and refectory, library, reading-room, common rooms etc.

The Chapel was attached to the main building but standing free and when in 1929-1930 the College moved to new buildings at Burcote, one and a half miles away, the Chapel was taken down stone by stone and rebuilt on the new site.

The SPG had written to the Principal, the Revd Francis Kirkpatrick, concerning me soon after my acceptance and in November I received a letter from him: 'I would be pleased to see you. When could you come?' The date I suggested was, he said, not very convenient as the College would be in retreat. Nevertheless the date was agreed and in due course I arrived.

I had no idea at that time that a retreat of the Catholic tradition imposed strict silence on all retreatants and noticed to my surprise that when at supper dishes were passed to the students, not one said thank you. Where were their manners? I audibly remembered mine. This secretly amused the students and one of them reminded me of it when I later joined the college. I explained my pristine ignorance. 'You must have thought us a very glum and silent lot,' he commented. I hadn't really. Everything was new to me and I had simply assumed that this was the kind of world I was entering.

I remember only one thing about the interview. The Principal was expounding on the need for humility in all who aspired to the priesthood when he suddenly stopped. 'You are smiling,' he said, 'Why?'

'I was thinking,' I replied, 'that you will have to knock that into me.'

'Well,' he responded, somewhat taken aback, 'at least that is honest.'

I assume that, for all my spiritual immaturity, I must have been much more self-confident at this stage of my pilgrimage than I am today. Certainly I was accustomed to making decisions without consultation. On trivial matters I would ask advice; but on matters of importance, no. The sin of pride? Or, maybe, of self-will, wanting my own way?

In January, I joined the College and took to its life as a duck to water. Everything was new, everything was exciting, and to my surprise we were not dragooned into believing anything. In matters of belief, we were simply presented with arguments for and arguments against and given long lists of recommended reading. I loved it.

The teaching staff comprised the Principal, a Vice-Principal (for most of my time the Revd Geoffrey Curtis, who later joined the Community of the Resurrection) and a succession of tutors, university graduates who came for a year for theological training (though they never attended any lectures!) and were responsible for coaching students needing to matriculate. These three were augmented by 'Pa' Creswell, the local schoolteacher at Clifton Hampden, who taught carpentry and building construction, and a Miss Nixon Smith from the Universities Mission to Central Africa headquarters in London, who came to help us once a week in phonetics and, if need be, in Swahili.

Poor Miss Nixon Smith, frail, aged and ex-missionary, her lectures were a light relief until one dreadful morning when she announced that she was going to set a test. 'It's not, dear boys, that I do not trust you, but I want to see how far you have got.' Alas, most of us hadn't a clue, and despite discreet help from the one or two who had – we cheated right, left and centre – results were dismal. And not a word of reproach from Miss Nixon Smith – only sadness. She was sure it was all her fault; she was sure we were not to blame. Soon afterwards her Swahili student, her one success, left, and she ceased to visit us.

Except on Sundays, we rose daily at 6.45 a.m. and attended Matins in chapel at 7.15 a.m. This was compulsory and should we fail to attend, we were required to visit the Principal in his study to explain. There was one let-out: we could apply to the Principal the night before for a 'morning in'. Few did. In three years I only applied once, went to bed and slept blissfully. Next morning the rising bell woke me feeling fresh as the proverbial daisy. I would have liked to rise and save up my exemption for another day. Like railway tickets. however, they were not transferable, so I lay in bed feeling cheated, my ticket wasted.

Matins lasted 20 minutes, and then there was silent meditation in chapel until Mass at 8 a.m. Breakfast followed at 8.40 a.m. and most students spent from 7.15 to 8.40 a.m. in chapel. I was an exception. On three mornings a week I slipped out of chapel at the end of Matins and betook myself at Dorchester to the banks of the River Thame and at Burcote to the banks of the Thames, in each case to a much-loved place of prayer, and there I kept vigil. It could be bitterly cold but neither frost nor ice would stop me, only rain. Huddled up on the fallen bough of a tree, I would watch the ever-flowing water, hear in the background the rustling of the breeze in the willows and keep my tryst with God. In this stage of my journey *Great Souls at Prayer* was a constant resource, so too were the books of Fr Andrew, SDC, and the *Book of Common Prayer*. I began to learn favourite collects, psalms and canticles by heart, and still after 60 years they thrill and sustain me.

At 10 a.m. came the daily one-hour lecture. If I remember rightly, the Old Testament on Mondays, the New Testament on Tuesdays, doctrine on Wednesdays, church history on Thursdays and either liturgy or ethics on Fridays. Coffee was at 11 a.m. and from 11.15 a.m. to 1 p.m,, from 5 p.m. to 7 p.m. and from 8 p.m. to 10 p.m. we were expected to be found in our rooms, following up references given in the morning's lecture, writing essays or doing required reading.

Evensong was at 4.30 pm and the day closed with Compline in chapel at 10 p.m. and lights out at 11 p.m. Silence reigned from Compline until after Mass next morning.

I liked all the lectures, but those on the Old Testament were a special joy. Once a closed book to me, it now revealed itself as the fascinating record of God's revelation of himself to Israel. It suddenly became alive. John Skinner's *Prophecy and Religion – Studies in the life of the prophet Jeremiah,* I loved passionately. 'I am a child, I cannot speak,' said Jeremiah at the time of his call, and I warmed to him. I too couldn't speak and I too knew it. To be assigned to speak in a college debate was a nightmare. I related to Jeremiah instantly.

'The Bible is the record of God's revelation to man.' The Principal emphasised this dramatically in his first Old Testament lecture. He always dictated his lecture notes and, having dictated the above quotation, he continued, 'And now underline the word "record" seven times.' And as we looked wonderingly at one another, he repeated, 'Yes, I mean it. *Seven times.*' God's messages to mankind, he told us, were not on tablets of stone or written pages but through the hearts and minds of his chosen servants. Those servants, he insisted, though sincere, could be mistaken, as also could be the numerous scribes who edited and supplemented their words in the ensuing centuries. So he prepared us gently for genuine textual studies.

Some 16 years later, when a chaplain on the North-West Frontier of India, I mentioned in a sermon H F Kirkpatrick's quotation and his insistence, 'And now underline the word "record" seven times.' Listening was a middle-aged free-lance evangelist, a Mr Nicholson, who, with his wife, shared our bungalow – wherein lies a tale. A little later he was taken seriously ill. He lay for days in a high fever and was not expected to recover – though happily he did. One morning in a weak and wavering voice he opened his heart to me. 'Mr Lovejoy,' he said, 'forgive me, but there is something you said in a sermon I can never forget. It continues to trouble me. You said that the Bible was not God's revelation to man, only a record of it. I have staked my life that every word of the Bible is true – and I still believe it.' And so, God bless them, do millions.

The afternoons at Dorchester were given over to shopping excursions to Wallingford, Abingdon and Oxford, all in cycling distance; and to sport: soccer in the winter, cricket and tennis in the summer, and rowing all the year round.

Village cricket was a marvellous institution. Social distinct-ions were forgotten – squire, parson and farm-hands all joined in and often beat us; we were a very small college. I remember one occasion vividly. Our hosts batted first and reached an average score, some 60 runs. Then we went in and wickets fell like ninepins to a demon fast bowler. We were something like 21 for 5 when to our astonishment our destroyer was taken off and we began to stage a recovery. During the tea break I asked an opponent why their best bowler had been taken off. 'Oh,' he replied, 'he's gone to milk the cows, He'll be back shortly!' He duly returned and in three or four overs we were finished.

In 1929 the College moved. A house once owned by Jabez Balfour, the financier, delightfully situated a mile and a half away on the banks of the Thames at Burcote, had come on the market and been bought by the College governors. It had spacious grounds, rooms easily divided and converted to serve the College needs and a covered tennis court. The College chapel was moved stone by stone from Dorchester-on-Thame, and a new block to enable the College to house 28 students was added.

The move went smoothly and I was assigned to help the Vice-Principal scrutinise and re-catalogue the library prior to its removal. Some books never used were detailed for sale. Thornton & Sons, Booksellers, of Oxford, showed interest and one afternoon Mr Thornton paid us a visit. There were many surprises. For some 20 massive but battered leather-bound sixteenth-century editions of the early Church Fathers we were offered practically nothing. 'Hardly worth the cost of rebinding,' was Mr Thornton's comment. While for a tiny early seventeenth-century *Voyages to the Americas* we were offered 35 pounds – a princely sum in 1929.

There was also occasional hilarity as, for example, when we found a nineteenth-century bishop's *A Journey Godward* catalogued under travel. The doctrinal section, however, provided our greatest merriment. Among the hundreds of books in this section was one entitled *Conversion and Redemption*. 'I've never heard of those two authors,' remarked Geoffrey Curtis. 'Let's have a look at it.' He opened it and then burst into one of his infectious giggles. 'Do you know,' he said gleefully, 'it's all about the Stock Exchange!'

In the summer of 1930 I passed my second-part General Ordination Examination but, being barely 22 and too young to be ordained, the SPG decided that I should be given the chance to graduate. Accordingly in the second half of 1930 I studied classical Latin and Greek and passed the required exams to qualify me as a Licentiate of Theology. In January 1931 I entered St Chad's College, Durham, to take the third year of their Bachelor of Arts Pass Degree – my L.Th. exempting me from the first two years.

The course had begun in September, so I joined it for the second term; completed its third term in June and followed

23

this by taking its first term in September and my finals in December. Besides Classical Latin and Greek, three other subjects were required. My chosen three were: Religious knowledge (jam!), Roman history and Greek education, and before going down in December I learned that I had passed.

Strangely, I took it all very much for granted, and my great surprise and joy was that in September, after only half a season St Chad's awarded me College colours for soccer. It was most unusual and of this I was, and am still, stupidly proud.

As regards ordination, I had become resigned. If it was to be, it would be.

On one occasion I had to present an essay to Dr A E Rawlingson, author of *The New Testament Doctrine of Christ* – required reading. As I was leaving his study he looked up and said, 'And why do you wish to be ordained?'

I could have replied, 'I don't wish to be. I have never wished it but it seems it's likely to happen.' However, I had no desire to go into details, so I simply answered, 'It's something to do.'

'That,' he replied, 'is a very inadequate reason.'

'Yes, I know,' I responded, 'but I think God is behind it.' And there we left it.

I returned to Dorchester Missionary College in January and the preliminaries for my ordination at Trinity began.

Living in Dorchester village was a retired army colonel who had farmed land in Western Canada. Also the Misses Hankey, whose brother was a priest; a lady with an un-house-trained and vicious parrot; and certain others who would invite college students to their homes on Sunday afternoons for tea. Over tea one Sunday afternoon, the retired colonel discovered that though I was due to work abroad, I was not as yet tied to any overseas diocese. He grew excited. 'Go to Canada,' he urged. 'Go to the Peace River country, my boy. God's own country!' It was where he had farmed.

When therefore, the SPG wrote saying they wished me to

24

do a two-year curacy in England before going abroad, it would give me experience and would enable me to register with the Church of England Pensions Board. When the time came for me to go overseas, had I any preference? I remembered the old colonel and wrote down 'Canada'.

More immediately I had to find a parish in England willing to have me. I answered one or two adverts in the *Church Times*. None seemed suitable. One vicar told me next to nothing about his parish but a very great deal about the prowess he had had at Cambridge as an oarsman! Oars and framed photographs of crews he had rowed in adorned his study, and one suspected that this was his life's one success.

Then the Principal at Dorchester called me to his study. He had received a letter from Fr Maxwell Fisher, Vicar of Holy Trinity, Hendford, Yeovil. The Dorchester student who had been with him for two years, Jack Charrington, was leaving – he had become engaged to a local girl. He asked if the Principal had any student whom he could recommend to replace him.

HKP, as we called him, spoke highly of Fr Fisher and I journeyed down to Yeovil to see him. He offered me the curacy but I turned it down. At Holy Trinity they used incense and holy water, they wore birettas and they crossed themselves and genuflected continually. None of which I was happy with – except in moderation. I did not feel I was able to stomach it.

Returning to College, however, I had second thoughts. I liked Fr Maxwell personally and, I reflected, the Principal thought highly of him. Were the incidentals, birettas, lace etc., so important? Next day I wrote saying if the title was still on offer, I would accept. I am glad that I did.

PART II

SUMMER GROWTH

5

I Serve My Title in Yeovil

Yeovil was in the diocese of Bath and Wells, and so on May 19th I presented myself at the Bishop's Palace adjoining the Cathedral in Wells, where the ordination retreat was to be held. The Palace was, and is, an architectural joy, surrounded by a moat and dating back to the thirteenth century. Sightseers would gaze fascinated on its turreted walls and on the swans gliding gracefully beneath. When hungry, the swans rang a bell provided for them under the drawbridge and food would be forthcoming.

Today the Palace, in common with all episcopal residences, is maintained by the Church Commissioners. Not so in 1932 – its maintenance was the responsibility of the resident bishop, and when the see fell vacant in the late 1920s, there was great difficulty in finding an ecclesiastical dignitary with the financial means to occupy and maintain it. Eventually Basil Wynne-Wilson, who had married a Miss Wills of the fabulously wealthy tobacco family of H O Wills of Bristol, had been persuaded to accept it and it was he who ordained me to the diaconate in 1932 and to the priesthood 12 months later. The story is that when Basil Bath and Wells had been consecrated and needed a motto for his espiscopal coat of arms, a clerical wag had suggested: 'Why not *God Wills?*'

I received no help worth mentioning from the ordination retreat. Silence was observed only from Compline until midday the following morning and we were all invited to play croquet on the Palace lawn in the afternoon. I remember chiefly dinner at night in the sumptuous banqueting hall, when we were waited on by seven or eight maids all dressed in episcopal purple; and the prayers attended by the ordinands and the whole domestic staff which followed.

On the Saturday night in the chapel the Bishop delivered his address, ponderous, academic and dull, but I do remember his text taken from Chapter 5 of the Book of Esther: 'And who knoweth whether thou art come into the kingdom for such a time as this?' Who knoweth? I prayed that I might be worthy.

Holy Trinity, Hendford, it was claimed, had been built in the nineteenth century by the gentry of Yeovil for their servants. They, the gentry, attended the ancient parish church of St John the Baptist, secure in their rented pews. Holy Trinity was a respectful 800 yards away – the 'upstairs-downstairs' syndrome.

Whatever its origin, by the time when I joined it Holy Trinity had become the Anglo-Catholic Church in the centre of the town and, as such, attracted Catholic-minded Anglicans from all walks of life. Nevertheless, it was an artisan parish containing within its boundaries all four of Yeovil's basic industries: Aplin and Barratt, manufacturing cheese and dairy products – Mr Aplin and Mr Barratt were local dairymen at the turn of the century; Petter's, manufacturing oil engines, Mr Petter being a former Yeovil ironmonger; and tanning and gloving. But in 1932 the Depression was biting hard.

Memories are of a young fitter from Petter's coming in to his wife and small child, whom I was visiting on a Friday night, and throwing down seven shillings and a few odd pence. 'That's my earnings, dear, to keep us for a week!' and of a woman sitting at home and sewing linings into gloves as she talked with me. Gloving was 90 per cent a home industry, and this woman received one shilling and a penny for sewing the linings into 12 *pairs* of gloves. By sitting up late she could earn up to 15 shillings a week in this way. I, as a deacon, received £220 a year. Fr Maxwell Fisher, 45 years old and married, had to keep a wife and four children and, withal, maintain a vicarage on £350 plus fees of, say, £24.

I was terribly green – 'O all ye green things upon the earth, bless ye the Lord' – acutely conscious both of my clerical collar and of my own inadequacy. Nevertheless, Holy Trinity people received me with most wonderful kindness. It is said that you never forget your first parish and I've never forgotten or ceased to thank God for the people of Holy Trinity, Hendford. I needed encouragement and they gave it me. Maxwell and Molly Fisher were particularly kind and I heard that Molly Fisher in later life said that she liked me best of all her husband's curates. Goodness knows why.

Typically, they asked me to lunch at the Vicarage both Christmases I spent with them. They were real family gatherings: Max and Molly, Molly's old father, Captain Levett, who in the previous century as captain of an Orient liner equipped with sails had sailed round the Cape; and the four children aged eleven years to three. After lunch, as in most Vicarage families, there was the distribution of presents. I was not forgotten, nor did I forget the family. John, the three-year-old, was a problem. In the end, I asked in the local W H Smith's for a book and duly wrapped it in paper. John, all agog, tore off the wrappings and then his face fell.

'Silly book,' he pouted.

'No, no,' exclaimed his embarrassed parents, 'Look, it's got pictures in it.'

'Silly book,' John persisted.

I was required to do 30 pastoral visits a week as a deacon and 40 as a priest, and each Monday morning I submitted my list and remarks to Max. A saving grace was that a visit counted even if the occupant was out, providing a visiting-card was left and, may I be forgiven, when my quota was short, I would sometimes make a hasty round of calls on parishioners most likely to be out, dutifully saying, 'Peace to this house and to all who dwell in it,' as I dropped my card through the letter-box.

One visit I especially remember. I was cycling down one

of the poorer streets of the parish, intent on visiting an elderly couple, both bedridden and entirely on their own and living in the wretchedest of conditions. In doing so, I passed a house on my left which was on my conscience and which I had passed many times before. Fr Fisher had asked me to call when I had time but had assured me there was no urgency. 'I really must call in some time,' I said to myself yet again when passing that afternoon. But the further I got from the house, the more insistent came the message. *No, go now.* In the end I cycled back and knocked on the door.

A frightened-looking girl opened it and on seeing me her face lit up. 'Thank you so much for coming,' she said. 'Who told you father was dying?'

She was alone in the house with him, and later I learned that in earlier years he had played the organ at Holy Trinity.

How does one account for such things? Coincidence? Conscience? The voice of God? I remember Archbishop Temple discussing such 'coincidences' in his *Christus Veritas* – required reading at College – and he says something like this: 'There may be underlying causes for such "coincidences" but I find myself that when I am close to God they happen; when I am self-absorbed they don't.' It is a very general experience. I only know that the incident recorded filled me with love and trust in the God whom I was beginning to see more and more as active in my daily life.

Another visit the consequences of which remain vivid in my memory occurred a few days before my second Christmas. I was asked to visit a widow in a more opulent part of the parish who, I was told in bated breath, claimed to be an atheist. I readily agreed to call because I thought I might be able to help. Unbelief? I too had passed through it all. Whether I helped or not I do not know, but at least I 'related' to her. She liked me and I liked her and before I left she gave me two pounds for Christmas toys for the poor children in the parish.

And another 'providence'. Just at that time my landlady had staying in the house a temporary boarder a little older than myself. He had just been appointed – surprise! surprise!

32

for he was very young – manager of Curreys' Store in the High Street. On hearing that I had two pounds, then a princely sum, to spend on toys, he at once offered his help. He had, he said, overstocked with children's toys and after Christmas would be selling them off cheaply. It was only three days to Christmas. I could have any toy in the shop at one-third its marked price! I had a lovely time: sizeable teddy bears and dolls for tenpence, large puzzles for sixpence and so on and so on.

But what I most remember was their distribution. We had in the congregation a girl in her twenties, the daugher of one of Yeovil's most respected solicitors. She was 'gentry' and quite beyond me – and, in any case, I was pledged to five years' unmarried service overseas – but if ever she spoke to me, if ever I even caught a glimpse of her, my heart fluttered. She was, I thought, the most wonderful creature in all creation. Hearing of the generosity of the disbelieving widow, she offered to drive me round in her car while I played Father Christmas. What perfect ecstasy! Peggy Painter! I still think of her.

Neither then nor now do I find preaching easy. I am so frightened of being boring, so conscious of the importance of what I have to say. During my first ordination retreat at Wells we deacons-to-be were given two hours in which to write a sermon on the Holy Trinity. There is a story of a boy creeping into a vicarage study and silently watching his father writing his Sunday sermon. After a while, 'Daddy, how do you know what to write?'

'God tells me.'

A further pause and then: 'If God tells you what to say, why do you keep crossing things out?'

In the Palace in Wells I kept crossing things out. I kept starting and restarting. In the end, with only half a sheet completed, I gave up.

I was still ordained, but perhaps a hint was dropped to my Vicar-to-be. In my first year I was only asked to preach once a month, and after my first sermon – on Sunday, June

5th, St Boniface's Day – he told me it was one of the best sermons he had ever heard. He was a dear! The more I think of it, the more sure I am that a hint had been dropped.

He himself had no difficulty whatever in preaching. One Sunday evening we were processing into church behind the choir when he whispered to me, 'I did ask you to preach, didn't I?'

Aghast, I whispered, 'No, you didn't. I'm sure you didn't.'

A pause. Then, as we approached the chancel arch: 'Don't worry. I'll do it.'

I offered to sing the Office for him but he said No. Perhaps he thought that singing it himself would be less distracting. Probably correct!

When the time came for Fr Fisher to ascend to the pulpit, he let himself go. I had heard it all before but he carried the congregation with him.

'Vicar was in good form tonight,' a member of the congregation said to me afterwards, and when I told him the circumstances he was lost for words.

We were given no practical training whatever in preaching at Dorchester Missionary College. All that was required of us was to read in our last college term a written sermon to the Principal for him to criticise.

Having read his sermon, one student, I am told, nervously awaited the Principal's comments.

'Well, it was sound,' said the Principal, and paused.

'What else?' asked the student.

'Nothing else,' replied the Principal. 'It was only sound.'

Maxwell Fisher's sermons may often have been only sound but such was his sincerity that his passionate love for our Lord came across and he carried his congregation with him.

During my two years at Holy Trinity, I forged a link with the Anglican Franciscans which still continues. The future Society of St Francis of Hilfield, Cerne Abbas, was just beginning. In 1921 Douglas Downes, Chaplain of Worcester College, Oxford, and acting Rector of St Aldate's, much concerned at the many jobless men then tramping the roads of Britain, was given Flowers Farm, Batcombe, by the Earl of Sandwich as a base for work amongst these homeless wanderers. Flowers Farm is today the Friary of St Francis, Hilfield, and in the last 50 years the Society has grown into a worldwide religious community. As I write, the First Order has 39 'houses' – 15 in England, 6 in the USA, 14 in the Pacific, 2 in Scotland, 1 in Africa and 1 in Northern Ireland – staffed by 135 Brothers plus 48 novices (37 in the Pacific Islands) and 40 Sisters plus 2 novices. The Second Order is an enclosed order for Sisters in houses at Freeland (UK), Stroud (NSW) and Mt Sinai (USA). The Third Order consists of men and women, ordained and lay, married and single, who live lives of simplicity in the world under a personal rule of life approved by the Order. There are, I understand, between 2,000 and 3,000 SSF Tertiaries scattered around the world today. There is in addition a much looser fellowship, the Companions, and until last year I was chaplain of the Companions in Kent.

In 1932 all this was in embryo. Brother Douglas had been joined by three other brothers: Arthur de Winton, Kenneth Hunt and Charles Preston, and in the nineteen thirties he and the other Brothers identified themselves with the 'Wayfarers' they sought to help, tramping with them on the roads, sleeping with them in doss-houses and casual wards, visiting them in prison and sharing their poverty. No earthenware at the Friary in those days. Only chipped enamel plates and mugs.

Besides the Brothers and Wayfarers there were in the early years others, Oblates, who without desiring to commit themselves to lifelong vows found shelter at Flowers Farm and shared the life and work of the Brothers. Market gardening, chicken-raising, bee-keeping, tailoring, jam-making and basketwork were all carried on, and on Yeovil's market days the Friars would man a stall in the marketplace to sell their wares. In their brown habits, white-knotted girdles and sandals they quickly attracted attention.

Flowers Farm nestles in the shadow of the Batcombe Downs some ten miles south of Yeovil. Fr Maxwell was on their Board of Governors, and the Brothers were often invited to preach at Holy Trinity. In 1933 Brother Kenneth conducted our mid-week Lenten services. He also took part in parish missions and was quite marvellous with junior children.

One story he loved to tell was of when he was taking a children's mission in the East End of London. A little cockney boy came up and asked him why he had three knots in his girdle. The three knots represent the three monastic vows of poverty, chastity and obedience. Brother Kenneth explained them very simply: 'This one,' he said, 'means "No money"; this one: "No wife"; and this one "Do what you're told".

All the little cockney boy could reply was 'Lummy!'

In 1933 the SPG again began to correspond with me concerning my future. As explained already, I had put down Canada as my country of preference. But Canada was then in the depth of the Depression and could no longer support the clergy it had – they were returning to England. So Canada, wrote the SPG, was out. However, the Brotherhood of the Good Shepherd in New South Wales had, they said, written to them enquiring if they had any unmarried clergy on their list whom they were prepared to 'second' to them for five years. There was not much difference, the SPG explained in the letter they wrote to me, between the prairies of Canada and the Australian outback! Was I prepared to go there?

I had not then, nor have I had since, any high opinion of my qualifications. If anyone has been prepared to have me, I have always been more than grateful. So I answered 'Yes' and went to see the Revd Fred Campion, then retired and living in Sussex, who in 1902 with Charlie Matthews and Reuben Coverdale, had helped to found the BGS in Dubbo. Fred Campion greeted me warmly, said I was just the kind of person the Brotherhood wanted, lent me a book *No Roads Go By*, and in general so fired my imagination that from then on the matter was settled and I began to read everything I could find about the outback of NSW. In particular, I read again Charles Matthews' *A Parson in the Australian Bush*, which I had first read soon after arriving in Dorchester. Now I pictured seeing for myself all the places it mentioned.

I had always wanted to travel and, consulting an atlas, I found that for this purpose Australia was ideally situated. Three routes all approximately the same length and all costing much the same were open to me: through the Panama Canal, via Cape Town, and via Suez and India. Jim, my brother, was in India on the staff of the Cambridge Mission, teaching history at St Stephen's College, Delhi, under S N Mukerji. Here was my chance to see him. SPG, generous as ever, granted me 38 pounds for my passage and 12 pounds for incidentals. 'Spend it how you like, but see that you are in Dubbo, NSW, before September 1st.'

How good God is! I decided to travel through France and Switzerland and to Italy, to board the Lloyd Triestino SS *Gange* in Venice on June 13th and reach Bombay two weeks later. I would then travel the 950 miles to Delhi by the GIP Express and after a few days there accompany my brother to Dalhousie in the Himalayas, where for four weeks we were to be the guests of Dr and Mrs S N Mukerji. Then down the whole length of India to Ceylon, spending a weekend en route with Canon and Mrs Manuel, friends of my brother, at Irrungalur, a village near Trichinopoly, finally joining the Orient liner RMS *Oronsay* at Colombo on August 9th. On August 29th the *Oronsay* was due to berth in Sydney.

My last Sunday at Holy Trinity was on May 27th. My stall was opposite the Vicar's and by Evensong I was, alas, so tired that during the Vicar's sermon I nodded off, only to be awakened with a start by Maxwell Fisher, who, wishing to emphasise some point, thumped the pulpit with a resounding bang. On the Tuesday evening was a farewell gathering in the hall, when presentations were made and nice things said.

'There is one thing about Holy Trinity,' said a church-warden with a twinkle in his eye, 'which I am sure Mr Lovejoy will never forget – the Vicar's last rousing sermon!'

The whole gathering collapsed in laughter. I had not realised till then how visible I had been in my stall to the congregation.

6

Bush Brother

Remarkably, considering my inexperience as a globe-trotter, when the RMS *Oronsay* glided into Sydney Harbour in the early hours of August 29th, I was aboard – and I was still at breakfast in the dining-saloon when Bishop Wylde and a friend came on board to greet me. Bishop Wylde had been Principal of the BGS a few years earlier and was now both Coadjutor Bishop of the Diocese of Bathurst and Rector of the Brotherhood parish of Gilgandra. His friend was a Mr Roxburgh of the Brotherhood Sydney Committee. I met the Sydney Committee later that day and next day the Bishop drove us 250 miles north-westwards, first over the Blue Mountains to Bathurst, and then to Dubbo, where we spent the night in Brotherhood House. Next day we travelled a further 50 miles to the north to Gilgandra, where I was to spend September in Bishop Wylde's care, working with Brother Howard (Howard Ellis) and Brother Harry (Tom Kitley), the object being that I might find my feet and get accustomed to the bush.

Before the beginning of the present century there was no Anglican ministry west of Bathurst apart from an occasional clergyman posted to Dubbo, 150 miles to the north-west, for the bush townships were too small and too scattered to support a priest. It was to overcome this lack that in 1901 the Brotherhood of the Good Shepherd had been formed. Also just beginning in Queensland were three other Bush Brotherhoods centred on Townsville, Charleville and Rockhampton.

Though quite independent, all operated on the same lines. In my day all Bush Brothers were unmarried priests, mostly from England, who promised five years of unmarried ministry in the bush in return for all expenses paid and a small personal allowance. In the BGS it was £40 a year plus £5 towards an annual holiday in Sydney. (In total worth £1290 today). Incidentals such as medical and dental care were free and, for those who came from England and had completed five years' service, their fare home. Hospitality in the bush was always gladly and freely given, and parishes which could not support a priest and wife could, with help from central funds, support two Bush Brothers, always providing two were available. A full ministry could thus be provided both for town and bush and, in the fellowship of the Brotherhood, isolation was overcome. In 1934 the BGS was responsible for five parishes on the Western Plains: Bourke, Brewarrina, Cobar, Nyngan and Tottenham; plus, nearer in, the parish of Gilgandra.

In October I was posted to Brewarrina, 60 miles east of Bourke on the Barwon River, the second largest of the six parishes and covering approximately 18,000 square miles, with a scattered population of less than 2,000, of whom 800 were living in Brewarrina. Besides Christ Church, Brewarrina, there were six bush churches in the parish: the Church of the Good Shepherd, Goodoga (76 miles from Brewarrina), All Saints, Angledool (110 miles), St George's, Lightning Ridge (120 miles), St Peter's, Cumborah (86 miles) – all north of the Barwon River; and south of the river: St John the Evangelist's, Carinda (80 miles) and St Mary's, Marra Creek (90 miles). A seventh, St Matthew's, West Bogan (76 miles), was built by the congregation during my ministry.

For my last two and a half years I ministered single-handed. Before that I had worked first with Brother Leyland Bird (later Canon Bird of Guildford) and then Brother John Linder (Brother Jack), who lasted only ten months.

On my own, I would spend the first Sunday in the month in Brewarrina, teach in the school and then leave that week to tour the northern district, holding services in homesteads, teaching in schools and visiting, spending the second Sunday in the month at one of the churches and being back in Bre, weather always permitting, by the Thursday. On the third Sunday in the month I took services in Christ Church and on the Friday began the southern tour, spending the fourth Sunday at one or other of its three churches. Returning from Carinda or the Marra, one passed no homestead after Yarrawin, 40 miles out. If it was night, as it frequently was, all was darkness until suddenly some three miles out the lights of Brewarrina appeared on the horizon. Home! But then the merry-go-round began all over again. On average I spent ten nights a month in the Rectory and the others in homesteads.

There was, mercifully, the occasional break. Once a quarter all the Brothers gathered from Monday to Saturday in Brotherhood House, Dubbo, for Reunion and once a year we journeyed to Sydney for the 12-day Sydney Campaign. Here, besides preaching at supporting churches on the Sunday, we visited and spoke at Church of England grammar schools and at drawing-room meetings in the suburbs. Those attending were generous to a degree. Collections of £120 were normal and at the larger meetings they often exceeded £250. (£5900 in today's money.) After the opening years, money was never the Brotherhood's problem. The problem was the finding of suitable young unmarried priests to serve.

The Brotherhood's Annual Meetings were held during the Campaigns and were great occasions, 400 or 500 supporters gathering. Occasionally, if I remember rightly, they were held in the Sydney Town Hall. The Principal, a Bishop, and two or three senior Brothers would speak. The rest of us just sat on the platform.

On one occasion Brother Ley spoke and waxed eloquent about the warm-hearted hospitality of the bush. To emphasise his point, he instanced a particular homestead. He had he said, counted it up and he had slept in five different rooms in that homestead. A questioning smile appeared on the faces of one or two in the audience. 'And that,' added

Brother Ley, 'is how you get to know people.' The audience collapsed and poor Brother Ley turned in all innocence to the chairman; 'whatever were they laughing at?'

At another Annual Meeting the main speaker was the Rt Revd John Oliver Feetham, second Principal of the Brotherhood and then Bishop of North Queensland. He sat next to the chairman and I was on his right. It was a hot night but Bishop Feetham, a cadaverous figure all in black, sat silent with a huge black cloak wrapped round him. His introducer kept referring to him as 'Bishop Fee-tham'. This was not the way he pronounced his name and he kept nudging the chairman and telling him in a stage whisper clearly audible to the first ten rows: 'Tell him Feet-ham. *Tell him Feet-ham.*'

Stories about him in his Brotherhood days abound. Perhaps the best is described by Ivan Southall in his book *Parson on the Track*. The occasion was a Sunday at St Mary's, Marra Creek. St Mary's is way out in the bush with no township near it but surrounded by numerous properties – properties were holdings of 12,000 acres upwards; 'stations' started at 100,000. In Bishop Feetham's time as a Bush Brother, settlers from miles around gathered quarterly for worship. They arrived early, some 30 or 40, for Holy Communion and then sat down for a picnic breakfast. This was followed by Matins at 10 a.m., a picnic lunch and Evensong at 3 p.m. For liquid refreshment they made enormous quantities of tea, boiling the water in bush fashion in four-gallon kerosine tins over an open fire. The tins were then carried to the congregation sitting on huge tarpaulins spread over the ground to deter the ants and to protect from dirt the Sunday-best clothes. On one memorable occasion the boy detailed to carry the tins dropped one at the edge of the tarpaulin. A flood of scalding water surged across the canvas in the direction of John Feetham, and the horrified boy was for the moment lost for words. Not so, John Feetham! He leapt furiously to his feet, clutched at his rear and bounded into the air again and again, shrieking 'Oh my bum! Oh my bum!'

As Ivan Southall remarks in his book *Parson on the Track* (Lansdowne Press, Melbourne, 1962), 'As far as the bush

41

people were concerned, this did not wreck his chance for immortality but assured it.' And for years the name of John Oliver Feetham was included in the *Australian Prayer Book Calendar of Saints and Heroes.*

Our seven bush churches were all of weatherboard with corrugated-iron roofs, lighted by pressure-lamps and furnished with altars, fonts, prayer-desks, benches and harmoniums. When Bishop Wylde came to consecrate St Matthew's, West Bogan, on September 9th, 1939, he congratulated the congregation in his sermon: 'Dear people, you have built this church with your own hands. Well done! You have paid for it yourselves. Again, well done! Now you have to pray in it, for until a church has been prayed in for at least ten years it is incomplete.'

On another occasion I remember him saying: 'Dear people, I know three reasons why you should not go to church: one, you are ill yourself; two, you have to look after someone who is ill; three, there is a drought and you have to scrub-cut to feed starving stock. Those are three good reasons why you should not go to church. I know *no* others.'

Bush churches were real houses of prayer but one always had to be prepared for the unexpected. One Sunday morning I was celebrating Holy Communion at the Church of the Good Shepherd, Goodooga, and some 20 people were present. In those days we always adopted the eastward position at the altar and during the 'Prayer for the Church Militant' I heard a car draw up outside. Imagine my surprise when on turning westward to invite the congregation 'truly and earnestly to repent of their sins', I found half of them had vanished. Had I done anything to offend them? I turned eastward and continued, and when I came to the distribution all were in their seats again. The explanation? The mailman had arrived and the absentees had gone outside to collect their mail.

Singing was always a problem. I was incapable of leading it. At Holy Trinity, Hendford, Mrs Priddle, the organist, gave up trying to teach me to intone the versicles in tune. In the bush, with no choir and frequently no organist, the situation could be desperate. I had, however, begun to learn the violin as a child and when in May 1937 I was moved for ten months to Gilgandra where there was a music teacher, I bought a violin and renewed my lessons. I never played well – far from it – but I could at least give a lead and after returning to Brewarrina my violin accompanied me on all my travels.

Bush services were mostly in homesteads and frequently a night's hospitality would be followed by a Holy Communion service in the cool of the morning. Evening services were happy occasions, followed by tea and cakes. In the hot weather they were held on the gauzed-in verandahs and one would note the different families converging. Headlights would appear on the horizon to the right. 'Good, that's the Priestleys coming.' Then more headlights to the left. 'Excellent, that's the Currys. They will be bringing their children.' Meanwhile table and chairs had been arranged on the verandah and I had set up my violin stand. Even more than in bush churches, one never quite knew what might happen.

In September 1938 when the car was out of commission, I began a cycle trip to the south with a 40-mile run down the railway line to Compton Downs near Byrock, where we had Evensong in Mrs Glasson's sitting-room. Mr and Mrs George motored across from the Wave Hill property with their three children and there were two fettlers' children from the railway siding present. These made up our tiny congregation. Also present amongst the furniture was a little blue children's chair, prettily painted. Unfortunately it had no sense of propriety. The service began normally but halfway through the congregation rose to sing the second hymn. I was preparing to play *Sun of my soul, thou Saviour dear* when, believe it or not, the little blue chair started up *Home, Sweet Home* in competition. (It was one of those children's chairs which play when you rise after sitting on them.) We quietly waited for it to finish as though this was the most natural thing in the world, then I put my violin under my chin again and we sang the second hymn.

On the Sunday following I took services at St Mary's, Marra Creek, and on the Monday continued my visiting, reaching Murrawombie station in the extreme south of the parish on the Tuesday afternoon. Murrawombie ran some 20,000 sheep and when I arrived the shearers had just finished work for the day, so after chatting and having tea with them I asked if they would like a service. Their rep said he would enquire and we fixed the time for half past seven. This was late for shearers, but earlier I had no chance, so the rep said. 'It's Tuesday, sir, and they will all be listening to *Dad and Dave'* (Australia's equivalent of *The Archers*).

However, at 7.30 p.m. some 30 of them trooped into the woolshed. I produced my violin and for a time we practised hymns, the rep meanwhile passing round a sheet of paper which the men were signing – a list of names and promises to give in lieu of a collection which the contracting boss would cash on application. This came to £1 9s 6d. We cleared the tables and the service started. I kept to Evensong but in a shortened form and spoke afterwards on 'Not condemning'. The hymns went with gusto. We were also very matey afterwards. One shearer produced a mandolin and another a Jewish harp and we had a singsong. One also asked, when I was talking after the service: was it still church or would it matter if they swore again? He was a wag, so I only smiled at him.

Ivan Southall in his book already mentioned makes great play of my incompetence in the bush and at the wheel, and you might imagine from what he writes that I was turning cars over daily. In all my five years in the bush I only turned two cars over, the first when stationed in Gilgandra parish, the second while in Brewarrina, and in the latter case the mishap had a silver lining.

In July 1939 I was travelling leisurely in Stephen (as the car was called) along the Castlereagh River road for a baptism at 'Brewon' at 3 p.m. Suddenly and without warning Stephen leapt out of the tramway-like dirt track to begin a mad career sideways over the paddock. Various thoughts flashed through my mind in quick succession: 'We'll turn

44

over – we must – glass!' The roof seemed to be coming down to meet me and there was the sound of glass breaking. And there I was, lying on the ground quite unhurt, only a little stiff in one leg; and there was Stephen lying on his side 30 yards away, bent and battered and looking deplorable – cab caved-in, windscreen broken, bonnet missing and the door, which had opened providently as we rolled over and left me on the ground, still gaping wide, protesting to heaven. Behind was a trail of cases, boxes, books, pickles, jars of jam, tools, accessories and whatnot, strewn in all directions in consequence of Stephen's somersaults. I collected my church bag, walked three miles to the homestead and was two hours late with the baptism. Investigating afterwards, we discovered that Stephen had rolled over three times before finally resting and that a blow-out was the cause of the mischief. Mechanically, Stephen was sound but the cab was so dented that I had to travel to Dubbo for Reunion four days later crouched in the driving seat, my head and shoulders leaning out of the crumpled door.

And the silver lining? After Reunion I carried on the additional 250 miles to Sydney to report to NRMA, the insurers. Even before the accident we had been wanting to trade in Stephen. He had done 44,000 miles – almost all over bush tracks – and was in need of various repairs. We were told we would be lucky to get £70 for him. However, the insurers offered me £106 in lieu of repairs, and the garage mechanic £30 for scrap. So we came out £60 to the good, and for £195, (£4,500 today) I was able to buy Phyllis, a smart Oldsmobile saloon with only 25,000 on the clock.

There was much uncomplained-of loneliness in the bush, and in saying so I am not thinking so much either of families in isolated homesteads living miles from any other human beings or of the boundary-riders' families in their isolated shacks, but of the *sundowners* who spent their lives, and sometimes lost their lives, tramping the bush and who received their name because as soon as the sun began to set they would present themselves at a homestead for food and lodging and, to my knowledge, never in vain; and of the *remittance men* whom one came across from time to time, paid by remittances from England to remain 'down-under'; and of the *pensioners* to whom the bush was home and who spent their closing years either 'sundowning' or, in the Lightning Ridge area, 'fossicking' in the waste heaps of abandoned opal mines, hoping to find among the discarded waste an opal, a 'pearl of great price' to provide them with comfort for their dying years.

But not only individuals, townships also died in the bush – worked-out mining settlements, and settlements rendered superfluous by the arrival of the train and the internal-combustion engine. With one such dying township, Gongolgon, 30 miles south of Brewarrina, I established a special relationship. By 1934 Gongolgon had outlived its usefulness. At the beginning of the century 'wool-growers' (lovely name) were grazing hundreds of thousands of their flocks on the Western Plains and in the shearing season teams of ox-drawn wool wagons would wend their way through Brewarrina to the railhead at Bathurst, 350 miles to the south-east. Gongolgon on the Bogan River was their first night halt. With the extension of the railway line to Bourke and Brewarrina all had changed, and the last Gongolgon pub had burnt itself down a few years before my arrival. 'He was a queer man, the owner,' I was told. 'When the pub began to burn we all rushed up to pull out the furniture but he yelled at us, "Put it back! Put it back! If you take it out I don't get the insurance"!'

Gongolgon in my day consisted of some half-dozen shacks, a school of eight children and a post office run for years by Mrs O'Sullivan and her daughter Rosie. Although a Roman Catholic, Mrs O'Sullivan had always the warmest welcome for passing Bush Brothers. On a journey to the south I was once bogged down eight miles out of Gongolgon and by the time I had footed it into the settlement it was late at night. However, a light was still burning in the post office, so I knocked and explained my plight. 'Rosie!' called Mrs O'Sullivan, 'Get out of bed and go across to your cousin's.' So Rosie appeared in her nightdress and walked across the 'common' to her relatives, and her bed was still warm when I slipped into it.

There were many Roman Catholics in the bush. When Bishop Wylde took a Confirmation he gave two addresses, the first before the laying-on of hands, explaining to the candidates what they were about to receive, the second afterwards explaining its implications. (He was so thorough that we Bush Brothers were wont to console ourselves if we had failed to prepare all the candidates as well as we would have liked: 'Well, no matter. The Bishop does it for us.') At the close of the service he would tell those present that he would like to have a short word with the candidates alone and the rest of the congregation would slip happily away for tea and cakes. 'I have just one final word to say to you,' said the Bishop when the candidates were alone. Guess what? 'Don't marry a Roman Catholic!'

Besides Christ Church, there was a small Roman Catholic school and convent in Brewarrina, run by nuns, and a Presbyterian church served monthly from Bourke, but although relations between the individual members of the churches were cordial there was no sharing of services.

Anzac Day, April 25th, is a great day in Australia. It commemorates the landing of the Australian and New Zealand Army Corps (the Anzacs) on Gallipoli in 1916, and on the morning of Anzac Day in Brewarrina there would be an Act of Remembrance in the School of Arts. (This was the public hall, but by the possession of 200 books it was constituted as a school of art and as such exempt from rates.) The Mayor and Aldermen, staff from the hospital, police, scouts and guides, schoolchildren with their teachers, former Anzacs etc., would all assemble and the national song *Advance, Australia Fair* was sung. The names of the Fallen were then read out and a two-minute silence observed. A trumpeter sounded the Reveille, and after the singing of the National Anthem, all dispersed.

One year my churchwarden, Geoff New, was Mayor and thought it wrong that throughout the proceedings no prayer was offered. 'We are all Christians. Surely at least we can say the Lord's Prayer together?'

We couldn't. As soon as Father Sullivan, the Roman Catholic priest, heard, he protested. 'It had been a civic ceremony. Now you have made it an Act of Worship. No Roman Catholic must attend.' Nor did they. Today, happily, in Australia as in England, things are very different.

But to return to Mrs O'Sullivan and Gongolgon. Bush postmistresses in those early days had formidable powers and no one dared offend. I was once passing through Hebel, just over the Queensland border, and called, as protocol required, on Mrs Geike, the postmistress, to pay my respects. While she was entertaining me to tea the exchange bell rang, and as it persisted I ventured to say, 'Don't mind me. Hadn't you better answer it?'

Mrs Geike glanced at the number ringing on the board. 'It's only Harry Smith ringing his girl,' she said. 'Let him wait!' It did not do to get across Mrs Geike! Mrs O'Sullivan was different, and so was Rosie, who succeeded her.

My 'special relationship' with Gongolgon was due to Mrs Meer Khan and her family. Mrs Meer Khan was a 'dinkie-dye' Aussie who had married in her youth a former Afghan camel driver several years her senior who, when camels went out, became a pedlar. He was away for months on end, driving his horse and van, and I never quite knew how his wife and family survived. Besides Mrs Meer Khan there were Mickie, Doris, Thelma, Alma, Betty and Barney. When I first met them Mickie was 16, a station hand and rarely seen, the others were aged 14, 12, 10, 8 and 5 respectively. None had been baptised.

They lived in a one-room cabin made of packing cases, a separate kitchen made of flattened kerosine tins, and a gum-tree shelter. But I was always welcomed and they were always clean. On my first visit Mrs Meer Khan said she wanted the girls baptised and over the next two years I prepared them for baptism and, later, Mrs Meer Khan and the four girls for confirmation. They were a lovely and united family.

The Confirmation took place in Brewarrina in September 1938 and thereafter I visited Gongolgon every other month giving my new communicants their communion. There were no other communicants in Gongolgon and in *In Journeyings Often* I have described a service held there early on Boxing Day morning 1938. We held it in the gum-tree shelter with an old pedal sewing-machine as an altar and with potato bags for kneelers. One or two had wooden crates to sit on. The circumstances were at least as humble as in the Bethlehem stable but there was much reverence, the linen I had brought with me was spotless, the silver chalice and paten shone brightly, and the lighted candles proclaimed the Light of the World.

Mrs Meer Khan's chickens came and went, and in fear that they might fly on to the altar, I delegated Barney to chase them off should they come too near. Being only five years old, he acepted the office with gladness. Unfortunately, his zeal outran his discretion, for during the Creed I heard what I suspected was a cuffing followed by what was certainly snivelling. 'But Brother Peter . . . *sob* . . . told me to.'

So my years with the BGS passed. There was a case, I am told, of an old lady in the USA who petitioned the Board for Matrimonial Causes for separation from her husband. 'But,' said the magistrate, 'you have been married to him for over 50 years. Why do you want a separation now?'

The old lady replied, so the story goes, in three words: 'Enough is enough.'

I could continue on and on with stories of my encounters and journeyings in the bush but 'enough is enough'. Before closing the chapter, however, I would add a word or two about that inner journey which engages us all.

I entered upon my ministry in Australia in fear and trembling. I have already told of the difficulty I experienced in expressing myself. At Holy Trinity I had spent not hours but days in preparing my fortnightly sermon. I had realised from reading how strenuous life in the bush would be, how constantly I would be on the move. How would I ever cope with the preaching? God provides. I had overlooked the fact that even when on my own and giving between 20 and 30 addresses a month, apart from the two-a-month given in Brewarrina, they would all be to different congregations. Normally two new sermons a month sufficed, and in general the more I preached a sermon the better it became. I was always nervous but the members of the congregations I preached to were unfailingly kind. They still are.

Gerard W Hughes' book *The God of Surprises* won the Collins Biennial Religious Book award in 1987. 'It is,' writes Gerald Priestland, 'one of the great books of spiritual guidance.' I have gained much help from it.

'If we insist that we must first prove that God exists before we turn to him, then we shall never find him,' he writes. 'And we shall never find him because we are trying to treat the God of Being as though he were an intellectual problem . . . such a God does not exist.' He emphasises that God is Mystery but 'If we turn to him, he will lead us.'

This I experienced as I began ministering in the bush. How was I going to cope? I just did not know but I turned to him and he enabled me. 'I will love thee, O Lord my Strength.' (*Psalm 18*)

The bush changes people. It changed me. Before beginning my training for the ministry, I had been full of self-confidence – I, Geoffrey, was in control. When I left the bush all that had gone. I had learned the lesson that St Paul himself learned from experience, that when we are weak, then we are strong. 'I can do all things through Christ who strengtheneth me.' (*2 Corinthians 12: 10; Philippians 4: 13*)

I also learned from the vastness and silence of the bush what Carlo Carretto learned from his life in the Sahara. As the desert, its sands and the stars became his first love, where, more than anywhere else, he could communicate directly with God, so 'the everlasting sameness of the never- ending plains' became for me.

When invited to a homestead for the night, you did not

50

normally appear till just before sundown, and I have a vivid recollection of pausing, having time to spare, some five miles from my destination for the night, the home of Arthur Hall, V.C., and his charming wife. I was feeling exhausted and I parked the car on the track, lay back in the seat and gazed at a red-soil tank. (A 'tank' is an earthen rainwater reservoir up to 6 feet deep and 40 feet square.) There was no sound, no movement save that of the pink and grey gulahs wheeling in the sun; but the scrub and the grass were green, for rain had recently fallen, and the sky was its lovely azure blue. I just gazed and gazed.

> The heavens declare the glory of God; and the firmament sheweth his handiwork. One day telleth another: and one night certifieth another. There is neither speech nor language: but their voices are heard among them.
>
> *Psalm 19: 1–3*

I was suddenly aware of God and of being at one with him. That 'direct communication with God' to which Carlo Carretto refers does not mean a hot line to heaven. 'There is neither speech nor language' but God's presence fills one. By the time I reached my destination I was remade.

By January 6th 1940 I had completed a thousand-mile Christmas trip, and having given Christmas Communion to all the churches and homestead centres in the parish, I prepared to say goodbye to Brewarrina, my five-year ministry fulfilled. I am sure there must have been a farewell party but I have no recollection of it. I only remember that when I was all ready to go, the last goodbye having been said and the parish car packed in readiness for an early morning start, that night it rained more than an inch and I was marooned! For two days I hid myself in the Rectory, letting no one see me. I felt a disgrace, a guest who had overstayed his welcome. On the third morning the roads could be travelled on and I slipped away.

I spent the rest of January in Brotherhood House in Dubbo, editing and collating, at the request of the Principal (Brother John Hudson, later Bishop of Carpentaria), the

51

reports I had submitted to the *Bush Brother*, the BGS quarterly, from 1934 onwards.

After I left these were published as a book, *In Journeyings Often*. It is now out of print but it is the source book for most of this chapter. Before it was published, however, I was again in Delhi with the Cambridge Mission and another chapter in my life had opened.

7

With the Cambridge Mission to Delhi

I left Dubbo in February and travelled down to Sydney. Intent on seeing more of Australia than New South Wales, I then went overnight by train to Melbourne and spent the next weekend in Adelaide as guest of Archdeacon Weston, an old Gilgandra boy to whom I had an introduction. While there I attended an evening meeting of the Australian Church Missionary Society (CMS) at which Bishop Baddeley of New Guinea was to be the chief speaker. I do not remember a single word he said but I have never forgotten his courage. That same day Bishop Baddeley had visited his dentist, who had pronounced his mouth septic. With presumably his approval he had there and then extracted all the Bishop's teeth. No temporary dentures had been made so the Bishop appeared on the platform toothless. He looked a sight and must have known that his speech was barely comprehensible. Nonetheless, he had been billed to speak, the large audience expected him to speak, and speak he did.

When, after officially retiring in 1973, I had completed 14 years as honorary curate at St John's, Sevenoaks, its Vicar, Fr Michael Shields, presented me with a beautifully bound *Daily Office Book* which was given, he wrote, in special appreciation of 'Work beyond the call of duty'. He and I had not always been of the same mind (to put it mildly) and I greatly appreciated his generous inscription. 'Work beyond the call of duty' expressed perfectly Bishop Baddeley's election to appear vulnerably toothless on the platform in Adelaide, and it was an inspiration.

53

From Adelaide I travelled by rail to Port Augustine. Here the fortnightly train to Alice Springs in the 'red heart of Australia' had steam up on an adjoining platform. How I wished I could have joined it! Alice Springs is now a popular tourist attraction, a city of 18,000 people. In 1940 it was simply a post on the Overland Telegraph line to Darwin, then a pearling village of only a few hundred people.

I stayed in my carriage on the Transcontinental Railway to Perth. The single-line track then ran for a thousand miles across the Nullabor Plain to Kalgoorie, and in the whole distance the only human habitations were the railway ganger camps spaced 80 to 100 miles apart. Here was true isolation. No roads went by and the camps' one link with the outside world was the 'Transcontinental', which passed each day going either east or west and halted to deliver mail and supplies and to pick up water.

At one camp were three cabins occupied by fettlers' families. The three wives came to their doors as the train drew in and each one had a baby in her arms, 'I suppose,' remarked one passenger, 'there's nothing else to do.'

At another halt a group of Aborigines had established themselves some 40 yards from the track and were selling artifacts. We wandered across and one passenger showed an interest in the boomerangs. Would it really return? The Aborigine threw it towards the train. It wheeled and returned to his feet. Still not convinced, the passenger asked for a trial. He held it as instructed, aimed it at the train and *crash*! Flying straight as a dart, it smashed a carriage window to smithereens!

I still had a weekend to spare before joining the RMS *Orontes* at Fremantle, and I spent it in Dalwallinu, 80 miles north-east of Perth, where a college friend of mine, the Revd John Hawkins, was Rector, and it proved a most enjoyable stay. I had shared a study with him for one term at St Chad's, and John would entertain friends for hours, reciting poetry, singing popular songs and telling anecdotes. What was he doing in this remote rural parish? For one thing he was bringing the gospel message and the sacraments and a degree of culture to his isolated parishioners. He had established a library and Bible and literary circles. Secondly, he was 'showing forth Christ'. To see and know John was to see and know his Master. He would spend hours in prayer, and it showed. And thirdly, like the fettlers on the Nullabor Plain, he was producing a family. I recall lines of nappies drying on the clothes-line. Later John returned to England and became an Archdeacon in the diocese of Exeter but while still in his forties died tragically (from a human viewpoint) of a tumour on the brain. I visited him a few days before he died but he did not know me. I discovered only this evening (16.2.95) that his second son, Richard, is now Bishop of Plymouth.

I arrived in Delhi in April, two days late. Having left the *Orontes* at Colombo, I was travelling third-class up to Delhi when, some 150 miles north of Madras, the carriage began to fill with Hindu villagers in festive mood. I enquired the reason of an English-speaking Pathan travelling back to the North-West Frontier and was told that they were village people on pilgrimage to a great Hindu festival then being held at Bhadrachalam on the Godavari River and that they would all be getting out at Dornakal. Bhadrachalam was quite close. Here, I said to myself, was something not to be missed, and at Dornakal I left the train with them.

Bishop Azariah, then the only non-white bishop in the Anglican Communion and of whom I had often heard, lived in Dornakal. His cathedral bordered the railway line and I made myself known to him. To my dismay, he informed me that it would take me a whole day to get to Bhadrachalam and a whole day to get back, and that it was a difficult journey. However, if I wished to go, his son Basil would be pleased to go with me. I think of Paul's words to Titus: 'A bishop, as God's steward must be hospitable'. (*Titus 1: 7*) How truly hospitable Bishop Azariah was.

By this time my train was well on its way to Delhi. I was bound to be one day late, so why not two? I accordingly sent my brother a telegram, which I heard later was not well-received as he had already laid on a dinner-party for me that evening. How was I to know?

That night Basil and I slept under the stars on the sands that border the southern bank of the Godavari River. We had for company thousands of fellow-pilgrims. There had been an outbreak of cholera at this particular festival some years earlier and every pilgrim had to be immunised against it. 'Come early,' the medical officer had advised us the night before, 'the needle is a bit blunt by mid-morning!'

Immunised, we waded the river early next day and visited the shrine. My chief memory is of the army of diseased, mutilated and naked beggars squatting on the steps and asking alms. Was it like this at the Gate of the Temple called 'Beautiful' in Jerusalem in the days of the apostles? (*See Acts 3: 1–10.*)

Since my previous visit to Delhi en route for Australia in 1934, my brother had returned to England to study at Westcott House in Cambridge. After 18 months he had been ordained and licensed to All Saints', Hertford, and he and a young Sunday school teacher, 13 years his junior, had fallen in love and married. He and Doreen were now living in the Civil Lines in Old Delhi and Jim was Chaplain and Vice-Principal of St Stephen's College.

I planned another six weeks' holiday in India as in 1934, but it was not to be. When eventually I left India four and a half years later, I left with a wife and child – all, strangely enough, a consequence of Hitler's invasion of Belgium. I remember the occasion well.

Delhi was then part of the diocese of Lahore. I was staying as a guest in Brotherhood House, Court Lane, and the Bishop of Lahore, the Rt Revd George Barne, was on a visit. We were at breakfast in the refectory when the Bishop arrived back in high dudgeon from an Indian Mass at St Stephen's Church in Chandni Chowk. The Bishop was an evangelical. Padre Godfrey Stokes, CMD, was an Anglo-Catholic to whom ritual and ceremonial were precious, and all had not gone well. The Bishop seated himself at the refectory table, ready to explode, when news came over the radio: Hitler had marched into Belgium! Padre Stokes was saved, all his enormities forgotten. Or were they? He left St Stephen's at the end of the year, never to return, and in 1942 joined the Anglican Benedictine Order at Nashdom. In 1984, at the age of 80 he became their Abbot and guided their move from Nashdom to Elmore Abbey in 1987, one of a great and immensely varied army of Christian witnesses nurtured in its day by the Cambridge Mission. Others, to mention but three, are Eva Fiennes, C F Andrews and S N Mukerji.

The collapse of the Netherlands, Belgium and France, plus Italy's Declaration of War on June 10th, changed all my plans. The Mediterranean was closed, all shipping had been requisitioned, and it was no longer possible for me to proceed immediately to England. At the same time, two English priests, Gilbert Hort and Kenneth Sharpe, due to join the Brotherhood, were stranded in England. Accordingly it was agreed with the Bishop that I should stand in for them, live in Brotherhood House and assist Christopher Robinson, Chaplain of Delhi and later Biship of Bombay, at St James' Church, Kashmiri Gate.

St James' was a church with a history. Around 1770, Hercules Skinner, a Scottish adventurer in the service of the East India Company, had a Rajput woman who had been taken prisoner in war placed under his protection. He decided that the best protection he could give her was to marry her, and she returned the compliment by bearing him three sons and three daughters. Their second son, James, was born in Bengal in 1778, and when 48 years old began the building of St James', Kashmiri Gate, in fulfilment of a vow.

James, like his father, became a soldier, a freelance mercenary, and in 1800, when in the service of Scindia of Gwalior, the small band of troops he commanded were annihilated by the overwhelming numbers of a rival Rajput ruler. Surrounded by dead and wounded, tortured by thirst and unable to move, James and his men lay on the battlefield from 3 p.m. on the day of the battle through a night and a day, praying for death. On the following night, barely alive, James made two vows: the first, which he didn't keep, that he would never go soldiering again; the second, which he did keep, that if his life was spared, he would build a church to the God of his Scottish forefathers. When 24 years later, he was a lieutenant colonel in the British Army, rewarded with wealth and honour and commanding his own irregular cavalry corps, 'Skinner's Horse', he fulfilled his vow and built St James', known for many years as 'Skinner's Church'.

When I joined the staff in 1940, the glory of Kashmiri Gate as a shopping centre was fading. Since Mutiny days the European population of Delhi was concentrated in the Civil Lines. Now it was moving out to New Delhi. The Church of the Redemption, now the Cathedral, had been consecrated, Connaught Circus had been completed, and the fashion shops of Kashmiri Gate were transferring thither their businesses. St James' nevertheless remained the church of the Europeans and the Anglo-Indians still living in the Civil Lines and the English-speaking church of the Cambridge Mission.

The Mission, founded in memory of the Christian martyrs of Delhi in the Mutiny of 1857–58, flourished. Its chief centres were the churches of St James', Kashmiri Gate, St Stephen's, Chandni Chowk, and Holy Trinity, Turkaman Gate, in the old city; St Thomas's New Delhi, and district churches at Jungpura, Gurgaon and Marauli; St Stephen's College, recently resited on the university campus outside the Civil Lines, St Stephen's Hospital in Tis Hazari; St Mary's and the Queen Victoria schools, St Mary's Home, and the United Christian School for Boys. At the centre of its life was the Cambridge Brotherhood in Brotherhood House, 7 Court Lane, and the St Stephen's Community (the 'Grey Ladies') then some 30 strong with their headquarters at the Kohti, Rajpur Road.

Christopher Robinson was Head of the Brotherhood and Cecilia Norris of the Community. Europeans and Indians served together in the work of the Mission and Indians were just beginning to play a major role, notably S N Mukerji, Principal of St Stephen's College, and A N Mukarji, later to become Head of the Mission and the first Bishop of Delhi.

During my time in Delhi I took a class on Religious Knowledge for Indian Christians in the College and Bible courses in the Kohti, but my main work was in helping Christopher Robinson in ministering to Europeans and to the congregation of St James'.

I revelled in cycling through the narrow streets and crowded bazaars, and Bible scenes were daily enacted before my eyes: the potters working at their wheels, making from the same lump of clay vessels both for beauty and for menial use and sometimes, when the vessel was marred in their hands, starting all over again (*Jeremiah 18: 1–6; Romans 9: 21*); and cobblers squatting on the pavements fashioning chappelis (sandals) later to be bargained for (*Amos 2: 6*); and all the time the haggling of buyer and seller as each sought to outdo the other. 'It is nought, it is nought, saith the buyer, but when he is gone his way, he boasteth.' (*Proverbs 20: 14*)

I gained my own experience of Eastern bargaining etiquette when I decided to get reprinted my Bush Brother experiences, published in Australia under the title *In Journeyings Often*. I discovered it could be reprinted in India at a fraction of its Australian cost and thought it might be appreciated by my Indian and English friends.

The Latifi Press in Old Delhi was recommended to me. Mr Latifi was a Muslim but he had beautifully rebound a Lectionary Bible belonging to St James' free of charge. He would not charge, he said for rebinding a holy book. His press was co-operative and did a splendid job. I had, however, to provide my own paper. I ascertained the quantity and quality needed and asked for an estimate from a paper-seller in Chandni Chowk. He quoted his price for a quire (24 sheets). 'And how much,' I asked, 'would you charge me for 2,500 quires?

'That is easy,' he replied, '2,500 times as much.'

'But,' I protested, 'surely you will charge less per quire if I order 2,500?'

'No, no,' he replied, 'the price per quire I quoted, that is the price. Either that or I give it to you.'

Dumbfounded, I replied, 'Well, that's very kind. Give it me.'

His reply was instantaneous. 'You are joking.'

I thought of Abraham's bargaining for the purchase of the cave of the field of Mach-pelah before Mamre from the children of Heth as a burying-place for Sarah. Ephron the Hittite answered Abraham, 'Nay, my lord, hear me; the field give I thee and the cave that is therein, give I it thee; in the presence of the sons of my people I give it thee; bury thy dead.'

And, I reflected, I suppose if Abraham had been as naive as I and had said that it was very kind of him, he would have got the same reply as I, 'You are joking.' But Abraham was more versed in the ways of the East. The offer of the field as a gift was only the opening gambit and if you read on in the story as given in Genesis 23, you will learn that Abraham eventually weighed over to Ephron four hundred shekels of silver and everyone was happy.

A similar example of Eastern courtesy and bargaining technique is to be found in the story of King David's purchase of the threshing floor of Araunah the Jebusite in I Samuel 24.

Among the cherished memories of my cycling days while with the Brotherhood was an incident in, I think, the Sadar Bazaar. The bazaar was crowded. I had to dismount and was slowly pushing my way through the colourful throng when I noticed perching upon a lower branch of a banyan tree in a corner of the bazaar a large kite viewing with disdain the crowds beneath. A diminutive Indian boy, perhaps eight years old, also noticed it. He had a catapult in his hand and hastened to find a stone. He fitted it and took careful aim. *Twang*! The stone landed right in the centre of the kite's breast. Was the kite upset? It just turned its disdainful eye on the catapult-owner and stayed precisely where it was. Exit the crestfallen 'David'.

A more serious memory is of my first Christmas in Delhi.

Imitation, they say, is the sincerest form of flattery, and an interesting feature of the first decade of the twentieth century in India was the manner in which both Bhuddism and Hinduism began following the example of the Christian missions in their care for the needy. The YMBA (Young Men's Bhuddist Association), started in Ceylon, was painstakingly modelled on the YMCA, and in Delhi the Hindu Radhakrishnan Mission was devoted, like the Cambridge Mission, to caring for the poor. Additionally, each Christmas they honoured the memory of the birth of our Lord, and in 1940 they invited a priest from the Brotherhood to attend their festival and speak. Christopher suggested I should go.

We sat on the floor of the shrine in their house. they in their saffron robes, I in my white cassock. Numerous candles burned and in the centre was a painting of our Lord, before which the monks made their offerings to the accompaniment of bells. When the time came for me to speak, I spoke to them on Anselm's dictum 'Either God or a not-good man'. I doubt if my words had much impact for in retrospect I have little doubt that they interpreted Anselm's dictum as 'Either *a* god or not a good man', and that would not in the least have troubled them.

Hinduism is a religion of 'gods many and lords many' and of many incarnations. Because God indwells his whole creation, God, Hinduism claims, may be rightly worshipped in everything he has made. Birds of the air, beasts of the field, fishes of the sea, trees, plants, planets, the elemental forces of nature all, claims Hinduism, can be rightly worshipped because God is in them; and the simple villager offers *puja* (worship) to whatever excites his wonder.

When my brother first came to India he brought with him his 350 cc Triumph motor cycle, his pride and joy. One day he asked his bearer to wash it down and to polish it. Going out to see how the work was progressing, he found his bearer, having completed his task, kneeling before his cycle and offering it *puja*.

On another occasion there had been a Roman Catholic

61

procession through the streets of Trichinopoly. It passed by Bishop Heber College, where Jim was a lecturer, and a college servant, hearing the drums and the music, went to watch. The climax of the procession was a cart drawn by oxen on which was a life-size crucifix with statues of St John and the Blessed Virgin standing beneath. On the servant's return Jim asked him what he had seen. 'I saw three gods,' he replied. 'Two men-gods and one woman-god.'

The saffron-robed monks at the Radhakrishnan Mission in Delhi had not and never had had any difficulty in accepting Jesus as a god.

As I see it, Christianity takes issue with Hinduism in four main ways:

(i) The uniqueness of the incarnation of our Lord. Jesus, in any real sense, is God's only son.

(ii) The forgiveness of sins. Because Christ died for us, sins, we believe, can be forgiven. This in Hindu eyes is immoral. Not even God, they claim, can forgive sin. Every sin committed must be paid for by the sinner either in this life or in a future reincarnation.

(iii) The lack of any real distinction between good and evil. God (Brahma) they claim is beyond good and evil. Radhakrishnan, born in 1888 and Spalding Professor for Eastern Religions and Ethics at Oxford (1936-52) and founder of modern Hindu Liberalism wrote (I quote from memory): 'I see a poor man passing and I say "God in the guise of a poor man". I see a sick man passing and I say "God in the guise of a sick man". I see a licentious man passing and I say, "God in the guise of a licentious man".'

(iv) The hope of eternal life. Eternal life (absorption into God) is for the Hindu the ultimate reward of countless reincarnations and few can expect to attain to it. For the Christian there is no reincarnation of the soul on earth, and eternal life (union with God, not absorption into God) is God's gift to everyone who believes.

As a priest licensed in the diocese, I was summoned to Lahore annually to attend the Diocesan Synod. The diocese was then part of the Church of India, Burma and Ceylon, and at my first Synod we were required to vote on how we wished future Bishops of Lahore to be chosen. There were various options: by the Metropolitan of India, by the Archbishop of Canterbury, by their advisory committees, by a diocesan committee and so forth.

Not at all abashed by my newness in the diocese, I rose to my feet to speak against the last-named option. 'This,' I said, 'is tantamount to a parish appointing its own vicar. It could be disastrous.' Bishop Barne, in the chair, just made a wry smile and lifted his eyebrows and the Synod collapsed in laughter. Poor greenhorn that I was, it was only later that I discovered that this was the method by which Bishop Barne himself had been chosen.

One other Synod memory, two or three years later. There existed in the Lahore diocese an Indian-Christian Evangelism Committee, and at this meeting they brought forward a motion. They had discovered in the diocese, which at that time embraced all India west of Delhi and all Kashmir and Pakistan, a small strip of land unclaimed by any denomination, in which the gospel had still to be preached. Would the diocese authorise them to make this their special field of mission for which they would be wholly responsible?

Various members spoke in support, but the Assistant Bishop of Lahore, the Rt Revd John Banerjee, a most missionary-minded Christian and beloved by all, kept his counsel. Finally Bishop Barne asked him to speak, and most of us imagined he would give the motion his enthusiastic backing. To our astonishment he spoke passionately against the motion. We had, he said, millions of non-Christians on our doorsteps. It was them we must evangelise. He had a great fear, if we passed the motion, that Indian Christians would salve their consciences by paying for someone to evangelise on their behalf in this distant part, feeling that they were now free of the obligation to evangelise the non-Christians, their neighbours.

In Matthew Chapter 23 Jesus castigates the scribes and Pharisees:

> Woe to you, scribes and Pharisees, hypocrites! for you tithe
> mint and dill and cummin, and have neglected the weightier
> matters of the law, justice and mercy and faith; these you
> ought to have done without neglecting the others. You
> blind guides, straining out a gnat and swallowing a camel!

Evangelism, like charity, begins at home, as the Decade of Evangelism is making clear to us. Yes it is 'without neglecting the others'. We still have duties to the greater world. Our love is to abound more and more with knowledge and all discernment till it embraces all mankind.

Conversions to Christianity in North India, in contrast to conversions in the South, were then, as now, rare. So rare that one elderly Indian pastor in my day confessed his sorrow on an episcopal visit. 'I seem, my Lord,' he is reported to have said, 'to have had little success in persuading unbelievers into the fold but' – and his face brightened – 'I have increased our congregation a little here in my own way.' He had reared a very large family.

Which reminds me of a paperback I once read concerning an Indian evangelist in the South. I have forgotten his story, and indeed his name – we will call him Ebenezer – but I shall never forget the title of the book: *Ebenezer, Father of Ten Thousand* by his wife!

Nonetheless, when the Church continues faithfully in its pastoral care, pastoral joys can come. One day a rough English 'Tommy' from the cantonment presented himself to me while I was doing duty in the Chaplain's office. He wished, he said, to get married. Some months earlier, it transpired, he had been solicited by an Anglo-Indian street girl. He had gone home with her. They had fallen in love and now he wished to marry her. She had given up soliciting and was living in desperate poverty and squalor. He was not entitled to marry and they would not receive from the Army either a marriage allowance or married quarters. But they earnestly desired to marry and I agreed to prepare them. They came regularly to classes, listened attentively to all I said and were clearly genuinely in love.

We had a parish worker on our staff at St James, Constance Mahy from the Seychelles, about whom I could tell many stories. She met them both, visited the bride-to-be in her 'home', and went to town collecting from the wealthier of our congregation clothes, furnishings, furniture – you name it, she begged it. To my disappointment I went down with a fever two days before the wedding and it was Gilbert Hort, newly arrived from England, who took the service. He too was enthusiastic: 'a lovely couple'.

Later, after being put on the strength and provided with married quarters, they were posted back to England and I received a grateful letter from him. All had turned out well and they were 'very, very happy'.

This was just before I left Delhi. Early in 1942, the Cambridge Committee had written saying that they had obtained passages for Kenneth Sharp and Gilbert Hort and both were hoping shortly to join the Mission. So once again, what next? India fascinated me, I loved its people and had no desire to leave. Again the Bishop came to the rescue.

He had in his pastoral care two categories of clergy: missionaries supported by societies in England and elsewhere; and chaplains paid for by the Government through the Indian Ecclesiastical Establishment (IEE), to which he himself belonged. So did all the Anglican bishops of the CIBC, (Church of India, Burma & Ceylon) including Foss Westcott, the Metropolitan. On one occasion Bishop Foss West-promised by being paid by the Government? He replied, 'Not at all. The Government pay me to criticise them. I am the

Government's Most Loyal Opposition.'

Bishop Barne's solution was that I should join the IEE as a temporary chaplain for the duration of the war. I gladly agreed. Earlier I had half-hoped that I might be invited to join the Brotherhood but no invitation came. In fact, the reverse. For two years I had attended the Brotherhood's Chapter Meetings. In 1942 there was a change of policy – I was no longer to be invited. Why I do not know but Christopher, who, as Head, conveyed the news to me, did so with so much embarrassment that I am sure that he was unhappy about it.

So the Brotherhood with its obligation to celibacy was out. I took it as a sign that I should think of marriage, and where was I likely to find a better partner in my ministry than among the members of the St Stephen's Community? I had met one of their members, a Marjorie Kellaway, occasionally at Jim and Doreen's. She was of my own age and had just completed her five years with the Cambridge Mission. I knew nothing really about her except that everyone seemed to like her and on her I focused my attention.

I prayed a lot and one afternoon, summoning up my courage, I rang the bell at the Khoti. Bea Mowll, sister of Archbishop Mowll of Sydney and one of the Community, opened the door. I asked if Marjorie was in and, if so, could I see her for a moment. The answer was in the affirmative and I was shown to her room. In my Diamond Jubilee sermon I describe what followed.

I am told that after I had left, Marjorie and Bea had a most unseemly giggle together!

But the seed had been sown and that summer I went for a month to Kashmir, camping with Jim and Doreen by the Dal Lake at Srinagar, while John Bishop of the Cambridge Mission with Mildred his wife and Marjorie lived in a houseboat moored alongside. Before the holiday ended Marjorie and I were engaged.

She had said 'Yes' when we were being paddled back to the camping-site in a Kashmiri *shikaree*, a flat-bottomed gondola-like punt, after a shopping expedition in Srinagar – very romantic – and next day in another *shikaree* we visited a dealer in precious stones whose shop bordered a waterway in Srinagar and who had been recommended to us by John Bishop. We stepped from the punt into his carpeted parlour and explained the purpose of our visit. We wished to buy an engagement ring and we thought, we said, of a white sapphire in the centre with emeralds each side. We sat with him on the carpet while he emptied a bag of white sapphires on to it, and when we had made our choice it was the turn of the green emeralds. The fourth finger of Marjorie's left hand was measured and a gold ring ordered. When we returned to Delhi, Marjorie was wearing it. Two months later, on October 8th, Bishop Barne married us in St James', Delhi.

The name Marjorie has its roots in a Persian word meaning 'pearl', and as you read on you will realise what a pearl she has proved.

8

Chaplain on India's North-West Frontier

In August 1942 I had learned of my posting as a temporary chaplain of the Indian Ecclesiastical Establishment. I was to go to Kohat in the North-West Frontier Province. My heart beat quicker. Christopher had often spoken to me of the Frontier, and when earlier a bus I had been travelling on from Kashmir had entered the NWFP just for a few miles, I had been immensely moved, expecting I knew not what. Now I was to live and minister in it! Why is God so good?

Kohat is a small frontier town some 40 miles south of Peshawar. I was to live in its cantonment, a headquarters of the Indian Army and Air Force, and to have spiritual responsibility for all Europeans in Kohat, in the cantonments of Thal and Bannu and in the outposts of the Kurrum Militia and the Tochi Scouts in the Tribal Territory of North Waziristan.

The Militia and Scouts consisted of frontier tribesmen – Afridis, Wazirs, Mahsuds and the like – encouraged to enter the Government's service by the comparatively generous pay offered them. They were carefully vetted and so distributed that in no battalion did any one tribe predominate. The battalions themselves were led by young officers of the Indian Army who offered their services partly from love of adventure and partly because the pay was extremely good.

Their forts were of the kind made familiar to English viewers by films of the North-West Frontier. In many cases these film forts are really forts of the French Foreign Legion filmed in North Africa, but no matter. They were much of

68

a muchness and all were built of mud.

So was my bungalow, 17, The Mall, in Kohat Cantonment. It was a large, airy building maintained by the Military Engineering Service, as was also the church, a temporary mud building replacing the 'Piffers' brick church burnt down a few years earlier. Also in my care were cemeteries in Kohat, Bannu and Thal, and all Christian graves. Soon after our arrival I saw an advert in the local paper by a freelance English missionary, a Mr Nicholson: *Accommodation urgently required in Kohat for English missionary and wife.* I at once offered two rooms in the bungalow. It was accepted with alacrity and I was soundly ticked off by the Station Staff Officer because of it. Only he could allocate accommodation in the cantonment. However, the Nicholsons were allowed to stay.

Behind the bungalow were the well and the servants' quarters. I inherited six servants from my predecessor, Padre Fish. A *khansamar* (cook), a bearer, a sweeper, a dhobi to wash our clothes, and a mali, Idi, to look after the garden. In the dry season, he would lead two bullocks every morning to the well to draw water to run in channels through the garden. Idi had no use for vegetables but loved flowers, yet he never asked me anything for seeds. The cantonment malis shared seeds among themselves. One season a garden-loving officer handed his mali some rare expensive seeds. Next season, to his surprise, he found them growing everywhere in the cantonment! Naaman begged two mules' burden of earth from Elishah after being cured of leprosy. Two loads of mules' dung sufficed to bring tears of joy to the eyes of my mali.

Our six servants lived with their wives and families in the compound, some 30 souls, all supported from my modest stipend. In addition under my control were three servants appointed and paid for by the Government; the church bearer, Karim Shah, and two cemetery malis, Jumma and Bahadur Khan. The latter were Pathans and striking characters. They kept their cemeteries in impeccable order and in season brought Marjorie bunches of roses from the bushes and loquats from the fruit trees planted in the cemeteries. All bore extremely well!

I saw little of the malis except on pay-day but with Karim Shah, the church bearer, I was in daily contact. Light-skinned and a Muslim, as were all our other servants, he was responsible for the care of the church and taking messages. He also accompanied me when on trek as my bearer. At first he was a bit of a mystery. He had dignity and authority and perfect manners, yet was uneducated as I eventually discovered.

It emerged in this way. One of his duties was to deliver the monthly church leaflet to all Christian families in the cantonment, but complaints began to come in that some families were being missed. When this continued, I decided to get Karim to make out a list and for an hour and a half I sat with him in the office, I dictating the names of the families he was to deliver to, he diligently writing the names down – or so I supposed.

When complaints continued to come in, I called him into the office and asked him to read his list back to me. He seemed unable to do so, so I summoned Akbar, the housebearer, handed him the list and asked him to read it. He looked at the hieroglyphics and his brow puckered. 'Sahib,' he said, 'it is nonsense.' Poor Karim! Rather than admit he was illiterate, he had simply doodled.

The mystery of his authority – he himself never stooped to clean the church; he always summoned minnions to do it for him – was solved when I was starting off from Kohat railway station on a trip to Bannu. As an IEE chaplain I had a first-class railway pass for all journeys, while Karim, as my bearer, travelled in the servants' compartment at the end of the carriage. Usually I travelled alone but on this occasion I had a Muslim Indian Army officer as my companion, who greeted Karim warmly. When Karim had disappeared and the two of us were seated comfortably in the wicker chairs provided by the railway, I questioned my companion concerning Karim. 'So you know my servant?'

'Oh yes,' replied the officer. 'I am only a village boy but

Karim Shah – he is one of the sons of the Prophet.' The officer was a university graduate. Karim was illiterate. But such was the officer's respect for Karim's lineage that he clearly looked up to him.

I much enjoyed my trips with Karim for they took me out of British India into the Tribal Territories, where there was neither law nor order and where every man did what was right in his own eyes. It was the first time that I realised that any authority, however bad, is better than no authority at all. There was no accepted body – often no body at all – to whom you could appeal for redress if you suffered injury or theft. You had to obtain any redress due to you, yourself. If your enemy shot your son, honour demanded that you should shoot his. If he stole your beast, you bade your time and then you raided his property, probably taking two beasts from him for good measure. In consequence every dwelling was a fortress and a man was never seen outside without a rifle over his shoulder.

At one Scout fort I was visiting, a *Subhadar* (non-commissioned officer) asked for weekend leave. His brother's eldest son had been murdered and he, the *Subhadar*, had been appealed to to 'redeem the family honour' i.e. to murder the murderer. He returned on the Sunday night and saluted the Commandant. 'Mission accomplished, Sahib,' he reported. Such was life in the Tribal Territories.

What, then, were the Scouts and Militia doing in it? Keeping watch for the Government.

The jacket of Charles Chenevix Trench's well-documented history *The Frontier Scouts* aptly describes the typical frontier tribesman:

> His most precious possession was a modern rifle; his pride to call no man his master; his pleasure to raid villages in British India, to snipe at travellers on the frontier roads and to pursue his blood feuds according to his tribal code of honour.

And the British Government made no attempt either to civilise or tame him. Providing he 'kept the rules', he was free so far as the Government was concerned to carry on as he liked. But supposing he didn't? Supposing he was suspected of harbouring enemies of British interests? Supposing he kidnapped and held to ransom British citizens or raided British India? Who was to bring him to justice and wean him from his wicked ways? The answer was the Militia or the Scouts, who were under the direct orders of the Political Officer.

And, as an IEE chaplain, so was I. This was a huge advantage. The regular Army Chaplains were under Army orders, and the Army was always ultra-cautious, only allowing its Chaplains on the Frontier to travel in convoy or protected by 50 rifles. On the contrary, when things were quiet the PO would let me travel on recognised tribal buses when and where I wished, and I could plan a trip with some degree of certainty. Travelling under Army orders was mostly by convoy, which meant that if, for example, I wished to hold services in Miranshah, I had to travel from Mirali by convoy, and the best I could do was to advise the SSO in Miranshah that I planned to travel on the first convoy from Mirali after such and such a date. All convoy dates were secret and supposing I arrived in Mirali just after a convoy had left, I could spend up to ten days kicking my heels in that very small Army camp.

When with the Delhi Brotherhood, I had been accustomed to wear a white cassock and sandals on all pastoral duties. In the hot weather one wore only a vest and shorts beneath and it was very cool. I continued the custom on the Frontier, but white soon got dirty so that travelling in Tribal territory I wore a cassock of coarse grey cotton (*mazri*) and instead of a topee a *pagri* (turban) of the same material. This was practical and meant that I did not stand out like a sore thumb when crowded in with Pathans on a tribal bus. I nevertheless still used a white cassock for services and for dress occasions.

Dinner in the evening in a Scout Mess was always a dress occasion. The Scout officers might be indistinguishable from their men when on a *Ghasht* (patrol) but at night they were English gentlemen, waited on by uniformed bearers, with tables lighted by silver candlesticks. They wore evening dress. A strange contrast, but even on the Frontier one had to maintain standards.

Miranshah, headquarters of the Tochi Scouts, was an interesting place. It was a typical Scout fort but large, and divided into two by a kind of Berlin Wall – in one half were the Scouts; in the other a unit of the Indian Air Force, and it was here that Aircraftsman Shaw (alias Lawrence of Arabia) hid himself when seeking privacy after the British Government failed to honour his promises to his Arab friends.

Beyond Miranshah was Datta Khel, surrounded on three sides by the Afghanistan frontier, and if there was ever an 'outpost of Empire' it was the Scout post there. On May 1st 1942, some four months before I was stationed at Kohat, the legendary Faqir of Ipi, egged on by Germany, laid siege to it and *The Frontier Scouts* gives a graphic account of the siege and of its relief after three months by an army brigade from Razmak led by a Scout platoon. A week later, headlines appeared in English newspapers: DATTA KHEL RELIEVED, and six months later, when all was quiet again, I visited Datta Khel in an Army convoy to report on the graves of the British buried there.

Two days after our first Christmas Day in Kohat, Marjorie accompanied me on a 110-mile trip up the Kurram Valley to Parachinar at the valley's tip, the headquarters of the Kurrum Militia and of the Political Agent. The Kurrum Valley was one of the quietest on the North-West Frontier and no special precautions were necessary. We travelled by bus, and after leaving Thal it seemed to me that the bus was making heavy going. It dropped from top gear to second and from second to first yet the road appeared quite level. And then I noticed the dams on the Kurrum River, alongside which we were travelling. The water in them was tilting upwards at an angle of 20 degrees! Then the penny dropped. The whole valley, road included, was rising at a gradient of one in five.

73

Parachinar, at an altitude of nearly 7,000 feet, was covered in snow. We spent the weekend in a very comfortable Dak bungalow, piling fuel on the welcoming log fire and I took Christmas services on the Sunday. It was almost a second honeymoon.

Once when I was ministering in Waziristan, Marjorie accompanied me to Bannu and stayed there with Mr Low, the District Commissioner, and his delightful family, but mostly she stayed at home in Kohat. However, she was never left alone in the bungalow at night.

Some years earlier an officer's wife, Mrs Ellis, and her daughter Molly had been alone in their bungalow after dark when Pathan raiders had murdered Mrs Ellis and carried Molly away to a hide-out in the mountains. She was eventually rescued by the courage of Nurse Starr of the Church Missionary Society, who, without military escort and accompanied only by a guide and her servant, was led on foot to where Molly was held and persuaded her captors to release her. It is one of the epic stories of the Frontier.

A consequence was, however, that thereafter no white woman was allowed to sleep alone at night in the cantonment. In the afternoon of my going on trek, a camel bearing the stick-guard's bedding would arrive at 17 The Mall, and the stick-guard themselves would arrive soon afterwards. Six aged pensioners, they slept on the verandah in my absence, doing duty two by two and spitting and coughing throughout the night. All this stopped when the Nicholsons came to share our bungalow.

In September 1943, Marjorie went on trek herself. Our first-born was due in October and it was arranged that she should go to St Stephen's, the Cambridge Mission Hospital in Delhi, for her confinement. She had herself worked for a short period at the hospital as Bible lady and the staff were her friends. On October 15th Peter was born. It was a painful delivery. Forceps had to be used and Marjorie was very weak afterwards. Six weeks later, accompanied by Peter and a nurse, she arrived back at Kohat. The servants gathered, congratulations were showered on her and all was triumph. He was a lovely baby. Indeed, when Miss Mahy, the parish worker at St James' of whom you have heard already, first saw him she held up her hands in amazement. 'But he is beautiful,' she exclaimed. 'I cannot understand it!'

Marjorie proved splendid as a chaplain's wife, and her ability to speak grammatically correct Urdu won her many non-Christian friends. In addition, she was always herself, natural and friendly, and she helped me out – as she still does – of many awkward situations. One example was the time when I entirely forgot an engagement I had made to meet a local Indian contractor at the bungalow. I arrived some 30 minutes late. Naturally, I was full of apologies but he dismissed them with a wave of his hand. 'No worry. No worry,' he exclaimed. 'While I was waiting I had very nice intercourse with your wife!'

About this time, my responsibilities in the Chaplaincy were changed. The Chaplain in Razmak took over North Waziristan and I became responsible for Dera Ismael Khan and Tank, the Army camps at Manzai and Wana, and the forts of the South Waziristan Scouts, in particular their headquarters at Jandola. The switch from North Waziristan enriched me with a whole series of new experiences and contacts.

Dera Ismael Khan (DIK) was 80 miles south of Bannu as the crow flies, but reaching it entailed a thrice-interrupted all-night train journey. Karim and I would leave Kohat at dusk, change at Jand and two hours later catch the Bannu train as far as Mari-Indus, which we reached about midnight. By this time I was undressed and sound asleep, stretched out on the sleeping-couch. Karim would wake me and I would transfer to an easy chair while Karim would make up my bed on a couch in the Mari-Indus waiting-room – or, if it was hot, on the platform itself. He erected a mosquito-net and when all was ready summoned me. Three hours on, my sleep was again disturbed. The train to Multan had arrived. Again the bedding-transfer operation. At daybreak we disembarked for DIK but DIK itself was on the further bank of the mighty Indus River. In the winter months the width of the Indus was no more than 800 yards and we bumped across a pontoon bridge in a railway bus. But when the spring sun had melted the Himalayan snow and the Indus was two miles wide, it was a different matter. We gathered on a jetty and awaited the arrival of an ancient paddle-steamer, not unlike the Mississippi show boats in the USA. Three hours later, hopefully, I was breakfasting in the Army Mess and my day had started.

Dera Ismael Khan was an important centre, the chief town in its district and the Army headquarters, and I would time my arrival to allow me one or two days' visiting before taking Sunday services at St Thomas'.

St Thomas' was a large Victorian mock-Gothic church, but except on special occasions attendance was voluntary and congregations small, and I was never sorry to continue 60 miles north-west to Tank, pronounced 'Tonk'. The Christian community there were few in numbers but very warm and friendly. The Political Officer had his headquarters in Tank and was in my time Gerald Curtis, whose brother, Geoffrey Curtis CR, had been Vice-Principal of Dorchester Missionary College in my student days. His wife Decima, 'last of ten', was a charming hostess, and while I was in Tank I was always invited to stay with them.

In the cantonment was a small Church Missionary Hospital run for years by 'The Three Ladies of Tank' – Dr Madeline Shearburn, Vera Studd and Ethel Haddow. They were a marvellous trio, and Pathans from miles around would come to them for treatment. Once a week 'Madie' Shearburn and her orderly would drive out in the Mission van to a district clinic. Now there is a saying on the Frontier: 'Take a risk once and you will get away with it. Take it twice and you chance your luck. Take it a third time and you're for it.' Madie Shearburn went at the same time and on the same day each week to the same clinic and was never harmed.

The value of her work was recognised and *Pukhtun wali* – the Pathan's code of honour – was sufficient protection. The story, indeed, is told that when the Second World War broke out and Madeline was stranded in England and unable to return to her post, urgent calls were made to the Foreign Office in London. She was of more value in maintaining peace in the district, it was claimed, than four battalions of soldiers – a few days later she was flown back to India by the RAF.

Getting to Manzai, my next centre after Tank, was not too difficult, but after that, unless the Political Officer gave permission, travelling was by Army convoy, and getting to Jandola and beyond that to Wana was often a problem. On one occasion the Frontier Police had a truck passing through and offered to take me on to Jandola for an extra two gallons of petrol. But would the Army give it? No. Giving petrol to the police was not provided for by Army regulations, but under them they were allowed to provide me with an armed escort. So an armoured car and two lorries, each manned by 20 sepoys were laid on, and Karim and I arrived at Jandola in style. Petrol consumption at least 12 gallons. No comment.

Stationed at Jandola was Dr Iliffe, the Scout doctor commonly called 'The Leech'. His wife, Vera, was a daughter of Henry Scott-Holland, later knighted, a CMS doctor who travelled the length and breadth of the Frontier giving sight to the blind by removing cataracts. She lived in DIK and was a faithful member of the church there.

One day Dr Iliffe came into the Jandola Mess, quietly amused. His help had been requested at a distant outpost and he had been travelling in a Scout truck carrying food and medical supplies when they were ambushed in a narrow ravine. They had turned a corner and found the road blocked by rocks. Hurriedly the driver put the truck into reverse while shots rang out on every side. *Bang, bang, bang*! from the mountain top. *Bang, bang, bang*! from the rifles of the guard squatting on the transport's roof. When out of range of hostile bullets, the truck slowed to a halt and a *jamidar* climbed down from the roof and saluted the doctor. 'Good shooting, sahib!' he exclaimed. 'None of us hurt; none of them hurt. Good shooting, sahib!' Maybe some of the Scouts were blood-brothers of the hostiles, in which case had there been casualties a blood feud could have followed.

Also amusing was another story related to me at an outpost. Carrier pigeons were employed by the Scouts for carrying messages and had to be trained. On one exercise some trainee pigeons were taken in a truck to a hilltop, ringed with a message and bidden to fly home. As they did, the truck too started for home and bets were taken on which would reach home first, truck or pigeons. It proved a dead heat. When the truck duly arrived the pigeons were found perching on the cab's roof!

Wana was not a fort but a large Army camp sited on a plateau at the foot of the mountains bordering Afghanistan's frontier. An intriguing feature as one approached the camp was a large white board beautifully lettered. It so intrigued me that I pulled out my camera. The lettering read:

WANA
GARDEN CITY AND MONASTERY
Paradise for the Married; Safety for the Single
BUILD YOUR OWN CELL!

During my chaplaincy, the General from DIK and a senior officer flew in to Wana and took their wives with them. The impact was considerable. Women walking around in Wana!

Wana was so inaccessible that the Indian Air Force stationed in Kohat offered to fly me out at Easter and Christmas to give those who wished the sacrament. They flew old Audax planes with open cockpits and I remember the instructions given me by the pilot on my first flight: 'Keep this blanket over your head – it will be pretty cold – and cling tightly to it. And keep your feet off those two wires [wire cables running along the floor of the cockpit] – they work the rudder!'

Those were the days! Later, Spitfires were substituted for the Audax but were never popular. They flew too fast. Helicopters – not then available – would have been ideal.

On my return flight, the pilot would circle low over 17 The Mall so that if Marjorie was about I could wave to her.

On one occasion I was walking back across the Tarmac with the Indian pilot when a bearer from the control tower ran to meet us and handed the pilot a message. He read it through and his brow puckered, 'Jesus Christ,' he exclaimed, 'I've got to go back again.' I continued on alone while he returned to the aircraft, and I reflected sadly. 'And Jesus Christ I suppose, is the one thing he has learnt from his Christian companions concerning Christianity – a new English swear-word.' How I hate the way we take God's name in vain. Muslims don't.

I have told you of the comings and goings of a journey by rail from Kohat to Dera Ismail Khan and of the good offices of Karim Shah in helping me to reach my destination successfully. Only when travelling back alone from Lahore after attending the Diocesan Synod in 1944 did I realise how much I owed to him.

On this occasion I reached Rawalpindi by a local train from Lahore to Peshawar and got myself and my baggage safely on to the platform. The branch line to Kohat starts from Pindi, and finding the Kohat train already drawn up on a side-platform, I climbed into an empty compartment, unpacked my bedding, undressed and made myself at home. We were not due to leave until after the arrival of the Frontier Mail around 10 p.m. But at 11 p.m. the train had still not started, so I slipped my white cassock over my pyjamas, slipped my feet into sandals and walked down the platform to investigate. Having found the stationmaster, I enquired how much longer it would be before the Frontier Mail arrived.

'It's very late tonight, sahib. Kohat train's not going to wait for it.'

'What!'

'No, it's starting any minute now.'

I turned about and strode as briskly along the platform as pride permitted. Ahead I could see the red rear light of the guard's van on the Kohat train. I walked and walked and walked and then I came to the end of the platform! The train had left.

The stationmaster was sympathetic. There was still another station on the main line before the Kohat line diverged. He would telegraph the stationmaster there to collect my luggage from the Kohat train when it arrived. I could pick them up on a local train to Peshawar due in three hours' time, and there were buses from Peshawar to Kohat. Simple. But naturally it did not work out like that. Such arrangements never do in India. The stationmaster at the next stop failed to locate my luggage and it travelled on to Kohat.

But all ended happily. At Peshawar I picked up with some British aircraftmen who took me to their station mess, and later that morning an RAF truck took me in to Kohat to the railway station. It was past midday but the train I had missed was still drawn up in the platform and my bedding, my luggage, my personal papers and my wallet were still undisturbed. Not a thing was missing! Throughout the whole time no one had realised that I was wearing only pyjamas under my cassock and that my sole worldly possession was a pocket handkerchief.

My two-year chaplaincy at Kohat was now nearly completed, and on its completion I was instructed to proceed to Risalpur, north-east of Kohat, but still in the North-West Frontier Province. Before I left Kohat, however, a shooting tragedy had cast a gloom over the whole cantonment.

In a bungalow on the Mall a few hundred yards from ours lived a British Army major, Henry Connolly, his wife Bibs, and their small son Michael. One morning Brigadier de Butts came hurrying to 17 The Mall to find me. Half an hour earlier Major Connolly, on duty, had slipped back to his bungalow and left his loaded revolver on the hall table.

Though warned never to touch firearms, five-year-old Michael had seen it there, picked it up and gazed down the barrel. There was a loud explosion and poor little Michael was dead. Bibs was out shopping and neighbours carried the little body into a bedroom and began clearing up all traces of the tragedy. They were just finishing when someone said, 'Quick! Here comes Bibs.' She was just entering the gate and I hurried to meet and, if possible, delay her.

For a few minutes I engaged her in casual conversation. Then she said she must get inside and I had to warn her that an accident had happened. 'Is it Henry?' she asked. 'Is it Henry?' and she pushed me aside.

Why did it happen? Why didn't God prevent it? One always asks such questions on such occasions. There is no completely satisfactory answer but in this case I like to believe that God did try to prevent what happened but came up against the stumbling-block of human free will. I like to believe that he was saying to Michael from the moment he picked up the revolver, 'No. No, Michael, it's not allowed. You mustn't,' but poor little Michael persisted.

He was a lovely little boy who for some unknown reason liked to be called Joey, and I remember how some months earlier I had taken a lesson in Sunday school on baptism and in it had stressed that we received our Christian names when christened. 'Before you were baptised,' I had said to Michael, 'God only knows you as your father's and mother's little boy – the new Connolly baby – but now that you are baptised he knows you as Michael.'

Michael was unconvinced. 'No he doesn't,' he replied. 'He knows me as Joey.' Poor Michael. Poor Joey. He is now with God himself in God's eternal kingdom.

In October 1944 we moved to Risalpur.

Risalpur, four miles north of Nowshera, had ceased to be an important chaplaincy. Before Army mechanisation, it had been a cavalry station, and a large garrison church, capable of seating 500, had been built in it. The cavalry had gone and a detachment of the Royal Signals and of the RAF were the main military presence, but there was no airfield and no hangars. The RAF personnel were cartographers engaged in producing maps for the RAF, more especially aerial maps of Japan now that Japan had entered the war against us.

Outstations of the chaplaincy were Mardan, once a cavalry remount station, and Malakand in the Swat Valley, headquarters of an Army brigade. These were 10 and 50 miles north of Risalpur. Further north still were Scout headquarters at Gilgit and Chitral.

Gilgit was politically in Kashmir but by mutual consent was administered by the NWFP. Within a radius of 65 miles from Gilgit are eight peaks of over 24,000 feet, including the beautiful Nanga Parbat (26,650 feet). Nowhere else in the world are there so many lofty peaks, deep valleys and long glaciers – except possibly in the neighbouring state of Chitral. The size of Wales, the state of Chitral possesses 42 mountains of over 20,000 feet! Both Gilgit and Chitral were snowbound by the time I settled in at Risalpur and to my great disappointment I was not able to visit them.

Christmas Day 1944, I spent in Risalpur. The garrison church at Risalpur was so large that I wondered how we could possibly decorate it adequately, but the church bearer and malis were well-trained. They cut down and decorated 20-feet fir trees to bring Christmas to the nave. (What did they do with them afterwards? I suspect they used them for firewood – one of their perks.) And they made the chancel glorious with six-foot poinsettias. Neither Marjorie nor I will ever forget them.

Holy Communion early in the morning was followed by a Christmas Day family service, and to wind up we held an open evening in our bungalow. 'Come and bring a friend.' About 15 came. Most were young marrieds, homesick for their families in England, and Peter, aged 15 months, was a great attraction. One by one, guests produced from their wallets family photographs. The evening proved a great success.

I went by bus to Mardan a few days later. Mardan's

importance lay in the past and there were only a score or so of Christians living there. Among them were Major and Mrs Christensen. Major Christensen was a wartime soldier who before being recruited had been pastor of a Lutheran mission running a small hospital in Marden. Although the area was normally peaceful, the hospital had been the scene a few years earlier of two vicious murders.

A local Pathan nurse at the hospital had become interested in Christianity and declared a desire to be prepared for baptism. One morning, members of her family stole into the hospital. They killed her and wounded another nurse who tried to defend her. Then, bent on revenge, they entered the Christensens' bungalow. The Christensens themselves were out but their three-year-old son and his ayah were within. The ayah fled and the murderers killed the little boy. Then they took flight over the frontier. The little boy's body was buried in the churchyard attached to the church and his still-sorrowing parents pointed out the tiny grave to me. He was their only child.

> Paul and Barnabas (says St Luke) returned again to Lystra,
> Inconium and Antioch, confirming the souls of the disciples
> and exhorting them to continue in the faith and that
> we must through much tribulation enter the kingdom of
> God.

Acts 14: 21–22

As it was in apostolic times, so it still was on the Frontier – and so it still is in many countries today.

Soon after arriving in Risalpur, I made my first visit to Malakand. The area was quiet and I travelled on a tribal bus. Colonel Middleton was in command and he and his wife made me welcome. There was no church building, and services were held in the Officers' Mess – Evensong at night and Holy Communion next morning. I paid a second visit in Christmas week, when a carol service replaced Evensong, and planned a third visit in February. But before this could happen, Marjorie and Peter and I were en route for England.

The Second World War was drawing to a close. In May 1943 the Axis forces in North Africa had surrendered. In June 1944 D–Day had dawned, and by September most of France had been liberated. I had therefore written to Thomas Cook in New Delhi to enquire about the possibility of a passage home as soon as hostilities ended. They replied that they had already such a backlog of bookings that it would take them at least two years to clear them. I must be prepared to wait.

As I wasn't, I wrote to the Deputy Chaplain-General of the Forces, Fr William Stephenson, whom I knew, enquiring about the possibility of my obtaining a chaplaincy on a troop-ship.

Fr Stephenson was, maybe, an unusual choice for a Deputy Chaplain-General for, although a cheerful person who got on surprisingly well with almost everyone, he was an Anglican High Churchman with very definite and unusual views. Himself a celibate, he believed that all who saw themselves as priests should be as himself, and used to refer naughtily to chaplains wives as concubines. 'And how is your concubine keeping?' he would enquire cheerfully of a colleague. It is said that he was challenged to try this with the Bishop but wisely refused.

He was also a firm believer in the truth of the Roman Catholic Church and had a statue of the Pope on his mantelpiece with a candle alight before it. 'And who would that figure be?' a stern Presbyterian chaplain is said once to have asked him.

'It is of the Holy Father.'

'And what would that lighted candle be doing?'

'It is in his honour. It never goes out.'

The Scotsman drew a deep breath and then blew. 'Ah weel,' he commented with quiet satisfaction, 'It's oot noo.'

In answer to my letter, 'Steve' replied that chaplaincies on troop-ships were always possible. When would I be free to leave. When I informed him that my chaplaincy with the IEE was only temporary and I was free to leave at any time, he told me to hold myself in readiness and that I should get any books I wished to take home with me passed by the Censor in Peshawar.

I still had with me most of the copies of *In Journeyings Often* which I had had printed in Delhi and some 200 miscellaneous books I had brought back with me from Australia. I therefore prepared to have them submitted to the authorities for censorship in Peshawar, but before I had done this I found a remarkable letter pushed under my office door. It was dated 18.12.44 and addressed to me:

Chaplain, Risalpur Cantonment: Subject: Religious Aid, and began:

'Respected Dear Father,
        With due respect and humble submission I beg to bring these few sentences to your kind notice for a merciful consideration and kind orders.

I sighed. Another begging letter! But it wasn't. Or at any rate, not of the usual kind. He begged me to help him become a Christian. Because he wanted to become a Christian, his whole family, he declared, were furious with him. They had kept him without money and without clothes and never let him out of their sight. They called him a *Kafir* – one who goes out of his religion – and refused to eat with him.

O Father, (he continued) I am just like a piece of flesh between a crowd of Bull Dogs and it is past my powers to describe all about my past two years . . .
    My health has left me so that I am like a thin bunyan tree. I am so weak that I cannot go out or fly away from these cruel hawks.
    This is all due to make me forget the remembrance of my Holy Jesus but I promise on my honour that I am ready to die facing many a trouble but quite unable to give up the remembrance of Jesus. I am a Mohomaddan by race and Indian by blood and belong to a respected Syed family. I pray you, Father, to assist me as one of

your meanest servants and keep me from these troubles.

P.S. Don't disclose this matter up and until I am converted. If not these cruel Mohammadans will put me to death.

Hoping to receive an immediate and merciful reply,

SYED SIBHAY MOHAMAD SHUDDAU'

What was it all about? I sent him a short note saying I would be pleased to meet him and would help him if I could, and in due course he presented himself on my doorstep. He was a thin and ragged figure of medium height, no darker than a Greek or Spaniard, and this was his story:

His father, he said, was a surveyor in Risalpur Cantonment who three years before had moved with his family to Bangalore in South India to take up work with his brother. For the first year all went well but then out on a shopping expedition he had happened to see a Roman Catholic nun cycling in her habit through the bazaar. He was so surprised he waved to her and to his dismay she got off her cycle and asked him, 'Do you know me? Are you a Christian?' They had formed a friendship and he had begun secretly to attend Sunday school classes at the convent. One morning he was followed. The storm burst and all the woes of his letter fell on him. This had continued for 18 months and then his family had decided to return to Risalpur. He still persisted that he wished to be a Christian and he was kept a virtual prisoner in his parents' home.

He seemed genuine and I felt bound to help him. At the same time it was quite clear that it would be safe neither for him nor for my family if he stayed in Risalpur. I thought inevitably of the Christensens in Mardan and of the nurse's grave in the churchyard there and of the grave of their little child. No, somehow Sibhay must be smuggled out of Risalpur, but where could he go? I sounded out Christopher Robinson of the Cambridge Brotherhood in Delhi and learned by return of post that they were ready, on my recommendation, to take him under their wing for a trial period. The sooner he went, the better. And so we made our plans.

By this time my books in eight tin boxes were ready for inspection by the Censor. An Army truck left Risalpur daily for Peshawar in the early hours of the morning and the Station Staff Officer agreed that I could accompany my books on it. I got word to Sibhay, and the night before we were due to leave he knocked on my window. I went to the door and gazed in amazement. Gone were his filthy rags. He was dressed quite beautifully. 'But how?' I exclaimed.

'They are my father's' he replied. 'He has lots of clothes. He will not miss them.'

This did not seem to me a particularly good way to begin the first stage of one's Christian pilgrimage but I let it pass!

We locked up the bungalow carefully and at daybreak next morning we left the cantonment, I in the cab beside the driver, my tin boxes, sundry Army supplies and equipment and Sibhay in the back. The truck, fortunately, was covered, so no one saw him.

At this stage of its journey from Delhi to Peshawar, the Grand Trunk Road runs parallel with the railway line, and halfway to Peshawar I asked the driver to stop at a wayside station and Sibhay descended. I had given him enough money for a ticket to Delhi but told him to buy a ticket not to Delhi but to an intermediate station, then change trains, buy another ticket and continue. One could not be too careful. He might have been traced to the wayside stop and his ultimate destination discovered. He said goodbye and that was the last I saw of him.

I am quite sure he obeyed the first part of my instructions – it was sensible. As to whether, having changed trains, he then bought a further ticket I felt less certain. In general then, and I suspect still, buying a railway ticket if one could avoid it was considered a needless luxury by India's poor.

When with the Cambridge Mission, I once criticised for carelessness a young Anglo-Indian Christian for having lost various valuable certificates. 'But, Father,' he explained, 'it was most unfortunate. I was on a railway journey and the certificates were in my box and suddenly a ticket-collector appeared at the end of the carriage. I had to leave the train quickly – it was still moving – and I had not time to take my box with me.'

I was a little apprehensive of any repercussions as a result of my helping Sibhay but I made my own St Paul's advice to the Philippians: not to be anxious about anything but with prayer and thanksgiving to make my requests known to God. Any day, the expected telegram could arrive.

It arrived on February 23rd. I was to report to Poona (Puna) transit camp in six days' time. We reckoned we must leave Risalpur by the afternoon train from Nowshera on Sunday the 25th and began packing frantically. Even so, at the start of the Sunday morning service in the garrison church we were only half-packed, so at its close I appealed for volunteers. As a result half a dozen RAF and Signal boys descended on the bungalow, and one by one the remaining boxes were filled higgledy-piggledy – clothes, pictures, china, shoes, blankets, what have you, in they went – and the boxes were corded. Two tongas were waiting at the door, the first for Marjorie, Peter and myself and our personal luggage, the second for the heterogeneous collection of tin boxes. Together we raced for Nowshera.

When we arrived the train was already in and about to leave. We bundled in, then sank back exhausted; and thus, with beating hearts we said goodbye to the Frontier, I with a sense of relief. Sibhay's father had learnt of my involvement in his son's escape. In fact, in what was probably a moment of foolishness, I had written telling him not to worry about his son, his son was safe; and I had half-expected him to present himself on our doorstep, maybe peaceably, maybe not.

Six months later, when Marjorie, Peter and I were settled temporarily in Tottenham, I received a letter from my brother Jim in Delhi. Independence was approaching and all Delhi – all India, he said – was in a state of turmoil. Servants were almost unobtainable. All the Brotherhood servants had given notice, his own were leaving at the end of the week and he was worried about Doreen, who was expecting a second child in the autumn. He concluded:

> As for Sibhay, you will have heard how he had to be sent to Calcutta because there was a price of Rs.700 on his head alive or Rs.400 if dead. He was traced to Calcutta, where the Oxford Mission thought well of him but it was too dangerous for him to stay with them. So he came back here and was baptised in St Thomas' Church, and left the same day under his new Christian name. I hear that he is now in Lahore working for the Civil and Military Gazette where Ted Tilt is keeping an eye on him.

And so he passes out of view. I still remember and admire him. He had left father and mother, his home and everything he had to follow Christ. I thank God for him.

We were several days in the transit camp but we welcomed the rest and the opportunity it gave to pack and repack our boxes and to paint our names on them, as required.

One evening word was given. We were leaving for Bombay next morning. The troop-ship we boarded there proved to be the *Capetown Castle*, the flagship of the Union Castle fleet fitted out for wartime duties. Few cabins remained; multi-bunk sleeping-decks were the norm. As Ship's Chaplain, however, I had been allotted a long, narrow cabin with a porthole, and Marjorie was able to prepare Peter's food on a small paraffin stove we had brought with us – illegally, we later discovered – and we travelled in comfort.

My duties were nominal. I was really only on board in case of emergencies, and we had none.

Our only excitement was after reaching Gibraltar. We found a convoy of some 20 ships awaiting our arrival, and sailed almost immediately, escorted by three destroyers. From now on we had to sleep in our clothes, always carry a life-jacket, ship's rations and a plastic flask of water, and wear an ingenious red electric lamp in a button-hole, in case we were thrown into the sea at night. I remember questioning member of the crew about the necessity of carrying drinking water. 'Surely the lifeboats will carry water.'

'Sir,' he replied, 'have you counted the number of lifeboats? And do you know how many passengers we are carrying? You've a hope!'

From time to time a destroyer would race off to a suspected danger spot and drop depth-charges, but the convoy never changed course and no one seemed particularly worried. Nonetheless we all gave a sigh of relief when in the afternoon of March 29th we berthed in Liverpool Docks. An hour later, to our amazement, we put to sea again. Night was coming on and we were safer, we were told, out at sea than in the docks.

We returned at dawn next morning and disembarkation began. It was the last Good Friday of the Second World War.

9

Tottenham Interlude

It was good to be back in England, even though an England still at war and one quickly noticed evidence of it. The buildings still standing were with rare exceptions unpainted and soot-begrimed, and everywhere one saw tell-tale empty spaces – bomb-sites cleared of rubble and made colourful by masses of pink willow-herb which seemed indigenous to them. Incidentally, though we did not know it at the time, we had arrived back in Liverpool three days after the last flying bomb landed on England. It fell on Smithfield Market and there were many casualties.

The *Capetown Castle* had on its passenger-list the Anglo Indian wives of not a few aircraftmen. In India, England had had no more devoted children. They had studied her traditions and her scenery, they had read avidly about her in magazines, and though they had only known of her by hearsay, they had always spoken of her as 'home'. As we entered the docks on March 29th, they lined the decks eager for the first glimpse of the 'home' of their dreams. It was a cold, dismal day. Did their hearts sink, one wondered, as they surveyed the grime and devastation which greeted them?

I myself had three pressing concerns. Settled in the train rattling towards London, Marjorie and I had time to consider them. We were back in England, yes; but we were homeless and practically penniless. I had no work to go to and Marjorie was four months pregnant. But blessed are the young in heart! We had no fears for the future and God saw us through in a quite marvellous manner.

We had planned to stay with Marjorie's brother and sister-in-law, Jim and Gwen Kellaway. Unfortunately, we found on arrival that Clair, their younger son, had measles, to which Marjorie must not be exposed, so we lodged two nights with a friend and contacted my father and stepmother by phone. They had been blitzed out of their home in East Sheen and moved into a small terrace house in London Road, Isleworth, which my father owned and which happened to be vacant. It being an emergency, they squeezed us in.

Marjorie's parents had also moved with her younger sister Thelma from West Norwood to Cinderford in the Forest of Dean. Her elder sister Dorothy, whose husband, Eustace Middleton James (always known as Billy), was a prisoner of war in Germany, had also moved with her two children to Cinderford to be near her parents. Dorothy had at once got busy – knowing Dorothy, you bet she did! – and a few days later wrote to say that a neighbour of hers, a Mrs Whittle, living with her two daughters aged 20 and 15, would be pleased to help. Mrs Whittle was a kind, motherly soul, an absolute dear, and although by the time we arrived Peter had developed whooping cough, she made not the slightest fuss and gave us the warmest of welcomes. She died in 1989 – God rest her soul.

With a roof over our heads, my next step was to seek means of support. I travelled back to London and reported to SPG. When they had seconded me to the Brotherhood of the Good Shepherd 11 years earlier, they had taken my name off their lists. They were ready to put it back again but said that with the war still on, all vacancies overseas were problematic and I would be well advised to seek temporary work in England. They suggested that I write to the Bishop of London and also to the Rector of Bedale in Yorkshire, who had recently written to them asking them if they had any missionaries home on furlough willing to help him for a few weeks in his Yorkshire parish.

I wrote to both. The Rector of Bedale replied saying

'Come at once'; the Bishop of Stepney, on behalf of his diocesan, to say that the large parish of All Hallows, Tottenham, was falling vacant at the end of April. The Priory, the Vicar's residence, would be unfurnished and must be kept vacant for the future incumbent. Could I be responsible for the parish during the interregnum and find my own accommodation? I replied, gratefully accepting.

By this time I was in Bedale. A Canon Hodgson was Rector. He was a bachelor and one of the few remaining 'squarsons' in the Church of England – squire of the village and also its parson. He drove about his parish in a pony and trap which were his pride and joy, and I preached for him at the VE Thanksgiving Service in St Gregory's, Bedale.

I spent six weeks happily with him, but early in June returned to stay with my father and stepmother in Isleworth in order to seek furnished acommodation for Marjorie, Peter and myself in Tottenham. I set out hopefully. There were several estate agents operating in the Tottenham area and I journeyed up from Isleworth seeking their advice. After just one day I realised that, short of a miracle, I would have to think again. Rented accommodation for myself, at a price, was, I was told, possible; rented accommodation for a family in a furnished house, out of the question. The war in Europe was over. Evacuated owners and tenants were flocking back to the cities to re-occupy their properties. Thousands were seeking re-accommodation. What hope had I?

And then I went up to London to attend the first of two SPG Annual Services in St Paul's Cathedral.

When we surrender our lives to God and put ourselves in God's hands, looking back on the past we can generally discern God's hand working in it. We exclaim with St Paul, 'Yes, all things do work together for good to them that love God,' and we give thanks and take courage. That is so when we look back. It is often not so easy to see God's hand at work in events still unfolding. When we do, we are brought to our knees in awe and humility. So it was with my house-hunting in Tottenham.

After attending the SPG service in St Paul's, I poured out

with the rest of the congregation into the courtyard and was standing looking vaguely around when a voice behind me said, 'Why, Geoffrey, what are you doing here?' It was Ethel Gotch of the Cambridge Mission to Delhi, home from India on furlough. I explained my plight – my hopeless house-hunting in Tottenham.

'Will you be coming here again tomorrow?' she asked. I answered 'Yes' and she replied, 'Meet me here at the same time tomorrow. I may be able to help.' She said nothing more and I was not unduly excited – so many leads in the past had led to nothing. But not this one.

She met me again in the courtyard the following morning and all was settled. We talk about 'Acts of God' as if they are invariably horrendous – droughts, floods, tornadoes, earthquakes etc., etc. Ethel Gotch recounted on that Thursday morning God working benevolently in a way which took my breath away then – and still does.

Ethel's sister and brother-in-law, a Mr and Mrs Green, had lived in Tottenham until blitzed out of their house two years previously. Then they had gone to live with another of Ethel's sisters, living alone in Palmer's Green. This sister had since had a stroke and could no longer be left. Meanwhile, the Greens' house in Tottenham had been repaired and a fortnight earlier they had received notice from Tottenham Council that unless they reoccupied within four weeks, it would be requisitioned. This was the last thing Mr and Mrs Green wanted, so would Marjorie and I occupy in their stead for the time being? It was less than 800 yards from All Hallows Church and completely furnished, even to a refrigerator – a novelty in 1945. They would be happy with 40 shillings per week rent, if we thought we could afford it! Our worries were over.

> Why art thou so full of heaviness, O my soul? And why
> art thou so disquieted within me? O put your trust in God:
> for I will yet thank him which is the help of my countenance
> and my God.'
>
> *Psalm 42: 6; 15*

94

Our days in Tottenham passed happily. It was a parish of 20,000 and had had at the beginning of the year a staff of three. These had all scattered and for the next six months I was fully occupied in pastoral duties, Sunday services and Saturday weddings. The 'boys' were returning from the Front. Their sweethearts were awaiting them, and if couples wished to live together society still insisted: first they must marry. The result was a flood of weddings. On no Saturday did I have less than two and on some I had as many as six.

At that time weddings had to be completed by 5 p.m. and on one Saturday I had five in a row at 30-minute intervals – a little like at the average crematorium today. At 2 p.m., however, the party due then, failed to appear. At 2.20 p.m. the guests due for the 2.30 p.m. wedding began arriving. Then at 2.25 p.m. the agitated 2 p.m. bride and bridegroom entered. Their taxi had let them down. Before we had sorted things out, the 2.30 p.m. bridal pair arrived and I suggested a double wedding. Neither side favoured one, so I told the 2 p.m. couple that the 2.30 p.m. wedding must go ahead as arranged but, fortunately, I would still be able to fit them in at 4 p.m. They sat silently at the back of the church for a while, then left. They returned looking much happier just before 4 p.m. and it was fairly obvious where they had been meanwhile!

Most couples were very well-behaved. Only on one occasion did I have to call a couple to order. They had clearly been drinking and despite my warnings continued whispering and sniggering, the best man being the chief offender. Finally, I left them standing at the chancel step and retired to my stall. After five minutes I returned and said, 'If you are prepared to behave, I am prepared to continue.' I had no further trouble.

I had a table and chairs placed in the study in the Priory and there I interviewed marriage couples and received callers. One morning a girl of 17 giving her name as Mary came to see me. She had, she said, been turned out of her home and had nowhere to sleep. I promised to do what I could, but when she returned in the afternoon I had still failed to find her a bed. I had phoned all the local hostels. All were full. I also phoned the local probation officer. He knew Mary's family well. They were hard-drinking and often in trouble with the law. He said that there would probably be fighting if Mary tried to return. 'We have a spare bed,' I told Mary. 'You had better stay with us tonight.'

She stayed on and we grew very fond of her. She worked for a car-spraying firm on weekdays and when not working, scrubbed the floors, which Marjorie was beginning to find difficult, did the washing, played with Peter and made herself invaluable.

She had one sister of whom she was immensely proud. As a family she explained, they were only working class. But not Ella! 'Ella's real posh.' She wanted us to meet her, so one evening we invited her to supper. I don't know quite what we expected. Someone rather loud and flashy, I fancy. But no. Ella was beautifully turned out. Her voice was pleasant and refined and she had both style and good manners. I happened to know that she had had an illegitimate baby – kept very quiet in those days. But when the conversation turned to having babies (not unnaturally, in view of Marjorie's condition), Ella never turned a hair.

'I think it must be lovely,' she said, 'to have a baby.'

She was a shorthand typist and engaged to her boss's son. I wished her quite genuinely every happiness and understood Mary's pride in her.

Later, Mary left spraying cars to become nanny to the child of a Doctor White in Southampton.

After she left, while I was still in charge of the parish, another unforgettable Mary came to spend a night with us.

'Mary Ball is paying Tottenham a visit,' said one of the churchwardens to me one Sunday. 'Could you and your wife put her up for the night? She's home from a mission hospital in China. Her parents were parishioners here and we've known Mary all her life but she is getting on now. She must be 50.'

Of course we said that we would be delighted, but inwardly we groaned; Oh dear, an aged missionary – it seemed like that to us, still in our thirties! But when the day arrived and a knock came on the door, Mary Ball proved dazzling – a mass of red hair and a vivacity which was infectious.

SPG later published a book about her, *Mary Who Couldn't Sit Still*, and it told the story of how when she was five and sitting with her elder sister in the pew of All Hallows, Tottenham, the second lesson had been from St Luke Chapter 1. Mary sat entranced, and when the reader came to the words of the Benedictus 'And thou, child, shalt be called the prophet of the Highest,' he paused and looked up, and it seemed to Mary that he was gazing straight at her.

'He means me,' she whispered excitedly to her sister, 'he means me! I'm to be a prophet of the Highest!'

'Not you, silly,' replied her sister scornfully. 'John the Baptist.'

But the memory remained and later Mary, trained as a nurse, was sent to be in charge of an SPG hospital in North China. She spoke of some of her experiences later that evening.

The hospital had been sacked more than once by the bands of brigands which at that time terrorised the area, and when Japan entered the war the Japanese took the hospital over, and Mary and her staff, together with other local missionaries, were interned.

The Japanese were not unkind but the rules were strict. Mary was concerned that the babies in the camp were not getting sufficient calcium, and to provide calcium they used to grind up the shells of eggs which a Trappist monk, against all rules, contrived to obtain for them. One day he was caught. The Commandant called together the prisoners. This, he declared was a serious crime and must be visited with the severest punishment. 'You,' he said to the prisoner, 'are sentenced to six months' solitary confinement.'

To the Commandant's bewilderment, the whole camp roared with laughter. Trappist monks are dedicated to complete silence 24 hours a day, and this particular monk's daily complaint had been that he was surrounded by so much noise. He wasn't used to it. If only he could be silent with God for a while! 'For so he givest his beloved rest.' *Psalm 127: 3*

We heard in September that Fr Wallace Clarke from the Blackburn diocese had been appointed to All Hallows and that he, with his wife and two daughters, would be moving into the Priory in six weeks' time.

Before that happened, however, we entertained another visitor and our second son was born.

The visitor was, like Jo Chapman, a friend of Marjorie's from her College of the Ascension days in Selly Oak, Birmingham. When in 1937 SPG had sent Marjorie to India and Jo Chapman to Burma, they had sent this other friend, Hope Onslow, to Canada to assist Monica Storrs and to be a 'Companion of the Peace'.

In 1929 Monica Storrs, the delicately reared daughter of the Dean of Rochester, himself born in Nova Scotia, had been persuaded by Eva Hassell to join her in ministering to the spiritual and physical needs of the settlers in the Peace River district.

'God's own country' was how the old colonel at Dorchester had described it to me. This may have been true of the Peace as it came tumbling down from its source in the Rocky Mountains to begin its long journey to Lake Athabasca, but by the time it had entered its more eastern stretches such a description was suspect. The district Monica Storrs came to in 1929 was an empty wilderness without towns, with few roads or schools; a land of hot, dusty summers and un-predictable sub-Arctic winters; an untamed land yet, withal, of unexpected grandeur.

Eva Hassell had founded the Peace Caravan Mission, and her caravans went wherever there were roads but there were isolated squatters and prospectors where no roads went by. Some had families and these Monica Storrs and her helpers visited, occasionally on foot but mostly by horse, and they became known affectionately by the people of the Peace as 'God's Galloping Girls'. In 1937 Hope became one of them. Now on furlough in England she came to stay with us in

Tottenham. With her in England was a Robert Symons.

In 1914, when he was 16, Bob had gone to Canada from England. He became a ranch-hand in the Cypress Hills in Saskatchewan and from then on, apart from war service, spent all his time on the prairies and in the Peace River district of British Colombia as cowboy, rancher, game-warden and naturalist. He met Monica Storrs and her 'Galloping Girls' and came with Hope to England in 1945 on a special mission. He wished to marry Hope – who wouldn't? – but for many years his wife in Canada had been a patient in a mental asylum with no hope of recovery. Since insanity was a ground for divorce in England but not in Canada, he had come to England.

Hope came from a county family, was a dedicated Christian, and had been strictly brought up. She was uncertain about marrying a divorced person and welcomed the opportunity of talking to me about it.

The Church of England teaching on divorce was stricter then than now and I put to her the official and, I believed, the scriptural position – that divorce was to be avoided because (i) it is the breaking of a solemn vow to God of faithfulness to a partner 'for better for worse, for richer for poorer, in sickness and in health' till death comes; (ii) because it breaks up families and is painful for any children; and (iii) because it is contagious – every divorce sanctioned makes another divorce more likely. I accepted then, as now, that the Church had no mandate to legislate for those not its members, but I put it to Hope that its own members were called to set an example; that in some cases divorce might be the lesser of two evils but it was always an evil; and that all that I said applied to anyone marrying a divorced person. She must do what she believed was right. It was obviously a matter for prayer.

In the event the decision Hope had in mind never arose. Bob Symons had become a Canadian citizen; insanity was not a ground for divorce in Canada and no English court could grant him one.

When in 1979 I was in the Northern Territory of Australia

and, as a temporary chaplain at Darwin Hospital, did regular ward visiting, I was surprised how often I got the answer 'As good as' when I enquired of a patient if he was married. This was the status Bob and Hope settled for, and they even persuaded an avant-garde Anglican priest in Cambridge – Canon Raven, no less – to read the marriage Service over them.

Robert's marital status was well-known in the Peace River district and many eyebrows were no doubt raised when, on their return from England, Bob and Hope set up house together. Nevertheless, they lived at peace with God and in great happiness. The Church, it has been said, is bound by the laws it enacts, but God isn't – and so it proved. When some years later the first Mrs Symons died, Robert and Hope married and Hope became Mrs Symons *de jure* as well as de facto.

Robert died in 1973 and Hope went to live in Stilton, a tiny settlement north of Regina, where she became Bob's executor, overseeing the publication in England of his many books. Among them: *Many Trials, The Broken Snare, Still the Wind Blows* and *Where the Wagon Led*, all illustrated by his own line-drawings and paintings. Hope was also responsible for the publication in Canada of The *Peace River Diaries of Monica Storrs 1929-31* under the title of *God's Galloping Girls*. Bob was collecting together the material on which the book is based at the time of his death. Its publication was Hope's tribute to him. In a small way what I have written above is my tribute to Hope.

After her stay with us in Tottenham, Marjorie corresponded regularly with her and she came to see us more than once when on visits to England after Bob's death. Her letters and her visits were always a delight. She radiated life and courage. She died of Parkinson's Disease five years ago, and the world is poorer for her going. Thank you, Lord, for her and for all she achieved in the life you gave her.

Thursday, September 13th, was a big day for Marjorie, for on it our second child was born. A week earlier Marjorie had entered the Salvation Army's Mothers' Home in Hackney and Peter had been entrusted to the care of a friend, Rose, whom he adored. But the 'Christopher-to-be' was slow in coming and so on the morning of the thirteenth, Marjorie was given an EMB (enema, medication and bath). It did the trick. When I paid my daily evening visit, I was told that she was still in the Labour Ward but I could visit her.

With some trepidation I entered but found Marjorie quite calm and collected. 'What was all this about the dreadful pangs of childbirth?'

I kissed her and then she said, 'What do you think of him?'

'Who?' I asked. I am not, I confess the most observant of men – some would say that was the understatement of the year! – and it was only then that I noticed that there was a cot at the end of the bed and in it my second-born.

He was baptised Christopher John in All Hallows Church a few weeks later. He howled the whole of the service! Wallace Clarke was officiating and after ten minutes of deafening noise he said to Marjorie, 'I shan't object if you take him outside till the actual baptising,' and Marjorie retired with her howling bundle into the porch. She returned when summoned and Christopher was duly baptised and signed with the sign of the Cross. Then it was to the porch again. At Dorchester Missionary College in a pastoralia lecture, the Principal had advised us: 'If at a Baptism a baby cries, do not raise your voice. The baby will always win.' Christopher certainly did.

He was being fed at the time on Ambrosia baby food supplied by the National Health and it wasn't agreeing with him. We changed, on advice, to cow's milk and all was well. Nevertheless, the first intelligible word he said was not the usual 'Mum' but 'More'. He was always hungry.

He was a most cuddly and lovable baby, with a turn for theology. He had a cat he adored and when he was just learning to speak, suddenly declared, quite out of the blue: 'Kitty no pray.' Pause, and then, 'Kitty can't. Kitty no hands.' You perceive the reasoning? It is bedtime and time for prayers. 'Christopher, close your eyes, put your hands together. . . .'

On another memorable occasion at breakfast he exclaimed, again quite out of the blue: 'You eat too much, you no go to heaven!' Had he heard of the sin of gluttony – he was always wanting more? Not at all. His reasoning was quite mundane. He repeated his statement: 'You eat too much, you no go to heaven,' and added, 'No, too heavy,' conjuring up a delightful image of angels struggling to lift Christopher skywards but failing to get him airborne.

Early in 1946 Fr Wallace Clarke invited Stephen Fell, a young priest from the Blackburn diocese, to join him, and I was strictly *de trop*. But Wallace Clarke was very kind and he allowed me to continue with him. Nonetheless, I had no wish to embarrass him and was in consequence very happy when a little later an opportunity came for me to work in Southern Rhodesia.

Donald Stowell, Wallace Clarke's predecessor, had left Tottenham to be Director of Missions in that diocese, and I had written to him regarding vacancies there. He replied saying there was an 'aching need' in the diocese for at least ten more priests. I took the letter to SPG, who said they knew Donald. The Diocese might need ten new priests, but they hadn't the money to pay even one of them. Nevertheless, it was agreed I could accept, and in May I received the offer to become Rector of Gatooma with Hartley and Priest-in-Charge of the St Paul's and Mhondoro Missions.

I had no idea what this involved or of the value of the stipend offered me. Marjorie and I simply assumed that the stipend would be sufficient and that God would give us strength according to our needs. So it always is for those who offer for service abroad in an unknown land – you never know until you actually arrive. It makes it all the more exciting. In September we sailed.

Before concluding this story of our stay in Tottenham, I would, however, add a footnote on a subject that occupied a good deal of my time and thought in the months before leaving – the subject of miracles.

102

As already explained, I had received a Bachelor of Arts pass degree as a result of my year at St Chad's College, Durham, in 1931. A Master of Arts degree did not follow automatically. To obtain it you were required to write a thesis. A fellow B.A., L.Th., of Durham, the Revd John Bishop, a contemporary of mine with the Cambridge Mission, of whom you have already heard, had qualified for his Master of Arts by submitting a paper on 'The History of the Urdu Language'. His success fired me. I had always been in two minds about the miracles in the Bible – how true were they? In what sense were we to understand them – and had wanted to study them properly. So I wrote to Durham University enquiring whether 'Miracles' would be a suitable subject for a thesis. The Theological Faculty replied suggesting the title of 'A Consideration of Miracle in Modern Thought', recommending certain books for study and requesting me in due course to submit an outline of how I proposed to proceed. I was to submit it to the Professor of Divinity, Canon Michael Ramsay, later to become Archbishop of Canterbury.

The outcome was a paper of some 9,000 words, and its writing had a lasting effect on my thinking. Where I had been uncertain, I was convinced; where I had been sceptical, I was believing.

Miracles, I argued, occurred constantly but were not against the Laws of Nature. How could they be? The so-called Laws of Nature were only man's viewpoint of God's unchanging will in creation. 'I am the Lord, I change not therefore you sons of Jacob are not consumed.' (*Malachi 3: 6*). Because of God's constancy, scientists, with God's help, are enabled to perform all kinds of wonders; through the fixity of creation, they attain their purposes. Through it equally, I argued, God is working his purpose out as age succeeds to age and, by the tranquil operation of his perpetual providence, answers our prayers and carries out the work of our salvation.

As to Bible miracles, each, I have come to believe, must be judged on its own merits. As a tale told and retold grows

103

in the retelling, so, no doubt, have the Bible's miracle stories. But they are rooted in truth, in some wonder in the hearts of the beholders which made them say: 'We have seen strange things today.' And the instinct 'This is God's doing and is marvellous in our eyes' was a right instinct. God is ever at work in his universe. It is only our eyes which are blind, our understanding which is faulty. 'Today if ye will hear my voice, harden not your hearts.'

My thesis was duly presented and accepted, but I had to receive my Master of Arts *in absentia*. When the next Convocation was summoned, Marjorie and I, Peter and Christopher were already in Southern Rhodesia.

10

First Months in Southern Rhodesia

SPG arranged for us to travel to Africa on the *Carnarvon Castle*, leaving Southampton for Cape Town at the end of September. Great excitement, of course, as relatives and friends saw us on to the boat-train at Waterloo. There was one final farewell at Southampton. We had boarded the liner and the gangways were about to be removed when a message came over the tannoy: 'Would the Revd and Mrs Lovejoy please go to the gangway area immediately.' What was this? Waiting for us was Mary, nanny to Dr White. She had heard that we were sailing to South Africa that day and had come to say goodbye. How pleased we were! Should Mary chance to read this, thank you and God bless you. And where are you now?

The *Carnarvon Castle* had been a wartime troop-ship and still awaited refitting. Men were bedded down in 'standees' (wooden bunks) on one deck; women similarly so on another. The only exceptions were mothers with children, who were grouped together in special cabins. In Marjorie's were five other mothers and 12 children, including several babies. Marjorie says crying was continuous throughout the night and there was little sleep. In comparison, we in the standees were fortunate and we slept the sleep of the just with no pricks of conscience, for husbands were barred from the family cabins after sunset.

We disembarked at Cape Town on October 12th. I can calculate the date because Peter was three years old on the third day of our journey up to Rhodesia. Children under three travelled free on all South African railways, which meant that we escaped paying for him – age is calculated from the day one starts travelling.

We enjoyed the journey. We slept once more as a family in a compartment all our own. Meals were brought to us and after the restrictions and rationing of England, food never tasted better – fresh tropical fruit for the asking!

A small group, consisting of my two churchwardens and the Methodist Minister and his wife, were waiting to greet us on the platform at Gatooma and we felt at once among friends.

All Saints' Church, Gatooma, was a pleasant brick-built church able to seat between 100 and 150 people and our Rectory, an aging weather-board bungalow was built in its compound. The parish was bounded on the south by the parish of Que Que and on the north by the parish of Hartley, of which I was also Rector and of which more anon. The eastern boundary was the Mhondoro Reserve and there was no official boundary to the west.

When Southern Rhodesia became a self-governing colony in 1923 roughly one-third of its total area of 150,000 square miles had been allocated to the European colonists (in 1946, 130,000); one-third to the indigenous Africans (in 1946, estimated at 1,800,000); and one-third remained unallocated. The western boundary of the parish impinged on this unallocated territory.

Mealies (maize) and tobacco were the main agricultural crops. Tobacco especially was booming. Fortunes were being made in a single season and more and more farmers were turning over to tobacco. But not all. I take my hat off to an old Scottish farmer in the Hartley parish who stoutly refused. 'What the world needs,' he said to me, 'is food – food for the hungry – and as long as I have breath in my body, it's food I am growing.'

Only a small area of a European farm was ever cultivated; the greater part was always undeveloped and some large properties, taken up by companies purely as investments for the future, were occupied only by African squatters and what the Bible calls 'the beasts of the field'. Rhodesdale, an estate of some 600 square miles east of Gatooma, was the home of elephants, lions and wildebeests.

Gold mines, some large, some small, abounded in the parish. The Cam and Motor Mine six miles east of Gatooma had been the largest gold-producing mine in the country and we held monthly services on it, but in 1946 its life was drawing to a close.

The parish still possessed, however, the richest gold-bearing mine in Rhodesia, the Golden Valley Mine 12 miles north-west of Gatooma and owned by John Mack. Here again we held services for the European employees once a month in the club-house.

When I arrived, the parish car was on its last legs (or wheels) and the Parochial Church Council suggested that I should approach Mr Mack for help in its replacement.

Mr and Mrs Mack of the Church of Scotland lived quite modestly in their home on the mine. They were elderly and childless and Mr Mack was immensely rich. I therefore put my case to him with confidence but came away empty-handed.

I had come, he told me, at a difficult time. He and his associates were planning to develop the Dalny Mine, which they had just purchased. Its development would cost hundreds of thousands of pounds. In addition, he said, he made all his donations to charity at Christmas. He had been looking into them and I would be surprised to learn how much they amounted to. I was surprised. 'They amounted,' he told me with bated breath, 'almost to £200!'

I contented myself by exclaiming 'Really!' But it was only that poor Mr Mack just didn't understand – in 1946 the Christian Stewardship movement had still to be born. John Mack was generous to his European staff and he cared within reason, I am prepared to believe, for his African miners. When he died, some ten years later, he remembered both Gatooma Parish and Gatooma Town Council generously in his will and both have reason to be grateful to him.

There were five service centres in the parish in addition to All Saints', but the only one with a church was on Mr Leonard Tracy's farm at Chakari, 20 miles to the west. Leonard Tracy was a leading churchman in the diocese and his two married sons Martin and 'CG' lived with their wives on the farm. Also his unmarried daughter, Bridget, whose responsibility and delight was the pigs. She adored them and stoutly defended them against all detractors – 'the cleanest and cleverest of all animals'. Shades of *Animal Farm*!

The little church of St Martin's in the Mealies, built of Kimberley (i.e. sun-dried) brick and thatched, was close to the homesteads and perfect in its setting. I remember, however, one visit in particular. I put out the prayer books and hymn books I carried round with me in a leather case and left the half-emptied case flat on the floor. When I went to retrieve it at the close of the service, it swarmed with termites. In the space of one hour they had eaten right through the leather case and were busy devouring the books left, which they appeared greatly to enjoy.

Termites, better-known as white ants, are voracious wood-eaters and do untold damage to unprotected buildings. On the credit side, they build huge nests in the bundu often 10 and 15 feet high, and soil taken from the anthills when mixed with an equal quantity of light, sandy loam makes excellent bricks.

There was no notice 'For Whites Only' outside All Saints' Church. There was no need. It was understood. Happily, all is changed now.

As explained earlier, as Rector of Gatooma, I was officially Priest-in-Charge of St Paul's Mission in Gatooma Location, but my duties there were minimal. Some years earlier the diocese had established the Mission by building a large tin church on a site provided by the Government, and by appointing and paying an African priest as its pastor. Fr Yacob Mwela had been this priest for many years and had built up a school of some 120 pupils who occupied the church on weekdays. He was energetic and capable and I left everything to him. At his invitation, however, I preached for him on a Sunday soon after my arrival and was so impressed with the singing of the choir that when Christmas drew near I invited them to sing an African carol as an anthem at our All Saints' Carol Service, thinking it might help to bring the two congregations together.

The plan was stillborn. A week before the service was due to be held Baba Mwela came to see me. His choir, he explained, did not want to come. They did not think they would be welcome. Later events showed me how right they were. Had they come they would have stirred up a hornets' nest. Today, thankfully, it is different. But in 1946 the Methodist and Dutch Reformed white congregations in similar circumstances would have reacted similarly. Only the Roman Catholic Church set a better example. Europeans and Africans did share together their small church in Gatooma, but even so there was a distinction – white sat on the left; blacks on the right. Language presented no problem. The Mass at that time, being in Latin, was equally foreign to both.

My main contact with Africans was through my superintendence of Anglican schools in the Mhondoro Reserve. The Reserve stretched from ten miles south of Salisbury in the north to opposite Que Que in the south – a distance of close on a hundred miles. At its broadest it was 40 miles wide, and the only European living in it was the Government Land Development Officer, Mr Micklethwaite, responsible for soil conservation and the dipping of the native cattle. He lived with his wife and young family some 50 miles east of Hartley on the road linking Hartley with Beatrice, and his eldest child, Anthony, attended Hartley Junior School.

To assist him, he had a band of African demonstrators, and together they ensured that no land was cultivated except in land designated 'arable' and that all cattle were dipped weekly.

Cotton was just being developed as a cash crop in the Mhondoro and all Africans were eager to grow it. Only Africans who employed good farming methods were given seed. They were also given 'Good Farmer' badges, and by such inducements and by the exacting of fines where necessary, the native reserves were being transformed. Stores, schools and agricultural shows were encouraged, and a start was being made in establishing clinics. African life in the Mhondoro was without doubt infinitely more wholesome than African life in the cities.

Primary education was also more available. Establishing any Government-recognised school in an urban area was expensive. All sorts of building regulations had to be complied with and all materials bought. Given goodwill, establishing a primary school in a reserve was comparatively simple. Bricks could be made on site; in 1946 grass for thatch was still easily obtainable, likewise poles; and almost the only materials having to be bought for cash were five-inch nails for the roof timber and either tar or cement for an ant-course. But the goodwill was essential – the bricks had to be made and baked, the grass had to be cut and bundled and the building erected.

Happily, the goodwill was mostly forthcoming. Every kraal wanted its own school and the 'New Deal' 1942 Native Education Act meant that once a school was built and recognised it was largely self-supporting.

But not every kraal could have a school because under the 1942 Act no school could be recognised if within three miles of another. There was intense competition, not only between the kraals, but also between the different denominations working in the Reserve – in the Mhondoro chiefly Anglican, Roman and Methodist – for not only had each school to be three miles from the next, it also had to be built on the 'building line' which divided the designated arable and pastoral areas.

When the Church Elders (the *vakuru*) came to me, pleading for a school, my first quest was always to find a site – rarely easy. In the case of St Lucy's, Mukerati, there were rival schools, one Methodist and the other Catholic, north and south of Mukerati on the 'building line', and the only point three miles from each was right in the centre of the kraal. I was perturbed but not the *vakuru*. 'Father, we will move our houses', and move them they did.

A year later, 10,000 bricks had been burnt and building was ready to commence. The bricks were made and burnt in a home-made kiln one mile away on the bank of the Sivandazi River, which bordered the Reserve. When the kiln was dismantled after three days' burning, as always some of the bricks were still only half-baked and black. No matter, they could be used for inside walls and for a teacher's house. The good bricks – of a pleasant sandy-pink hue – had to pass a further test. Dropped one on another from a height of three feet, neither must break.

Schoolchildren carried the bricks from the kiln to the building site. On a visit, I noticed a small child of eight carrying only two bricks on her head. The normal load was three and I suggested she carry another one. Poor little mite, I had no idea how heavy they were.

The parents built the school themselves – a simple thatched building, 24 feet by 16 feet – which served as the church on Sunday and the school from Monday to Friday.

I found a teacher for them, a school-leaver from the kraal, David Mukerati, who had just completed Standard six at a Central primary school, and on the opening day 27 children were enrolled. David was a nice lad, and without any training whatever did well. Poor David. A year or two later he went to Salisbury during a school vacation and died there in mysterious circumstances. Some said he had been mugged and murdered. Then the search for another teacher began.

The 1942 Native Education Act required me as Superintendent to do a full day's inspection of every recognised school four times a year. What did such an inspection entail?

School began by the ringing of the bell. This was roughly an hour after sunrise. Life in a reserve was still basic. No villager possessed clock or watch, and time was indicated by reference to the height of the sun. 'We will meet when the sun is so high,' and an arm indicated the height. But as soon as the sun rose, life began. Men left to see to the cattle, women to draw water from well or river, and the children of the more enlightened parents left for school; for some a three- or four-mile journey. At the first stream they washed.

When the head teacher judged a sufficient number of his children present, one of them would ring what served as a bell, more often than not a three-foot length of railway line hanging from a tree – how obtained, goodness knows; my schools in the Mhondoro were all more than 30 miles from a railway track! As the metallic clanging continued, the children present left off playing and lined up in rows before the church, according to their classes. The head teacher and I then inspected them.

One morning it would be clothes. They wore their oldest clothes, often rags, when at home, but they came to school in their Sunday best, and by the end of my time in Africa many schools were boasting uniforms.

Another morning it would be equipment, and they had to show their exercise book and pencil and 'reader' if they possessed one.

Sometimes we inspected heads, ears, teeth and finger-nails. They kept their teeth clean with twigs and their finger-nails pared with safety razor-blades. These had many uses and the boys carried them loose in their trouser pockets!

Inspection completed, all marched into church for assembly, and 30 minutes of religious instruction followed: two mornings on the Catechism, two mornings on scripture and, on Friday mornings, hymn-singing, which was always popular. Academic studies followed: arithmetic; vernacular reading and writing; English reading and writing; and what was loosely called 'history/geography'.

I spent my time checking the registers, seeing the exercise books were properly marked, listening to the teachers and occasionally questioning the children.

The teaching medium was English and listening could be fascinating. One lesson on hygiene was on the danger of bilharzia – a prevalent wasting disease caused by drinking infected water. The teacher concluded the lesson something like this: 'So what have we to do before we drink any water?

Yes, we have to boil it. Do I always? Do you always? No we don't. But should we? Yes we should.'

In another lesson a mistress was doing her best to explain about the rising and setting of the sun: 'The sun appears in the East, it travels right across the sky and then it disappears beneath the horizon in the West. And what happens next? During the night it travels back under the earth to appear again in the East next morning. Isaac! You are smiling. Don't you believe that?'

'No, Miss.'

'Then what do you think happens, Isaac?'

'I think, Miss, that God makes a new sun every morning.'

Confusion of teacher.

The last hour of schooling was practical. Government regulations laid down that every recognised school must have five demonstration plots each of at least one-quarter of an acre. This was to teach the proper rotation of crops, normally: mealies with manure, mealies without manure, ropoko, groundnuts and cotton, Ropoko was invariably a poor crop and as its chief use was in the brewing of native beer, I was glad to learn, when visiting another mission, of an alternative – munga. I brought back a small bag of seed with me and gave it to the head teacher of one of my larger schools. It was not accepted with any enthusiasm but I insisted it should be sown. When its shoots began to appear I asked what munga was used for. I was told 'It is used, Father, for making beer but it does not make as good beer as ropoko!' End of experiment.

Other practical activities were (i) growing vegetables in the school garden, which had to be near a stream or well (ii) woodwork: making stools, yokes, or smaller objects with sharpened hoes (adzes); these were finished off with razor-blades or broken glass (iii) baskets and mats made from sisal grown in the school compound (iv) pottery with local clay (v) sewing – but a shortage of mistresses made this difficult.

Around 1 p.m., school ended and the children made their way home, unless, that is, there was organised sport in the afternoon. In any case, it was only after they arrived home,

113

having been up some eight hours, that they had their one meal of the day! This meal would be a bowl of thick *sudza* (cooked mealie-meal) plus a 'relish', generally vegetable; a meat relish was a luxury. The *sudza* was eaten with the fingers, hence the importance of paring their nails. Teachers and the occasional family would begin the day with a gruel of mealie-meal and a mug of tea, but this was unusual.

As soon as the children had left I had my own lunch, generally corned beef and potatoes followed by fruit and tea, and a meeting with parents and teachers if there were problems or if new buildings were planned. I collected fees and book-sales from the headmaster and paid the teachers their wages, An ETC teacher (holding an Elementary Teacher Certificate) received five pounds per month plus increments, and an untrained teacher who had attained Standard 6, three pounds per month. A teacher who had only passed Standard 5 (frowned on by the NED) received two pounds.

On these trips I was mostly accompanied by Baba Elfric Matimba, who rode beside me in the cab, first, of the Gatooma parish pick-up and later, of the Hartley Mission truck. I was responsible for education and Baba Matimba for pastoral work in the Mhondoro. He was a priest of the old school, hard-working, experienced and devoted to God and his people and to the Church in which he had been reared. Although his education had stopped at Standard 4, his English was good. I grew very fond of him and shall always be grateful for all he taught me.

On one occasion he confessed to me that he was feeling old and that cycling was becoming a burden. I rather laughed off the idea, for although he might do one hundred miles on a trip, it would be spread over many days and he would rarely average more than ten miles daily.

'In any case, Baba,' I said, 'how old are you?'

That was hard to discover, for he was born long before any African births were regstered. 'I must be 60,' he replied.

On another occasion he was asked why he was a Christian. 'I am a Christian,' he replied, 'because my parents were

114

Christians before me. If they had not been, I would not be alive today.' And he explained that he was one of twins, and when he was born, according to tribal religion, twins were unlucky and both were killed.

While the medium in the schools was English, church services were in the vernacular – the unified Chishona introduced by the Government. It is a most difficult language which I never mastered. A word's root comes at the end, not at the beginning, and meanings can vary according to the pitch of the voice. Even more confusing 'b' and 'd' have different meanings when pronounced 'explosively' (breathing out) and 'implosively' (breathing in). Pronouncing a word implosively entails much lip manipulation which no European can easily achieve, and which has, I fancy, resulted in the thick lips of the Bantu tribes.

Elfric therefore interpreted for me when speaking in church or addressing parents. As, however, his English vocabulary was limited, I was reduced to speaking with great simplicity, which was an excellent discipline.

One meeting with parents I shall never forget. It was after dark and I was sitting in my hut when Baba Matimba entered. One of the teachers had made a village girl pregnant. The case was being heard in the headman's house and both parties wished me to be present.

As School Superintendent it was no direct concern of mine. Had the girl been a school pupil and had the teacher been found guilty, it would have been. I should have had to dismiss him and report the case to the Education department, who would have banned him for life from any further teaching. They were very strict. But in this case the girl had left school many years before, so it was essentially a matter between the boy and the girl's parents.

However, besides being Superintendent I was also Priest-in-Charge of the Mission and both parties were Christians, so I brought along a chair and a pressure lamp and listened.

The boy had admitted responsibility but had refused to marry the girl, and the whole question was one of damages. All Africans desire a son to perform their funeral rites when

115

they die, and the teacher had agreed to the asked-for damages of four head of cattle, but only on the condition that he was given custody of the child when born, should it prove to be a boy. If it proved to be a girl, the mother-to-be could keep it. The bargaining continued and Baba Matimba kept me informed of its progress.

The girl was sitting on the ground beside her father – the only female present – and suddenly the enormity of it all struck me. Here they were arguing about what should be done with the child when born and the mother-to-be was not even being consulted!

I whispered to Baba, 'Ask the girl what she wishes to happen to her child.'

His reply stunned me. 'It's nothing to do with her!'

I insisted nonetheless that he ask her, but of course he was right. Her reply when elicited was: 'It is as my father wishes.'

In 1945 a woman was a minor all her life and had no legal rights. Until she was married she was the property of her father, and on marriage became the property of the husband. The husband-to-be had to pay *lobolo* (bride-price) to her father and, should she fail to produce children, her husband could return her to her father's kraal and demand the return of his *lobolo*. Under Native Law women were simply chattel.

Happily, all is now changed – one of the blessings of independence. To its credit, Robert Mugabe's government has insisted on the freedom and equality of women. They now have the vote, can own property and are persons in their own right. All unpopular legislation. For a period *lobolo* itself was forbidden. But it is one thing to pass a law; it is quite another thing to try to enforce it, and such was the pressure of public opinion that *lobolo*, with legal safe-guards, has now been reinstated.

Little racial tension existed in 1945. As explained earlier, Europeans were in control and whites were whites and blacks were blacks and never the twain shall meet.

The Government doctor in Gatooma was Dr Alan Knight,

116

a relative of Archbishop Knight of the West Indies. The Community of the Resurrection at Penhalonga had an African priest among its members, a Fr Rakale, who had been trained in England and was everywhere respected, so I thought. In the winter of 1947 Dr and Mrs Knight invited him to stay with them, and it seemed to me, here was a chance for me to take a Sunday off for once.

I announced that he would be taking the 8 a.m. Holy Communion at All Saints'. Only a handful, led by Dr and Mrs Knight, attended, and afterwards Mrs Peel my PCC Secretary and a regular communicant, confessed to me that she had not felt able to go: 'I know it's prejudice and I know I'm wrong, but I just felt I could not take Communion from an African. I wouldn't have been able to concentrate on what I was doing. I should have been bristling all inside.'

At heart, she knew that she was wrong. Others on the PCC were not so generous. Their attitude, expressed or un-expressed, was: 'We've been taken on the hop this time; but it must never happen again.'

The following winter Fr Rakale was again the guest of Dr and Mrs Knight. By then I had left Gatooma and was living in Hartley, but my successor also invited Fr Rakale to celebrate for him. The All Saints' PCC was split down the middle and half resigned.

On a happier note is the report of a sixth-form debate which took place about this time at Penhalonga, then one of only three African secondary schools in the colony. The motion was: 'This house believes that the Government has done more for the African than the Church has.' The chairman's summing up was masterly:

'The Church,' he said, 'is our mother, she cares for us. The Government is our father, he pays the bills!'

And it is a fact conveniently forgotten by many present-day black nationalists that at that time the White government was spending more on African education than on any other one item in its budget – more than on defence, on security or on communications.

117

In 1947, Gatooma was honoured by a royal visit. King George VI, Queen Elizabeth, Princess Elizabeth and Princess Margaret were touring Central Africa and a whistle-stop call at Gatooma was on their itinerary.

On April 10th, at the time scheduled, the Mayor, aldermen and Town Council assembled in the forecourt of the railway station, together with the local notables, the police and the schoolchildren. A few months earlier Marjorie had started a government-sponsored nursery school with the help of Mrs Finch, the wife of a bank official. Their tiny tots were given pride of place. African schoolchildren from the location were also present but rather in the background.

The visit lasted no more than 20 minutes. The Mayor and his wife and the aldermen and their wives were introduced to the King and Queen. The Queen said a few words to the schoolchildren, and then they were off again. The royal coach had darkened windows but not quite dark enough. Through them we saw George VI stagger to a couch and slump into it. Never strong, he was already an exhausted man. But the Queen, now the beloved Queen Mother, gracious as always, stood smiling and waving at the door of the carriage as the train moved off.

As April 21st 1947 was Princess Elizabeth's 21st birthday, all schoolchildren were given a day's holiday. In no way was I able to communicate this in time to the children at our schools in the Mhondoro – posts were erratic and there were no telephones – so I gave the holiday to them on my next trek.

'Had they heard of Princess Elizabeth?' I asked. 'She had just become 21. To become 21 was a great occasion among Europeans. Because it was, there would be no school tomorrow, it would be a whole-day holiday.'

The reception was mixed. The teachers grinned from ear to ear; the faces of the children fell. They would much rather be at school than sitting about in the kraal or herding goats.

Another visit later in the year created much less excitementbut was more prophetic of the future. Joshua Nkomo, father

118

of African Nationalism in Rhodesia, arrived in Hartley on a tour through the Mhondoro.

He arrived in a cavalcade of new Mercedes – the gift, no doubt, of a foreign power – but his message fell for the most part on dull ears. Independence had yet to become a burning topic, and the resplendent Mercedes limousines created more attention than his words. 'Africans owning limousines? What next?'

Nonetheless the 'wind of change' proclaimed by Harold Macmillan in South Africa in 1960 was already a gentle breeze beginning to make itself felt in Southern Rhodesia.

11

Rector and Missionary in Hartley

After a few months in Gatooma I was quite clear that to minister adequately in two European parishes and at the same time meet the ever-growing demands of African education was beyond me.

White clergy working in the diocese of Southern Rhodesia were of two kinds: either they were full-time missionaries supported by SPG in England and in charge of central mission stations, mostly in rural areas, or they were priests appointed by the diocese as Rectors of European parishes. Those parishes were responsible for their support, which, in 1946, entailed the provision of accommodation and transport and a basic stipend of £400 p.a. The latter was required to be paid into the Diocesan Stipends Fund plus a quota of about ten per cent for diocesan 'overheads'. Rectors received monthly stipend payments from the central fund, and if parishes got badly in arrears with their quota their rector was removed. Hartley had been a parish when Gatooma was only a railway siding, and my workload at Gatooma would be resolved if Hartley could once again be established as an independent parish.

The problem was: Could Hartley with its tiny population be persuaded to accept the responsibility of having a rector of its own? It was asking a tremendous lot of them. Currently they were paying the Gatooma PCC £100 p.a. for providing a monthly service of Holy Communion in St Edmund's Church. With this, Hartley was perfectly satisfied. In addition their PCC had let their badly neglected Rectory to the

Electricity Supply Commission, and this brought in a small but useful income. The PCC was, for the most part, sceptical of the whole project and I might well have despaired had I not felt my own position so desperate. I knew I just could not cope, as things were, indefinitely. As so often, it was 'over to God'.

At the meeting of the Hartley PCC called to consider the proposal, I had one trump card up my sleeve. In order to enable Hartley to establish itself, the Gatooma PCC had offered to pay £200 of Hartley's first diocesan quota of £400. But the meeting opened disastrously – or so it seemed.

The minutes of the previous meeting having been read and passed, the Treasurer presented his statement of accounts for the previous month. Among the expenditure was an item, 'Floor polish two shillings and ninepence', which Mrs McGoven, a new volunteer on the church cleaning rota, had submitted. It would hardly be an exaggeration to say all hell broke out. Every volunteer who had ever polished the church floor had provided her own floor polish. Why had Mrs McGoven been paid? Could the church afford it?

My heart sank. With such an outcry over a matter of shillings, what hope had I of persuading them to accept the responsibility of finding some £600 a year for a rector for whom most saw little need?

But the PCC had exhausted itself. When the time came they listened quietly while I assured them that with God all things were possible and I was confident the money could be found. When the vote was taken, they voted *nem con* for the proposition. As I have said before, 'God works in a mysterious way his wonders to perform.' Unwittingly, Mrs McGoven had been his instrument.

Problems nonetheless remained. I informed the diocese and they agreed to the re-establishment of Hartley as an independent parish responsible for the work in the Mhondoro Reserve and, as expected, they offered Marjorie and me the choice of staying in Gatooma or of moving to Hartley.

While Gatooma was a 'desirable' parish, I suspected that there could be some difficulty in finding a priest for Hartley.

121

Moreover, I felt responsible for the Hartley venture and looked forward to continuing my work in the Mhondoro Mission. Marjorie agreed, and three months later we moved.

Before this, alterations and repairs had been made to the Rectory. It had only two bedrooms and we needed a spare room for visitors. This we obtained by partitioning the dining-room. There was a large gaping hole in the floor-boards of the main bedroom, which the previous tenants had concealed by their bed, their chief fear being that their baby might crawl though it! This we patched up. One of the two small vestries in the church we fitted out as my study.

There was no indoor sanitation or sewerage in Hartley. In lieu thereof a PK (Kitchen Kaffir for *piccaninny kaia* i.e. 'small house') of corrugated iron stood on the edge of the compound, its bucket being emptied weekly by the Council's night-soil collector. The Council did, however, provide piped running water and we had hot and cold taps in both kitchen and bathroom, the hot water being supplied by a chip boiler in the compound. The bathroom housed the Rectory's show-piece: a home-made concrete bath. No need for pumice-stone; the surface of the bath sufficed! A shallow earthen trench dispersed the waste water over the compound, and a few months after our arrival a pawpaw seed established itself in the trench, sprouted and grew. Within a year it was six feet high and within two years it was yielding abundant and delicious fruit.

The Rectory's real problem we only discovered later – the roof-timbers above the bedrooms were bug-infested. The dirty creatures mostly kept to the rafters but in season would sally forth through cracks in the wooden ceiling and climb down the strings of the mosquito nets. In those days there were no pesticides strong enough to exterminate them and wooden huts would normally be burnt down. This was not possible in the case of the Rectory, and we soon came to accept the situation, catching and burning the bugs as they appeared. They were little worse than the ticks which infested the animals. We had a lovely red setter which we had brought with us from Gatooma – a stray which had been wished on us – and de-ticking him with tweezers and throwing the ticks into an open fire was a regular and distasteful business.

We moved to Hartley in February 1948 and an urgent priority was to make the parish financially viable. In the next 12 months I visited every farm within its boundaries and succeeded in establishing three new centres for monthly services: Makwiro, Rutala Hills and the township of Norton. In addition there were already established centres on Gadzema Mine and at Concession Hill.

Norton was 50 miles to the north and only 16 miles west of Salisbury where the residents and local farmers shopped and banked. Norton being 70 miles from Gatooma, previous Rectors of Gatooma-with-Hartley had never attempted pastoral work in the district. If they wished for services there was always the cathedral. A junior school existed but was never visited. Here was a pastoral opportunity. Mr Hall, the recently appointed headmaster and his wife, were most welcoming and I often stayed with them on my weekends in Norton. It was agreed that I should spend one weekend a month in the township and district, and normally I spent the Friday morning teaching in the school, on the Friday afternoon and Saturday I visited, and on the Sunday morning I gave the township a Communion Service. By 1950, Norton was a centre second only to Hartley in importance. While at Norton, Marjorie with the Bishop's permission took Sunday Morning Prayer for me in Hartley and, on occasion, courageously deputised on the church's old-fashioned 'squeeze-box'.

Fr Osmund Victor, Provincial of the Community of the Resurrection in South Africa, was Dean of the Cathedral in Salisbury and in 1948 I invited him to preach at our Harvest Festival in Hartley. He arrived by a local train early on the Sunday morning and I was at the station to meet him. Hartley had no platform to alight on; one descended down carriage-steps on to the rich red soil. Fr Victor stood on the top step

123

and surveyed what there was to see of Hartley. 'What a dorp!' he exclaimed. 'What a dorp!' I kept silent but my hackles rose. Hartley was my choice and I liked Hartley; but an impartial visitor would certainly have sided with Fr Victor.

It is very different now but in 1948 Hartley was a dying township. Besides the church, it still retained a junior boarding-school, a police station, a Government doctor, a Women's Institute and hall, a butcher, a garage, two European stores, three other stores and an open-air swimming-pool; but little else. Some 20 European bungalows remained but not a few were empty and falling down.

It is different today because in 1948 cotton was booming and W Whitehead & Co. Ltd, the Lancashire cotton-weaving multinational and a subsidiary of Lonrho, were seeking to establish themselves in the colony. The Hartley Town Council had offered them a site, two miles from the township, and a public meeting was called.

The Council Chairman, Dr David Carnegie – the Government Medical Officer – commended the sale to the meeting. To my astonishment not a speaker from the floor supported him. It would change, they said, the character of Hartley. They liked Hartley as it was! David in the chair was splendid. He never lost his cool and replied fully and sympathetically every question asked him. At the close, I proposed a vote of thanks to him and the Council. It was never seconded. Nevertheless, a year later Whitehead's opened in Hartley and Hartley has never looked back.

David Carnegie was a descendant of Robert Moffat, father- in-law of David Livingstone, and David and Betty, his wife, had charm. They were of our own age and we became firm friends. David, however, had his own methods as a medical practitioner. On one occasion we met on the doorstep of an elderly spinster who had phoned for David to visit her sister, who wasn't well. Inside, her dog came grovelling to meet us. It looked very sick and David was much concerned. 'What's wrong with its ear?' he enquired and he bent down to examine it.

'I did not call you to examine my dog,' said its owner starchily, 'I phoned you to visit my sister.'

On another occasion, Marjorie phoned him to come and see Peter. 'There's no need,' he replied, 'I'll send round a prescription.'

'But,' protested Marjorie, 'I haven't described his symptoms. You can't know what's wrong.'

'Oh yes I do. All the children have it. I'll send something round.' Which he did, and Peter recovered.

My African work in the Mhondoro expanded steadily. Fr Elfric Matimba lived in the centre of the Reserve, about 30 miles from Hartley and only a few miles north of the road from Hartley to Beatrice, and, as already mentioned, I took him with me on my school inspections whenever possible. Nevertheless, reaching him in the rainy season could be hazardous. Not only was the road ungravelled, the drift across the Sivandazi River bordering the Reserve was always chancy. In the dry season the Sivandazi was dry or just a trickle, but after a downfall – and on one occasion two inches of rain fell in just 20 minutes – it could be come a raging torrent. At such times one had to wait patiently on the bank until the water fell, usually only a matter of hours.

One day, I was waiting none too patiently in the Mission truck for the water to fall, when a bulky well-dressed African came cycling down the road. Seeing the height of the water, he squatted down on the bank, glancing constantly down the road behind him. After a while a village woman, whom I took to be his wife, came trudging along, a bag of mealie-meal on her head. She dropped her burden, picked up her lord and master's cycle and carried it across the torrent. She returned, her lord and master climbed upon her shoulders and she carried him across too. On her sixth and final crossing she carried over her mealie-meal and proceeded on her way!

Education for girls was generally unpopular, the prevailing view of the African male being that education was bad for them: 'It makes them cheeky,' they would say. Nonetheless, chivalry was not unknown and I was often impressed by the courtesy of my teachers. Once when I offered two young teachers, male and female, a lift in my truck, the boy said, 'She must sit in front. She is a female.' I was much encouraged.

Giving teachers lifts provided them with an opportunity to relax and for me to get alongside them, and simple remarks made on such occasions were sometimes memorable. As an example, 'Mr Jack Tarr is a good man. I hope we Africans do not make him a bad man.'

The said Mr Jack Tarr was a white farmer who had taken up undeveloped land on the Reserve's western border, and quickly won the respect of Africans. He built a school for his worker's children, and on one occasion when some Africans from the Reserve brought to him – on a bicycle! – a desperately sick relative, Jack left his work and drove the African, for whom he had no responsibility whatsoever, 50 miles to Gatooma Hospital.

Yes, Mr Tarr was a good man. Would the Africans make him a bad man? Not the Africans he had helped, but there were others. Just as there are good Europeans and bad Europeans, so there are good Africans and bad Africans, and my teacher's fear was that in season Africans from the Reserve would help themselves to his mealies, break down his fences and steal his sheep.

I valued African travelling companions for more than just their company – they knew the Reserve tracks better than I. But even Baba Matimba sometimes got lost.

St Saviour's, Marisamuka, was a centre well off the beaten track, and on one of my trips Elfric lost his bearings. All he could say was that he thought it was somewhere off to the left. To our relief, while we were still stopped and deliberating, a villager appeared out of the *bundu*. He had just come, he told us, from Marisamuka and it was not far down the track by which he had approached us. What 'not far' meant was anybody's guess, so I pressed Elfric to enquire further.

'How many miles was it?'

'He doesn't know what a mile is.'

'Then ask him,' I said, 'how long it took him to get here.'

'Not long.'

'But how long? How many minutes?'

'He doesn't know what a minute is!'

It was brought home to me how necessary accepted standards are. Without them we have nothing to go on. 'Break down, Lord, the banners of Satan. Set up everywhere the standards of Christ.' So be it.

We had no choice but to take the villager at his word, and fifteen minutes later we were at Marisamuka.

In his book *The Primal Vision*, Bishop John Taylor writes of the 'powers of pure malevolence' which haunt the lives of Africans, especially to be feared if those recently dead died in anger, or by suicide, or who had been denied the proper rites of burial. The fear was everywhere.

In Hartley, an African in charge of the lift at a local gold-mine was accused of murder. When one whom he believed to be his enemy was being hoisted to the surface, he had reversed the lever and sent him and the cage crashing to the bottom. His defence? He had to do it. His enemy had put a spell on him and was slowly killing him. Only by killing his enemy could he save his life.

My only direct contact with this darker side of African life occurred at Marisamuka. The school's headmaster, Wilbert Ndoro, was a devoted Christian and Catechist. He had, as his assistant in his school, a young African who had passed his Standard 6 the previous year. Although Wilbert had years of teaching experience and was married with a family, because he was only a Standard 6 teacher, he was receiving no more from the Government than his young unmarried assistant, namely £36 per annum. When, therefore, an NED circular announced that the Department were prepared to regrade Standard 6 teachers of proved experience and ability, I immediately applied on behalf of Wilbert.

It so happened that on the night before the inspector was due to assess him, I was staying at Chipashu. To reach

Marisamuka from Chipashu by car is 18 miles because between them flows the Umfuli River, but as the crow flies they are only a few miles apart. It was in the dry season when the Umfuli was fordable and I wanted to make sure that all was well at St Saviour's. I therefore borrowed a cycle, waded the Umfuli and reached the school soon after the normal time for assembly. No assembly had been called, the children were running wild and the second teacher explained in despair that Wilbert was in his house saying he was unwell; he would not see the inspector.

I summoned Wilbert, and clearly something was seriously wrong. His eyes were rolling and his limbs shaking. What possessed him?

To practise exorcism in England, the Church of England requires special training and the Bishop's Licence. I had neither but it was an emergency. Our Lord in the gospels had cast out demons and had given the disciples power over evil spirits to cast them out. I sent up an arrow prayer and took Wilbert's quivering hands. I looked him straight in the face and told him with all the authority I could command: 'Look at me.' He did, and we stood looking into each other's eyes for perhaps half a minute, though it seemed far longer. Then I said something like this:

'In the name of Jesus Christ, I command you, evil spirit, to come out of this his servant Wilbert. (Pause) I command you no more to enter into him.'

Amateurish perhaps, but suddenly to my joy and relief Wilbert's whole expression changed. His eyes had already lost their glazed appearance; now his quivering stopped. 'Thank you, Father,' he said in a changed voice. 'I am all right now.' Was it just nerves or something more?

He returned to his house, collected his register, blew his whistle and the school assembled. He impressed the inspector and obtained his regrading. Meanwhile, I was back in Chipashu.

When I paid a return visit to Zimbabwe in 1972 and revisited St Saviour's, Wilbert was still there. He had retired from teaching but was still the Church Catechist – unpaid, but taking services Sunday by Sunday, preparing candidates for baptism, visiting the sick, doing the work of an evangelist, making full proof of his ministry. The love of God shone from him. On Catechists such as he the Church in Zimbabwe was built. God bless him.

Wilbert was never ordained, but many headmasters in those days were. Today that involves making a very considerable sacrifice. The wife of a married Anglican priest in Zimbabwe has to work if they are to support a family. But in 1946 it was otherwise. A priest's stipend then was on a par if not higher than that of a primary school headmaster, and his standing far, far higher. If, then, you had found God in your life, to apply to be trained for the priesthood was natural, and splendid priests most of them became. I remember with affection Julius Murumbedzi, of whom I write later, Elijah Cirimuuta, Langton Machiha, Noel Bororwe, Amos Matanda, Gabriel Mashingayidze and Michael Zambezi. With all except the last I still correspond, though all except Gabriel are now, like me, retired.

The old-time African priest was a Father-in-God to his people and his word was law. The Christian faith was everywhere outwardly accepted as true – it was the religion of the whites they argued – whites were very clever. They knew everything – and even older Africans, wedded for life to the beliefs and customs of their ancestors and prevented by fear and by the foreigners' insistence on monogamy from accepting the 'New Way', would look wistfully Christwards. They longed for education for their children, helped to build the Mission schools and when Mass was held flocked into church.

Rules were strict. They could attend the reading of the Word and preaching but not the Holy Mysteries themselves. After the address Baba Matimba would stand on the chancel step and order all not baptised to leave. Often a pause would follow and he would repeat in stronger voice, 'All except the baptised must now leave,' and slowly, reluctantly, those

129

not baptised would shuffle away.

Some did offer themselves for baptism, but in my time three-quarters of those baptised were schoolchildren. They were admitted automatically as 'Hearers' on reaching Standard 1. Two years of instruction in the scriptures, the Shona Catechism and church worship followed. The Shona Catechism was a comprehensive manual divided into three sections; section one for Hearers; section two for Catechumens; and section three for confirmands. I have a copy before me as I write and this is how it begins:

1. 'Who made you?' 'God made me.'
2. 'Why did God make you?' 'God made me to know Him, to love Him here on earth and to be with him for ever in heaven.'
3. 'Who is God?' 'God is the great unseen Spirit, the Maker of all things.'
4. 'Is there only one God?' 'There is only one God.'
5. 'Where is God?' 'God is everywhere.'
6. 'Is God eternal?' 'God is eternal. He is without beginning and without end.'
7. 'Does God see and know all things?' 'God sees and knows all things, even our secret thoughts.'

All excellent. But it was recited parrot-fashion, and what was really believed in those bright-eyed little black heads was anybody's guess. Religion is caught, not taught.

After two years as Hearers, they were admitted to the Catechumenate.

The children of Christian parents in good standing were entitled to be baptised in their local church as infants, but it was then comparatively rare and more than 90 per cent of baptisms in the Mhondoro took place at a great corporate Act of Witness held annually at St Andrew's, Chipashu.

For practical reasons this was always held on a Saturday during the Easter school holidays – the rains were over, the rivers were low and the weather cool; schoolchildren were free to travel and it was a between season, agriculturally.

The previous six days would have been spent giving the candidates their final preparation. Those coming more than 30 miles would have started on the previous Friday or Saturday and, like Galilean pilgrims going up to Jerusalem for the Passover, would have journeyed leisurely, greeting their friends en route and camping at night. All pilgrims brought their own provisions, blankets and cooking utensils with them.

Monday to Friday followed a uniform pattern: worship at daybreak followed by catechising and instruction; afternoons in 'practical Christianity'. All except the very old were allotted a task, some making bricks, some cutting grass, some digging latrines – for conditions at Chipashu were primitive. Then came the evening meal and, as darkness fell, singing and dancing.

Let me describe my visit to Chipashu in May 1948. I arrived around 10 a.m. on the Saturday morning and found the candidates packed into the church, singing and receiving final instructions. Then the service started. After the opening hymn and prayers and the reading of the gospel, the candidates filed out of church and were marshalled with their friends and sponsors for the procession to the river half a mile away. A Crossbearer and two servers were in front, then came all who were Christians, and finally the candidates. I followed in the rear. We walked slowly, singing the Litany, but when we came to a path forking to the right, the candidates took it while the rest of us continued straight ahead.

'Where have they gone?' I whispered to my companion.

'You will see.'

Eventually we came to the river-bank and halted. And then I saw the long line of candidates, some 150, marching towards us on the opposite bank of the river – they had crossed it lower down.

Opposite us they halted, and Baba Matimba, cassock tucked up, entered the water and addressed them, the river at this point being about 40 feet wide and two feet deep. In words translated from the *Book of Common Prayer*, he questioned them:

'Do you renounce the devil and all his works?' (They knew what this meant. It meant renouncing witchcraft, casting spells, invoking the spirits, polygamy – the old religion). 'Do you renounce them?'

'We renounce them all.'

'Do you believe in God the Father? In Jesus Christ? In the Holy Spirit? Do you accept the teaching of the Church?'

'We do.'

'Do you wish to be baptised?'

'We do.'

'Will you keep God's holy commandments?'

'We will.'

And then they filed forward: boys first, then the girls, then the men, then the women. They waded through the water to where Elfric and a server were waiting, each holding in their hand a card on which was written their Christian name-to-be. They handed the card to the server, who read out the name on it to Baba Matimba. We will say the name was 'Petros'. Elfric took the Petros-to-be by the hand.

'Petros, I baptise you in the name of the Father' – and he plunged Petros beneath the water. 'In the name of the Son – and he plunged Petros down the second time. 'In the name of the Holy Spirit' – and Petros was plunged down for the third time.

After he had been plunged down the third time, the water running from his face, Petros groped his way to the bank holding up his right hand, and another hand came down from the bank to grasp it, the hand of his sponsor. He was pulled up the bank and led behind a grass enclosure.

The candidates had come in old ragged clothes, representing the unclean heathen life they were leaving behind. Now they put on clean new clothes and the white baptismal robe which symbolised the new life they had entered.

When all were baptised, we formed up in procession again. This time the newly baptised followed immediately behind the Cross, and as we processed, guess what we sang? *Onward*

132

Christian soldiers marching as to war.

Inside the church, the newly baptised were given candles. ('Handed' might be the more appropriate word; they had paid 3d for them on arrival at Chipashu.) 'These,' they were told 'are to show that you have passed from darkness into light.' And St Andrew's Church, normally dark, became a mass of twinkling candles. So, with the Reception into Church, the service ended and the merrymaking began.

The Confirmation and First Communion of those baptised at Chipashu in May 1948 was held the following year and was typical of many. The Bishop of Southern Rhodesia, Bishop Edward Paget, came by train to Hartley, and together we travelled out to Chipashu, arriving just before 3.30 p.m. The 152 candidates, their sponsors and their friends were waiting to welcome us, and since St Andrew's was far too small for such an occasion, the Bishop confirmed the candidates, row upon row of them, in the open air, anointing each with oil and addressing each by name as he laid his hands upon them.

The sun was beginning to set before we had finished. The weather was good and most were camping out, and the scene that night was unforgettable. Above were the twinkling stars and beneath the flickering light of some 30 camp-fires, each reflecting the eager animated faces of boys and girls, all chattering excitedly together and huddling for warmth around the glowing embers.

Next morning those newly confirmed made their First Communion. It was cold and blustery, so we had the service in church, somehow managing to pack in all the candidates and a few more besides. The Bishop spoke on the importance of worship and emphasised that, necessary as schools were (schools were almost a *sine qua non* for the African), they were not as necessary as churches. 'Education uninspired by religion only makes clever devils. Worship is paramount.' And so the Eucharist was celebrated and the holy food offered and received.

On this occasion, however, the service over, a further ceremony followed. A large and shapely stone had been

133

*d*ragged to the church on an ox-sleigh. The Bishop was asked to dedicate this stone as the foundation stone of the new St Mark's Central Primary School to be built on the banks of the Umfuli River 15 miles to the west.

Its building was to be a landmark in the history of the Mission and in the next chapter I tell the story of its building.

First, however, a domestic postcript. Early in 1948 Marjorie again became pregnant. We arranged for her, when the time came, to go to the Queen Mary Nursing Home in Gatooma, and on Saturday night, November 6th, her pains began in earnest. I dressed hurriedly and delivered her safely to Queen Mary's. Later that night, I and a nanny roused Peter and Christopher and drove them some 20 miles through Mopani scrub to Mopani Farm where Gus and Nan Van Lingen, good friends of ours, were waiting to receive them. Finally, as Sunday began to dawn, I arrived back at Hartley just in time to take the 8 a.m. Holy Communion. That is my story. Marjorie's is different. She would gladly have changed places. Antony Hugh was born later that afternoon.

12

Early Days at St Mark's

At my first Teachers' Conference in the Mhondoro in December 1946, I had asked the teachers what they considered to be the most pressing need of the Mission. They had answered unanimously: 'A central mission station.' The largest of their schools could only teach up to Standard 3. Like other missions, they needed a central primary school teaching up to Standard 6. 'When our children have passed Standard 3 there are often no places for them in other mission schools.' I found that this was true, and began searching in earnest for a site in the Reserve to fulfil their need.

In the early days of the British occupation, the British South Africa Company had allocated huge tracts of lands to the Church for its work among native people, and on these lands the Church had built its central mission stations. St Augustine's, Penhalonga, had been established in 1896, St Faith's, Rusape; St David's, Bonda; St Columba's, Bulawayo; St Mary's, Hunyani and All Saints, Wreningham (later Daramombe) soon afterwards.

But those days were over. There was no longer suitable empty land at the Government's disposal. Land for a mission centre had either to be bought at a price from a European Farmer bordering the Reserve, or, if in the Reserve itself, to be offered by the villagers.

In 1948 the diocese was, as always, financially stretched. The Diocesan Synod had even discussed engaging no more married priests from England, owing to their cost. Money from the diocese for buying land bordering the Reserve was out of the question, and so I began the search for any land in the Reserve itself which might serve our purpose. Towards the end of the year I found a possible site.

The Sivandazi River, a tributary of the Umfuli, formed the western boundary of the Reserve for most of its course, and just before its junction with the Umfuli was a small triangle of Reserve land completely empty. Why, I never discovered, unless it was because it was of the rich red soil preferred by European farmers. Africans liked sandy loam soil because it was easier to work.

I saw Mr Sisson, the Native Commissioner in Hartley. He said that I would have to get the consent of the villagers, and in July 1949 Mr Sisson, an interpreter, myself and the local villagers met. Africans were so hungry for education that I expected no opposition. To my surprise there was, and when the Commissioner put the question to them: were they prepared to allow the Mission to use the land for a central school? they said no.

'That's that,' said the Commissioner to me, and was about to dismiss the meeting when to my surprise 'Paraffin', who kept a small native store on the main road near the suggested site and who, till now, had said nothing, spoke up.

'First,' he said, 'let us go and look at the site.' And to this they agreed.

Their idea of a central mission site was the traditional one. They imagined it as embracing thousands of acres. When they realised that I was only asking for 50 *morgen* (110 acres) and that no local villagers would be forced to leave, they changed their minds and agreed. But it was touch and go.

The diocese had asked the Society for the Propagation of the Gospel for help. In December 1949 we received a grant from them of £2,000 towards the building of St Mark's, and in the following spring work began. We had fenced the site by March, and after Easter, Howard Majoka, a Standard 5 teacher from St Luke's, Chikoware, 5 miles away, was seconded till the end of the year to superintend the building work and to enlist and organise voluntary labour. He and four villagers arrived in May. They cleared ten acres of land, and in June parties of villagers arrived to cut grass for thatch and to make bricks – we needed more than a hundred thousand.

Later that summer, Wilson Nzobo, a local builder, 'one whose heart God had touched', was taken on, and by December four oblong 'dormitories' (28 feet by 14 feet), an office, three teachers' houses and my own house were completed. In all this God worked with us.

In January 1951, in one of the so-called dormitories, the embryo primary school opened with an enrolment of 28 children and two teachers, a Julius Murumbedzi as headmaster and Howard Majoka as his assistant. Julius had come straight from the newly opened St Patrick's Teacher Training College outside Gweru. He was full of enthusiasm and immensely likeable. He received only five pounds a month from the Department, and thinking he might like to earn a little extra in his spare time, I asked him if he would like to paint the iron window-frames in the buildings being erected. He readily agreed and I asked him what would be a fair price – would 18 pence a window be fair?

'Oh no, Father,' he replied. 'I will do it free to help the Mission.'

He was later ordained, and when Marjorie and I were living in Sevenoaks, USPG paid for him to attend a post-ordination course in stewardship and evangelism at Marjorie's old college, the College of the Ascension, in Birmingham. Flora, his wife, accompanied him. Though officially retired, I was then on the staff of St John's, Sevenoaks, and in November Fr Michael Shields, its Vicar, invited Julius to preach at the Sunday morning Parish Mass. He made a deep impression, and he and Flora won many friends. On returning to Zimbabwe, he was made Diocesan Missioner and Steward-ship Adviser; also Archdeacon and Vicar General of the diocese in the Bishop's absence.

And he had begun his schooling squatting on the mud floor of a pole-and-dagga school in an African reserve, taught by an untrained catechist and equipped only with slate and pencil! But it never turned his head. Today he is Priest-in-Charge of St Michael's, M'bare, the Harare parish embracing Runyararo, Barbara Tredgold's dream-child. He is still recovering from the effects of an horrific car crash a few years back which left him unconscious for weeks, hovering between life and death, but continues to witness by his life to the grace of Jesus Christ, the love of God, and the power of the Holy Spirit. Flora teaches and is a leading light in the Mothers' Union.

For the first five months of 1951 I had to help me in Hartley two old friends of Bishop Paget from his Transvaal days, a Revd and Mrs Steer. Mr Steer had just retired, and before returning to England wished to see something of Southern Rhodesia. He had offered help at his own expense to any priest in the diocese needing assistance, and the Bishop kindly put us in touch. Mr and Mrs Steer stayed at the Hartley Hotel and Mr Steer proved a quite wonderful colleague. I doubt if I could have coped without him, and I made a secret vow that if it were at all possible on retirement I, like Mr Steer, would offer my services free to any priest in need. By the grace of God this I have been able to do.

Throughout 1951 the usual pattern of Sunday services in the parish continued, and sometimes when taking a Sunday afternoon service on a farm I would take Marjorie and family with me. I would drive the parish truck, with Marjorie on the passenger seat, Antony on her lap, and Peter and Christopher standing each side of her. No seat-belts in those days!

A much longer journey was in May 1951 when we all spent the inside of a week at Daramombe. Looking to the future, I was anxious to learn all I could about the running of a central mission station and had written in March to Fr Reg Clark, its priest-in-charge, asking if I could spend a week with him in May, possibly bringing my family with me. He had replied on April 6th:

138

We do hope you and your family will be able to come as suggested. My wife is expecting a baby about the end of April, perhaps earlier – but if the babe decides to be awkward and time his arrival with yours, then the Gilberts, the Ibbs and Miss Russell will take you over. We are all anxious for you to come. He then gave travelling instructions.

We went by public transport, all five of us, taking over 12 hours on the journey. Leaving Hartley by train at 5 a.m., we reached Salisbury by 8.30 a.m., and at 9.30 a.m. boarded the Salisbury – Fort Victoria native bus. After seven tedious hours we reached Enkeldoorn, where Reg Clark collected us. The baby had arrived on time.

There was much to see, learn and talk about, and inevitably children and babies figured in the conversation. On one occasion Marjorie and I described the hassle of Antony's birth. Reg's only comment was: 'You were lucky – you made it to Hartley. Our last-but-one was born in the mission truck on the way to Enkeldoorn. I had to act as Mary's midwife.' Thereafter Reg had a special love for his third-born.

Although a naturally shy person, Marjorie was an ATCL (Associate of Trinity College, London) for dramatic art, and once on the stage threw off all inhibitions. She had taken the Gatooma Amateur Dramatic Society by storm with her portrayal of the scheming sister in the comedy *Fresh Fields* 'she outplayed us all' and on August 15th, 17th, 18th, she produced *Fresh Fields* herself in aid of Norton and Hartley church funds, again playing the role of the scheming sister, ably supported by David and Betty Carnegie. I acted as prompter. (What do you do if one of the cast picks up the wrong cue and jumps two pages?)

A week later we left for a fortnight's holiday in the Vumba, a holiday resort south of Umtali and on the borders of Mozambique, where Archdeacon Wood had a holiday cottage which he kindly loaned to us. It was the season for pineapples

139

and there were these luscious fruits growing in the cottage garden.

Another memory is a four-mile walk along the shady paths of an under-cliff to the Vumba Hotel. It was the time when the financier Clarence Hatry's Photomatic empire collapsed. The manager of the Vumba Hotel happened to be named Hatry and I remember a customer at the bar remarking upon it: 'No connection, I hope, of that bastard who has just done the British public out of millions?'

'Sir,' came the cool and courteous reply, 'he is my father.'

I am trying to be perfectly honest in these memoirs but sometimes with passing years impressions and reactions change. While at Vumba I wrote my letter for the September/October issue of *The Hartley and Norton Church News*, and in it I summarised the current position as regards the parish and the Mission. It is very factual, as well as revealing my own heart-seachings, so I give it in full.

Dear Church People,

Some of you may have noticed a 1948 Peugeot half-ton vanette standing for the past two weeks in the shadow of St Edmund's Church. It belongs to the Mission and is the first outward sign of a coming event which will mark yet another step forward in the history of both parish and MIssion – their coming separation, the one from the other.

ST MARK'S MISSION

I have from time to time mentioned in this leaflet the work of St Mark's Mhondoro Mission, and most of you have known that since coming among you I have had African as well as European work to attend to; but not many of you, I think, have guessed the extent of that African work, nor of how much of my time it has taken away from the parish. Statistics may be dull but at least they can convey a lot in very little space, so here are some statistics of the Mission: 20 centres with regular Sunday services, 14 churches, 15 schools, 1 African priest, 50 African schoolteachers, 1,200 confirmed Christians, 1,700 school children and an African monthly pay-bill of over £200.

The nearest centre with a school is 28 miles from Hartley, the furthest is 90; and for all these centres I have been for the past three years ultimately responsible. For their administration and finance I have been entirely responsible. Yet my main work has been, in theory, the care of souls in the Hartley parish, a European area.

It has proved an impossible burden and has been fair neither to parish or Mission. For some 12 months, accordingly, your Parish Council has been petitioning the diocese for a separation of these two quite distinct spheres of the Church's work, and had the Mission any similar body able to make its needs known, it would have done the same. It has desperately needed for many years past a central mission station in the Mhondoro Reserve with a resident priest-in-charge, and the good news from the point of view of both parish and Mission is that it is shortly to have one. As a result of a generous grant of £2,000 from the SPG in England, the central station-to-be of the St Mark's Mission is slowly taking shape on a 50-*morgen* site in the Mhondoro Reserve.

We were allocated the site two years ago and work began in earnest on it in May last year. Today three dormitories, two teachers' houses and the Mission office are approaching completion, and my family and I expect to move out to camp in two of the dormitories in about six weeks' time, and from then on I am to concentrate on the work of the Mission.

HARTLEY PARISH

It is not, so far as we are concerned, goodbye. We do not expect to leave Hartley until the end of October, and even after that I shall be coming in to take Sunday services until my successor is appointed.

And we are not leaving the district. St Mark's, where we are going to live, is only five miles from Bougainvillea Farm, and Hartley will remain our shopping and banking centre.

141

We shall very much look forward to seeing you at St Mark's once we are settled in; and as soon as our real house is built, we shall look forward to returning some of the hospitality we have received. Only the foundations of the house are in so far, but we hope to press on quickly with its building, and being on the spot should make a very great difference.

It is for this reason that we have decided to go so soon, but we also feel that it is for the good of the parish that the parish should be recognised as vacant and that the separation of the parish and Mission should come quickly. It constitutes a big step forward for the parish, the Mission and ourselves.

In some ways we look forward to it – it will be good only to have one job, not two, and to be able to concentrate upon it; the past three years have been a constant tug of war between the just demands of both Mission and parish. There is also a certain thrill about a pioneer work such as ours will be at St Mark's, and it is what we have always wished to do.

On the other hand, it means a big reorientation of thoughts and ways, a real striving to know and love and understand the African, a ministering of the Word and Sacrament which is the same and yet different (for the seed must be suited to the soil it is sown in). And for all these things I ask your prayers.

Some people welcome change. I never do, and every new step I take, I take in fear and trembling, feeling quite insufficient. My feelings as regards this coming new step are no different, yet I believe I am called upon to take it. And so I take it in confidence that God's grace will be sufficient and that it will be for the benefit of all his work in this portion of his kingdom.

May his kingdom come, in our hearts, in this land, and in all the world, increasingly. . . .

The move to St Mark's took place towards the end of October. All our worldly possessions were loaded on to a five-ton lorry, and two hours later we distributed them into two of the dormitories and the Mission office. Marjorie cooked on a wood-fuelled kitchen range and water was drawn from the Umfuli River on an ox-sleigh. It was emptied into tanks and treated against bilharzia – a kind of tapeworm which infects, with few exceptions, the rivers in Zimbabwe.

The morning after our arrival Marjorie was scrimmaging under a wardrobe and let off a mighty scream – a small snake was sleeping there. But this was nothing compared with the scare we got a few days later. Marjorie and I decided to take a stroll by the Umfuli in the cool of the evening. Between the river and the Mission's northern boundary was a stretch of no man's land varying from 20 to 120 yards, according to the winding of the river. A track ran through it and we were sauntering along this track when we heard a sudden swishing through the undergrowth. What was that? A little later came a second swishing, and this time we saw – a huge crocodile was making for the water's edge. We beat a hasty retreat. What scared us most was the speed with which it shot away from us. In captivity crocodiles crawl from place to place slowly, ponderously. The one we had disturbed darted away at the speed of a lizard. 'Never be scared of a crocodile,' I once read, 'all his terrific jaw-muscles are geared for closing. For opening his jaws he relies on gravity. Just hold his upper and lower jaws together and he is helpless. But beware of his claws.' I repeated this to Marjorie, who was not amused.

In November we had visitors. 'Ronald' and 'Gladys' came to visit us from Daramombe. Ronald, a 30-year-old B.Sc. and AKC. of King's College, London, had been recruited by SPG to be the first headmaster of St Mark's, and he and Gladys had been at Daramombe for three months learning African ways. Now they wanted to look at their home-to-be. I liked Gladys, and was impressed but not attracted to Ronald, and this impression was confirmed when they moved into St Mark's early in December. Ronald was critical of Daramombe and had not a good word to say either for it or St Mark's. We had cleared and fenced the site, built four teachers' houses, four dormitories, a mission house and office, ploughed and planted ten acres of land and still had a small cash balance in hand. What more he could have expected me to do with £2,000 I cannot imagine. Marjorie and I were due to go to England for six months' furlough in February, and Ronald would be in sole command at St Mark's till our return. Let him have a go! He could change a lot in six months. Meanwhile, I had work to do for I still had Hartley parish to care for; I returned there each weekend.

Christmas 1951 was memorable. I was in Norton for Christmas services on the 23rd and 24th, and on Christmas Day itself took a Christmas Communion in Hartley at 8 a.m. and a Family Carol Service at 10 a.m. Then I started back for St Mark's.

It was a time of great rain, and when I reached the Sivandazi I found it running swiftly and quite impassable. I knew that Marjorie was expecting me back for Christmas lunch, to which Ronald and Gladys had been invited, so I parked the truck on the roadside above the drift and prepared to swim for it. A small African boy on the further bank tried to dissuade me: 'No, no, Father, too deep.' (He didn't realise I could swim.) I stripped, packed my clothes in a plastic bag, tied it on my back with a belt and waded in. I was not troubled at the thought of crocodiles – the river was running far too swiftly. Nonetheless, halfway across fear seized me. The plastic bag started to slip off my back and I had a ghastly vision of 'Father' creeping into St Mark's clad only in msasa leaves. It would never be forgotten! But I was spared. With my right hand I held the bag in position and with my left hand and feet I dog-paddled; and so I arrived, like Paul's ship-wrecked mariners off the coast of Melita, 'safely to land'.

I found Marjorie almost in tears. The wind was contrary, smoke was everywhere and the kitchen range refused to get hot. Eventually we sat down to a half-cooked Christmas lunch at 4 p.m.

Christmas over, preparations began for the new school year. The kraal schools needed new equipment, and new teachers

144

must be signed on; registers must be made up. My time was fully occupied and everything was made more difficult by heavy rain. Ronald made frequent trips into Salisbury. The NED were not 100 per cent happy about St Mark's opening. Classrooms had still be be furnished, and would sufficient pupils register? But eventually they agreed and authorised Ronald's salary for a year.

In Hartley the old Rectory had been sold for scrap for £100. Whitehead's new weaving factory was operating and Hartley flourished. The parish had raised £1,168 in the previous 12 months and had put aside £337 for a new car and £400 towards the Rectory rebuilding. It had, however, failed to meet its diocesan quota of £500 by £166 and the diocese was unhappy – 'the quota should have been a priority'. I had too much to do to be greatly worried. The 1951 acounts had to be audited and passed, plans for the new Rectory had to be agreed and arrangements made for the maintenance of Sunday services during our furlough. I had also to pack.

To cap it all, in January came the official opening of St Mark's, an important occasion and not without its embarrassments. At 2 p.m. a mixed gathering assembled. Representatives from the dioceses, the NED, and the Native Department were present and a varied assortment of European farmers, white parishioners, African teachers, children and well-wishers.

The afternoon began with a conducted tour of the site, and when passing the quite modest teachers' houses one white farmer remarked for all to hear: 'Fancy building houses like that for *munts*'. Embarrassment number one. The speeches followed, comprising the usual compliments, well-wishes and thanks. Refreshments in the open air had been planned but, alas, a drenching shower intervened and the African teachers packed into our house for shelter, but one or two of the white farmers said No, they were not going to mix socially with blacks, and they persuaded the others. So embarrassment number two: blacks in the house, whites sheltering on the verandah.

But it was not for long. The shower was a brief one and as soon as it was over the Europeans wisely made for home. If the Sivandazi had risen they would have been marooned for the night.

Even Archdeacon Wood, Vicar General of the diocese and representing Bishop Paget on furlough, had to bid a hasty farewell, and a long talk I had wanted to have with him concerning the future of St Mark's and Ronald and myself could not take place. I should, I know, have gone to Salisbury to see him, but the next ten days were hectic ones. We had our furlough passage booked on the RMS *Stirling Castle* sailing from Cape Town on February 22nd, and there just didn't seem time. 'Leave it till we return,' said Marjorie. I was hard-pressed for time, so I did – but it proved a tragic mistake.

We had in any case to leave Hartley earlier than expected. Normally it was a four-day train journey to Cape Town but torrential rains had fallen in the Union and in many places tracks had been washed away. Our travel agents told us that we should leave Hartley no later than the sixteenth. Accordingly on February 15th we prepared to travel in to Hartley. We had loaded our luggage on to the ox-cart and were about to clamber in ourselves when Mr Micklethwaite, the Land Development Officer from near Chipashu, arrived carrying a rowing-boat on the top of his truck in case the Sivandazi proved unfordable. Strictly speaking the boat was not necessary as the water rushing over the drift was only two feet high. But Marjorie had crossed the drift in the ox-cart in similar circumstances a fortnight earlier to be photographed for her passport, and she had hated it. So we transferred to the rowing-boat and crossed in style.

In one respect our leaving early proved fortunate. When we signed in at the Hartley Hotel that afternoon we heard that King George VI 'had slipped quietly away in his sleep a few hours earlier'. A surprise. Cut off from news in the Reserve, we had had no idea that he was dying. I hurriedly arranged a memorial service for him to be held the following afternoon in the WI Hall.

That evening we had supper with Richard and Peggy Ball. Richard was Bank Manager and Church Treasurer in Hartley, and 18 months earlier Peggy had had to go into hospital for the removal of a cancer. A few days later her distressed husband had phoned me up. (I was still in Hartley.) Peggy, he told me, was home. When the surgeon had opened her up he had found the cancer so deep-rooted that he couldn't operate. They had just sewn her up. She couldn't last more than six months. The surgeon hadn't told her, but he said that Richard must. 'I just can't,' said the harassed voice. 'Will you?'

I found Peggy dressed and cheerful. I said that I was glad she was home again. Had they said anything to her about the operation?

'No,' she replied, 'but I know what you are going to say – that they say I am going to die; that I have only a few months to live. I'm not going to die – not yet. They said the same about my sister and she lived another five years!'

When six months later Peggy went back to hospital for a check-up, the cancer had disappeared. And the medical explanation? 'You simply can't account for these things. Sometimes, just occasionally, exposing the cancer to air seems to kill it.' Yes perhaps, I said to myself, but only when there is faith and prayer.

A few years later Richard retired and they went down to the Cape to live.

The children hadn't accompanied us to the supper at the Balls'. We had left them in the care of Trudy Lannigan, wife of the hotel manager. She was not an Anglican, she was, I think, a Swiss Lutheran, but she was a very good friend and our children still remember her because each Christmas she wrote to England for a Beatrix Potter book to give to them.

Early on the morning of February 16th we left Hartley on the boat-train for Cape Town. Mr Ball, the Van Lingens, and a few other friends saw us off.

13

'All Thy Waves and Storms'

The railway journey proved uneventful. All the wash-aways had been repaired and we arrived at Cape Town on February 9th, three days before the *Stirling Castle* was due to leave. However, it had already berthed and we were allowed on board, so we had three days' accommodation free by courtesy of the Union Castle Line. The first day we spent shopping; the second on the sands in Table Bay – a new and lovely experience for the children.

We had one minor scare. While shopping in a large departmental store in Cape Town, a voice came over the Tannoy: 'Are Mr and Mrs Lovejoy in the store? Their little boy Christopher is in Barclay's Bank across the road saying he is lost. Will they collect him, please.'

Three-year-old Antony we had on reins under tight control but, unnoticed by us, Peter and Christopher had wandered off 'exploring'. They had become separated and Christopher, finding himself opposite an exit and seeing Barclay's Bank across the road, where I had just previously cashed a cheque, had made his way to it, thinking we might return. Never again, we vowed, would we let him out of our sight. Christopher himself, a matter-of-fact six-year-old, seemed quite unconcerned.

The *Stirling Castle* had been reconverted from its role as a troop-ship and we had a cabin to ourselves. The voyage should have been a happy one. Unfortunately, Marjorie went down with a bout of asthma soon after we sailed and spent most of the voyage in the sick bay. She was well enough, however, to go ashore at Las Palmas, where we took on many crates of tomatoes. We were hoping to buy butter, still rationed in England, but the price was prohibitive. The 'eye-catchers' were large beautifully dressed dolls in which a brisk trade was done. We regretted having no small girls in our family.

We berthed in Southampton on March 8th, and after the ambling nature of the South African railways we found the speed with which the boat-train crashed over the points at perhaps 30 mph terrifying.

It was early spring and the London parks were glorious with daffodils. We were spending our first four weeks in England at the Church Missionary Society's London hostel in Leigham Court Road, Streatham, for missionaries on furlough, and two days after our arrival Marjorie and I reported at SPG House in Tufton Street. We were warmly welcomed and I was asked to be the fifth member of an SPG team doing a fortnight's deputation work in the Lichfield diocese.

An airmail postal service was now operating between Southern Rhodesia and England, and as we left the Secretary handed me a letter from the diocese marked 'to await arrival'. I opened it on the top of the bus taking us back to Streatham and glanced at it casually, thinking it was to do with the business details of our furlough, Then I read and reread it, my heart beating. It was a very long letter and I could not believe my eyes. My whole world was collapsing around me. Marjorie, of course, wanted to know what it said. 'Not now,' I answered. 'Wait till we get home.'

The letter dated 3.3.52 was from the Venerable EDK Wood, Archdeacon of Mashonaland and Vicar-General of the diocese, Bishop Paget, the Diocesan, being on a tour of Central Africa prior to a short visit to England.

This is not going to be an easy letter for me to write [he began] or for you to you to read; but I hope that our past friendly relationship, which I so much appreciate, will help me to write and you to read as we ought.

149

He then went on to say that he regretted having had to leave so hurriedly after the official opening of St Mark's but that the short talk he had had with me and the copy of a suggested 'Constitution and Rules' for the running of St Mark's which I had handed to him then had led him to believe that there was little chance of a happy partnership between Ronald and myself. Further thought and other considerations, he wrote, had quite convinced him.

This suggested 'Constitution and Rules' to which he had taken exception I had, in fact, worked out with Ronald. When Ronald had visited St Mark's the previous November, he had been harshly critical of Daramombe, its staff and its running. The priest-in-charge, he said, was always interfering with the running of the school, the atmosphere was bad and it was the same on every mission station in the diocese. (How he knew that I couldn't imagine.) 'Hadn't they any sort of constitution?' I had asked, and he had replied that they had talked of drawing one up but that nothing had come of it. 'Ought we to have one?' I asked. He agreed that we should try, and it was this suggested constitution, worked out with him, that I had handed to the Archdeacon.

Admittedly, Ronald's and my relationship had become somewhat strained, but I was tired, he was new, and I hoped that after my return all would be well. And I had some sympathy for him. He had been recruited by SPG to be the headmaster of a new central primary school still being built. The usual blah: it was a challenge. Its success would depend on him. He would be in complete control. They hardly seem to have mentioned the Mission as a whole, or that I was responsible for its churches and primary schools, and that I was living at St Mark's with my family and that St Mark's was our home. Whatever the truth, Ronald clearly resented our presence on 'his' station and wanted us out. That, I believe, determined his attitude and actions.

The Archdeacon then went on to say that I had been most unfortunate in my relationship with my parishioners in Hartley and had 'alienated the sympathies of most of the Africans for whose benefit the Mission had been started'.

I read and reread the letter. I just could not believe it. As regards the parish, at no time had there been any open criticism, and the PCC meetings had always been friendly ones. The parish finances spoke for themselves. The income in 1947 had been only £198; in 1951 it reached £1,168; and congregations had grown. I am ready to believe, however, that among non-churchgoing parishioners there was criticism.

When I revisted Zimbabwe in 1972 to take charge for six months of the parish of St Bartholomew's, Rusape, a young Dutch Reformed minister had just arrived in the township. Because he championed the rights of the Africans, the Afrikaners in the district had not a good word to say of him and labelled him a 'nigger-lubber'. When I moved from Hartley to St Mark's I suspect many whites in the parish so labelled me. 'If he wants to go, let him go. He seems to prefer them to us.' Alas, my leaving them was bound to hurt, even though it proved, as I predicted, for the ultimate good of the parish.

'But', wrote the Archdeacon, 'I had also alienated the sympathies and support of most of the Africans for whose benefit the Mission had been started.'

'Only a European,' wrote Baba Matimba, 'could have said such a thing.'

I had no doubt who that European was. 'Beware of that Ronald,' a friendly white farmer had said to me. 'He's dangerous.' Unhappily, I paid no heed to the warning. I stood well with the diocese, so I thought. Marjorie and I had certainly served the diocese wholeheartedly for more than five years, and it never occurred to me that should matters between Ronald and me come to a head, they would listen entirely to one who had only just arrived in the diocese, and never even give me a hearing. But so it proved and it was that which hurt.

In St John 7:51 Nicodemus is recorded as protesting to the Sanhedrin concerning Jesus: 'Does our law judge any man before it hear him?' Those words echoed and re-echoed through my mind. To have been taken into the diocese's confidence would have made all the difference.

151

Some ten years ago I met Ronald again. It was at a meeting of the Transvaal, Zimbabwe and Botswana Mission at the Royal Foundation of St Katharine in London. For three years after I left he had done great things at St Mark's Mhondoro. It had received NED recognition and had flourished. After three years, however, he quarrelled with the diocese – why, I don't know – left St Mark's and entered the Government Education Service. He returned to England and was ordained to the diaconate, and to the priesthood 12 months later, becoming a 'non-stipendiary minister' in the Oxford diocese and then, in 1985, Rector of Swyncombe with Britwell Salome in the same diocese. He retired three years later and went to live in Leeds, and we are no longer in touch.

When we met at the Royal Foundation of St Katharine he was quite unselfconscious and greeted me warmly, and I responded likewise. Another wound healed. So be it.

But the six months which followed our return to England in 1952 proved the most painful of my life. I remember sobbing my heart out on my bed. The whole world seemed an empty void.

God of his goodness has endowed me with a generous heart. It is natural to me to like people and to wish to help them. Now suddenly all this changed. Something within me seemed to have snapped. I looked out on a cold and cheerless world. I felt at one with the hippy and the drop-out. I knew now how they felt. I regarded those about me as enemies. If they could hurt me they would. It was the same when an airmail letter arrived from Zimbabwe. I would turn it over and look on the back for the name of the sender. Another from the Archdeacon? It would be in reply to mine. Please, please, Lord, I prayed, don't hurt me any more. It will finish me.

One thing upheld me at this time. I shall call it 'the tranquil operation of God's perpetual providence mediated through Christ's Body the Church'.

As already mentioned, we were staying at that time at a CMS house in Streatham and were within walking distance of St Peter's, a church of the Anglo-Catholic tradition with a daily early-morning Eucharist. There were never less than six persons present, sometimes as many as 15, and every morning I was one of them.

There were no greetings or welcome. We came in silently, sat by ourselves, and left without a word. No one ever spoke to me. On one occasion the Vicar happened to be standing by the door as I left. He did choose to ask me where I came from, and when he heard asked me in to coffee. I was longing to unburden myself but he never gave me a chance. He spoke the whole time, telling me the history of St Peter's and what, under God, he had been able to achieve. Then he arose, held out his hand and said goodbye; and that was that. But it didn't matter. The opportunity his church provided for me to join in its worship morning after morning began the healing of my soul.

As you will have gathered throughout this period my belief and trust in God and his love and care never wavered. I had been ordained 20 years and had experienced, in success and failure, in darkness and in light, his guiding and upholding hand. My darkness now was always lightened with the ray of hope. And so it is mostly when Christians say they cannot believe. Their doubts are intellectual; they cannot understand with the mind. 'If there is a God, why...?' is the typical question. They wonder with their minds but in their hearts they believe. Only rarely does their disbelief go deeper. An illustration will explain.

Once, while training for ordination at Dorchester, I had been kneeling in the college chapel watching the celebrant. The Principal was facing east, as always in those days, and, hands uplifted, was reciting the Eucharistic Prayer. And I remember thinking to myself: 'there he goes on, acting as if someone is there, thinking he is being heard. And he isn't. There's no one there'. That was fundamental doubt. I no longer doubted. I was sure. But I had never discussed it with him. I had kept my thoughts to myself. I didn't believe. I was different and that was all there was to it. It wasn't discussable.

That phase passed. How I cannot recall. What God wanted me to do, I did not know. But at least I returned to belief in him. Somehow God brought me through.

So he also brought me through in 1952. God was. I knew it in the deepest part of my being and I no more questioned his sovereignty or love than I did his existence. At the same time I never imagined for a moment that what he had allowed to happen to me was really his will.

When Jesus told the parable of the tares in the field, the farmer's servants ask, 'Sir, did you not sow good seed in your field. How then has it tares?' The farmer replies, 'An enemy has done this.' What had happened to me was, I was sure, the work of that Enemy of whom our Lord often warns us.

In addition to 'the tranquil operation' of God's perpetual providence mediated to me through the worshipping congregation at St Peter's, I saw God's hand also in a chance encounter I had on the precincts of Charing Cross railway station. Bishop Paget had arrived in England and I was on my way to see him when I bumped into an Indian Ecclesiastic Establishment chaplain whom I had met in Delhi. We exchanged a few pleasantries and then he burst into a dreadful harangue against the IEE. Having, so he said, been promised the Chaplaincy of New Delhi, he had accompanied the government to Simla for their summer session. The summer over, he had returned to the plains, only to discover that in his absence the Chaplaincy of New Delhi had been given to another. And he was bitter. He was more embittered than anyone I have ever met. I am going to meet Bishop Paget, flashed through my mind. Whatever else I am, let me not be bitter. And God kept me from bitterness.

Time is a great healer, and the last and most substantial ingredient in God's healing process was a holiday spent with my family in idyllic surroundings in Wiltshire.

Mr and Mrs Fitch of Marden Manor near Devizes had at their entrance drive two semi-detached cottages, one occupied, one vacant. Mrs Fitch and her daughter were regular churchgoers, and Mrs Fitch had persuaded her husband to offer the empty furnished cottage to missionary families on furlough. For eight weeks we were the fortunate family.

Peter and Christopher had been looked after for a month at the CMS home for the children of returned missionaries at Farleigh, near Horsham. They were happy there but we missed them. Now the family could be reunited. We went by taxi to Farleigh and then on to Marden.

Cigarettes were hard to come by in England in 1952 and very expensive, and so, although not ourselves smokers, Marjorie and I had taken up the offer of buying a thousand duty-free cigarettes before disembarking at Southampton. When we offered our taxi-driver a hundred cigarettes as a tip, he was overwhelmed!

I do not remember a wet or cloudy day at Marden. In our memory the sky was always blue, everything was green and all nature sang.

Peter and Christopher had by now missed three months' schooling, so we enrolled them at Churton Primary School, a mile away, and every morning they walked unaccompanied over the fields to school. Peter was eight and Christopher six. We never worried. We were home again and England was a safe and happy land.

Marjorie and I spent much of our time letter-writing, mine mostly to friends in Zimbabwe, hers to friends in England. She wrote that we had decided to remain in England for the sake of the children. This, maybe, was in modern parlance 'economical with the truth', but the real truth was too difficult to explain.

One of her letters was to a Julian Casserley. He had been a curate at St Luke's, West Norwood, before she left for India and she was godmother to his eldest son, Richard. Julian was now Rector of Mamhead, a small parish in the Exeter diocese, and a lecturer in theology in what was to become the University of the South-West. Later, he joined the staff of the General Seminary in New York and he and his family became citizens of the United States.

In June 1952 he was preaching a special course of sermons

155

on Sunday evenings at St Marychurch, Torquay, and afterwards the Vicar, the Revd. afterwards Prebendary, Peter
Vokes-Dudgeon would invite him back to the Vicarage for
supper. On one such occasion Peter Vokes-Dudgeon mentioned that he was looking for a curate. His present curate, Fr
Wittey, in charge of the district of Shiphay Collaton, had been
offered a benefice in Carlisle and had accepted. Had Julian
any suggestions? Marjorie's letter had just arrived and Julian
immediately recommended me. It was clearly 'meant' and
within a week all was settled: when Fr Wittey left, I was to
succeed him. 'There is a divinity that shapes our ends, rough-
hew them as we will.' Once again God was shaping mine.

I love and memorise the words of scripture and at different
times in my ministry different texts have echoed and re-
echoed through my mind. When in the last weeks before my
furlough the pressure of work threatened to overwhelm me
and I felt completely drained, I would think thankfully of
the words of the writer of the Letter to the Hebrews in
chapter 5 verse 9: 'There remaineth a rest for the people of
God', and would take courage.
   In the distress recorded in this chapter, I found myself
repeating time and time again the words of Psalm 42 verse
9: 'All thy waves and storms have gone over me', and I felt
at one with the writer; and at one, too, with Jonah, who
according to the writer repeated the same words from the
belly of the whale, As I got less and less desperate I would
half-smile to myself as I repeated them. 'All thy waves and
storms have gone over me – but God has been my helper.'
   A Prayer Book Collect equally helped me in those first
despairing days at Streatham. The Feast of the Annunciation
March 25th occured then, and St Peter's being a 'high' church
observed the octave. Repeated every morning, the lovely
Collect for the Annunciation became enshrined in my heart:

We beseech thee, O Lord, pour thy grace into our hearts; that
as we have known the incarnation of thy Son Jesus Christ by
the message of an angel, so by his cross and passion we may be
brought unto the glory of his resurrection.

'Dear Lord,' I said to myself, 'Me too: by thy cross and passion to the glory of thy resurrection.'

Going to Shiphay was to be my resurrection.

14

Shiphay Collaton

All things work together for good to them that love God
Romans 8:28.

At the turn of the century Shiphay Collaton was a small hamlet one and a half miles west of St Marychurch and with only the village of Cockington between it and the sea. Together with the even smaller hamlet of Edginswell, it was part of the parish of St Marychurch and was ministered to by an officiating parson driven over on Sundays to conduct Morning Prayer in a simple little stone building donated by the Kitson family which served both as church and school. The Kitsons, bankers in Torquay, were the local squires.

Then after the First World War, Shiphay became a select suburb of Torquay, referred to, so I am told, as 'Snobs' Hill' by irreverent bus-conductors.

After the Second World War came further development. Torquay Corporation started building and in 1952 some 500 council houses had been built and occupied and a further 1,000 were planned. Shiphay's population meanwhile had risen to around 4,000. At first the news of the proposed building plans brought dismay, but the new estate proved to be a model of its kind. Almost all the houses were semi-detached; all roads were tree-lined; and there was great variety of design, three-bedroomed and four-bedroomed houses standing cheek by jowl. The occupants were similarly mixed. Tenancies were restricted to married couples with two or more children of school age or under. In consequence, one could have schoolteachers and bank clerks in one pair of three-bedroomed semis, and next door, in the four bedroomed semi, rough labourers from Ireland with children everywhere. Yet it worked well. It was a happy and harmonious community.

'All things work together for good to them that love God.' Looking back, I see our days at Shiphay in New Testament terms. We were reliving, so it seemed, the life of the early Church after Pentecost. Everything we did God blessed, and one felt the Holy Spirit himself was in charge. One thing would lead to another, and we had all the enthusiasm of the first disciples. My predecessor, Fr Witty, had been indefatigable in visiting and I inherited from him a mixed grill of men and women of every age dedicated to God and his kingdom. And, as after Pentecost, their number was forever growing. As we grew so our needs grew, and as each need arose, so each need was satisfied.

The first pressing need was for a new church hall. When Marjorie and I arrived in 1952 the Torquay Town Council had built an infants school on the new estate. The small school previously housed in the church had closed, and the partition previously dividing church and school had gone. The old schoolroom now constituted the nave, and a modern brightly coloured reredos stood behind the altar in the chancel, its centre panel depicting our Lord's baptism by St John. The old school fireplace in what was now the nave had been bricked up but its stone mantelpiece remained. It looked, to my eyes, incongruous, but when I suggested removing it I was stoutly opposed. It was needed, I was told, by the flower ladies for their vases. So the mantelshelf remained.

On the same block in Cadewell Lane as the church was the 'church room', a small wooden hut complete with kitchenette, toilet and stage. A Sunday school for children up to 12, run by Miss Hopkins and Miss Martin, met there on Sunday afternoon, while older children met nearby in Elsie Beck's cottage in Water Lane. On weekdays the room was let to various local organisations and used for church social functions. But it was glaringly inadequate.

Across the road from the church and up a bank was a strip of land belonging to the church, given over to allotments. Soon after our arrival the church committee obtained the help of Mr Palmer, a local retired architect, to draw up plans for a hall on this site, and in April 1953 we launched a novel scheme to finance its building. The estimated cost of the hall was £2,000 and we proposed raising this by issuing 2,000 Shiphay Church Hall Building Bonds of £1 each. Each year, 100 bonds were to be repaid, together with a bonus of four shillings. The bonds and their repayment were guaranteed by the St Marychurch PCC since our building committee had no legal status. All the bonds were quickly snapped up. The turf for the hall was cut on November 1st, 1953 and the hall was completed the following September. On October 27th, 1954, in our new church hall, the first drawing of 100 bonds was the climax of a social evening.

In February 1954 came the Mission to Torquay. Preparations for it had begun in 1951 while we were still in Zimbabwe, and Fr Peter Vokes-Dudgeon had told me about it as soon as I was appointed to Shiphay. All Anglican churches in Torquay were taking part, and each church was to find its own missioner. Preparations and publicity were to be united efforts.

I thought at once of Brother Kenneth, SSF. Was he still at the Friary? Did he still take missions? Would he remember me? The answer in every case was Yes, and so began a most useful link-up between Shiphay and the Franciscans. Three 'outreaches' were planned: a Teaching Mission for the faithful in 1954; a Children's Mission the following year and a full-scale Parish Mission in the fulness of time as indicated by the Holy Spirit.

The Mission to Torquay opened on Sunday, February 7th. Brother Reginald, SSF, was to assist Brother Kenneth. He arrived on February 11th and we had a 'Meet the Missioners' Social the following day. On Sunday the 14th the Bishop of Exeter commissioned Kenneth and Reginald in the church at

160

3 p.m., and at 6.30 p.m. was the Opening Service of the Mission. Holy Communion was celebrated each morning throughout the week and a Mission Service was held each evening at 7.30 p.m. During the day the Missioners visited. Our own particular mission closed on the Sunday but a closing United Service of Witness and Thanksgiving was held in the Torquay Town Hall at 7.30 p.m. next day.

The Mission to Torquay had three consequences for us in Shiphay: (i) The introduction of a Parish Communion at 9.30 a.m. each Sunday. (This was just being introduced in many parishes by the Parish and People Movement) (ii) The moving of the time of Sunday school from 2.30 p.m. to 11.15 a.m. to coincide with the time of Sunday Morning Prayer and (iii) Most significant of all: the presentation of 15 children and 29 adults at a Confirmation held at All Saints', Babbacombe, on June 6th.

The moving of the time of Sunday school to the morning revealed a further need. Once a month the children and their parents were to join with the Matins congregation for a Family Service. The Sunday school enrolment now exceeded a hundred. We put in extra seating for this service in every possible space; even so, it was a colossal crush. Sunday school numbers continued to rise, and so in May that year I journeyed to Exeter to see the diocesan architects. Mr Gundry, the junior partner, saw me, and when I explained the position to him he asked what funds we had available to meet the cost. I answered quite truthfully that all we had was £192 in a Post Office Church Building account. He nonetheless agreed to proceed.

The total cost was provided in a providential way. Up to 1954 the Church Commissioners' income was restricted by law to the payment of clerical stipends, but in 1954 the law was changed. They were given permission to make limited grants for the provision of churches in new housing areas. In 1955 the Exeter Diocese was promised a grant of £10,000 for this purpose to any church ready to build. We were the only new housing area in the diocese with plans already drawn up, and so we were promised the whole grant – sufficient, it was thought, to meet the total cost. It wasn't. In my experience architects invariably underestimate, but 12 months later we were given a further diocesan grant to enable us to complete. This we owed to Mr Wallis, the diocesan treasurer, who was enthusiastic for the scheme and our very good friend.

When the need is real, God answers prayers. It was the same when the time came for tendering. The architects had to submit three tenders to the diocese. Whom did we suggest? At the Building Committee meeting the names of two local firms with good reputations and known to be competitive were quickly put forward. Then someone suggested Narracott's. We drew in our breath. Narracott's were the most prestigious – and expensive – builders in Torquay. Nevertheless, their name went forward, and when the tenders were opened theirs was the lowest! During World War Two, St Marychurch church had been totally destroyed by a bomb on a Sunday afternoon. Narracott's had recently completed its rebuilding and were anxious not to have to disband the team. So Narracott's became our builders.

It was a tremendous year. The Holy Spirit gave us no breathing-space whatever. Shiphay Collaton was planned to become first a conventional district, separate from St Marychurch, and finally a parish on its own; but before this could happen not only had our church to be enlarged but also more suitable accommodation had to be found for its incumbent.

Our new church hall was still being built when in August 1954 Shunem Guest House, on the north side of Cadewell Lane and not a hundred yards from the church, came on the market. In every way it was eminently suitable to be a vicarage: two large living-rooms, three double and two single bedrooms, a large garden with a croquet lawn, a small chalet suitable for a Sunday school class, a garage, even a conservatory with established grapevines. The owners, Mr and Mrs Arden, were anxious to sell. They were asking £3,700 but eventually came down to £3,500. But 37 Marldon Road, where we were then living, was only valued at around £600. Where was the balance to come from? Fortunately a Mr Green of the Halifax Building Society was on the PCC. The society, he told us, did not normally give advances on Church property, but if four individuals could be found to guarantee the advance, it would be considered. On Monday, October 18th we moved into Shunem, and even before that, on July 16th, I had been made Priest-in-Charge of the Conventional District of Shiphay Collaton.

There is one Shunem story I would like to add. To the left of the house was a huge elm tree which in a gale could have demolished Shunem. The Church Council decided the threat must be removed and we were told there was an Australian tree-feller living in the pre-fabs at the back of the house. We besought his help. One morning he arrived armed only with a rope and axe. He slung the rope into the tree and clambered up some 15 feet. Then he got busy with his axe. Chip-chop, chip-chop. Bystanders were abused in the most lurid language. 'The B . . . B . . . Bs, they only want me to fall.'

He never stopped and that afternoon he dropped the tree exactly where he wanted on the croquet lawn, making no dent in it whatsoever. Next morning he returned and, spurning a mechanical saw and using only his axe, he hewed the branches into manageable pieces.

The year before a smaller tree endangering the church room had been taken down by a tree firm for £65. Our Aussie friend had to be persuaded to accept £5 with which to drink our health.

There was further progress on all fronts in 1955, the most important impetus being the Children's Mission. Br Kenneth was bringing with him Celia Matthews, a parish worker with Fr Charles Shells ('Seashells') of St Anne's, Wandsworth, as assistant. 'I'm all right with juniors,' Kenneth explained, 'but I can't cope with infants. Celia can.' And so it proved.

They spoke at Shiphay Primary School on Thursday, April

28th and at Torre Junior School on the Friday. On the Saturday there were 'Meet the Missioners' parties and the Mission itself opened on the Sunday.

Brother Kenneth recounted the adventures of *Billy and the Pirates*. He was tremendous. Billy's 'friends', duly enrolled, had their secret sign and their password, and numbers grew steadily throughout the week. There must have been at least a hundred enrolled by the end of the Mission and our Sunday school never looked back.

Celia was equally good with the infants. On only one occasion did she fail to cope. She had great difficulty in getting her story of *The old woman who lived in a vinegar bottle* off the ground. Living in a vinegar bottle set on fire the imagination of the tinies. Up went the hands. 'Please, if she lived in a vinegar bottle, how did she hang pictures on the wall?' 'Please, Miss..?' 'Please Miss..?' Celia vowed she would never tell that story again.

As a consequence of the Mission, our Sunday school enrolment rose to nearly 300, with an average attendance of about 200, some meeting in the church room, some in the chalet, some in the vicarage, and the greatest number in the hall. They were divided into 25 to 30 classes and we were fortunate in always being able to enlist sufficient teachers to take them, many being trained teachers. Others we had to train ourselves. All our children lived in the parish.

The great annual event was the combined junior and senior Sunday school outing in July. Twice we also took the infants and went by train to Dartmouth and then up the river by boat to Totnes. Twice we took juniors and seniors to Dartmoor. For these visits Wallace Arnold Tours would provide us with coaches. On our first visit in 1955 they supplied us with six. Not all were their own and one might have come straight out of a museum – very tall, wooden seats, large wheels. One almost expected solid tyres! I wondered whom we would be able to persuade to ride in it. Each coach had a teacher in charge and was given a name, and this coach we handed over to a marvellous character,

Percy Scragg, both churchwarden and choirmaster. Percy labelled his pre-historic wonder 'Dan Dare' after the comic-strip space-hero of the day and the children queued to ride in it.

Parents and children brought packed lunches with them. We provided drinks for the day – between 40 and 50 crates of mineral water! In the afternoon we organised sports, and at their close set up trestle-tables for sandwiches, cakes and other refreshment. There was bedlam. As soon as the food appeared, the children pushed and shoved to get nearer the tables. 'Sit down!' I shouted. 'Sit down. You will get nothing until you sit down.' And suddenly my mind went back to St John's account of our Lord's feeding of the multitude in the wilderness:

> And Jesus said 'Make the men sit down.' Now there was much grass in the place, so the men sat down, in number about five thousand.
>
> *John 6: 10*

Now I knew why he said it.

In order to have races and games, we always chose places on our Sunday school outings where there was grass, but on Dartmoor the grass always merged into the moorland. On our second visit, in 1959, two of our more adventurous juniors unbeknown to me, went scavenging in it and came back delighted with a piece of shrapnel. I told them to throw it back.

I was travelling with them in one of Wallace Arnold's newest coaches and the driver was I thought, excessively nervous about getting its coachwork scratched by the bushes in the narrow lanes.

A week later a police inspector and a sergeant called at the Vicarage. The father of one of the lads had discovered his son and two friends throwing a hand-grenade to one another in his garden! Questioned, they had confessed that they had smuggled it home from Dartmoor. The father had taken it to the police station, where bomb experts had declared it 'live', and the policemen wanted to know where they had found it. I pleaded ignorance, but described where

165

we had been, and on our next visit to Dartmoor we found the whole area wired off and a warning notice erected: DANGER! KEEP OUT! UNEXPLODED SHELLS. The story was headlined in the *Western Gazette* and even found its way into the national press.

I thought of the coachdriver so anxious not to get his coach scratched and all the time driving with a live hand-grenade hidden in a knapsack nesting on his luggage rack!

'Make the men sit down.' Earlier another New Testament verse had taken on fresh meaning for me. The Torbay Hospital was sited in the parish and had its own chaplain, but I was honorary chaplain to a small isolation hospital on the Newton Road and held ward services in it one Sunday a month after Evensong, when members of the choir accompanied me.

On weekdays I would take Holy Communion to individual sick patients. One such patient from Chudleigh was there for many weeks, having been found to be a cholera carrier. He had been in India during the war and, unknown to anyone, must have become a carrier there. Now an outbreak of cholera in Chudleigh had been traced to him. I visited him regularly and gave him Communion by intincture – that is, I did not let him touch the pix but dipped the wafer into the wine and placed it straight into his mouth.

On one visit, in a moment of absent-mindedness, I gave him the pix to drink from. He handed it back to me, some wine still remaining. It was consecrated. I could not throw it down the basin. What was I to do with it? I should, of course, have handed back the pix to him to drain but that course never occurred to me. I said a silent prayer and consumed what was left.

When our Lord appeared to the disciples after his resurrection, Mark records that he said to them: 'These signs shall follow them that believe. . . . They shall take up serpents; and if they drink any deadly thing, it shall not hurt them.' I had not thought much of the text till then. Now, as I drained the pix, I was grateful for it and its promise.

There was another text – words of St Paul – I did not, but might have, applied to myself during our years at Shiphay. The words in his second letter to the Corinthians in which he pleads with them not to receive God's grace in vain and describes to them his circumstances and the circumstances of his fellow workers. They seek, he says, to give no offence in anything but in all things to approve themselves as ministers of God;

'as sorrowful, yet always rejoicing; as poor yet making many rich; as having nothing, and yet possessing all things.'

2 Corinthians 6: 10

When Fr Vokes-Dudgeon had offered me the curacy at Shiphay, all he had been able to offer was a house and £350 pa – not enough, he admitted, for the five of us to live on. Although later he was able to augment this with a grant from a clerical charity, the Curates' Augmentation Fund, the whole time we were at Shiphay we were desperately poor. We never thought of buying new clothes – we clothed ourselves from jumble sales and we obtained all our holidays by exchanging work and houses. It was nearly always with a married priest with a family, and the children loved it – new surroundings and a whole new cubby-hole of toys to play with! Television was still a novelty and there was even television in one parsonage we occupied.

Another treat for them was the Christmas pantomime on the pier in Torquay. Miss Blakeney-Edwards, an elderly and rather lonely parishioner, would buy the tickets and come with us, and she did us proud: front seats, sweets, ices at the interval, even a taxi to collect us and bring us home.

Parishioners were good to us. Do you know how to make a tough boiler chicken tasty and tender? Bob Dunning, the butcher, told us. Instead of stuffing it with fresh parsley, egg and breadcrumbs, you stuff it with raw potatoes. It roasts beautifully.

Our friends were delighted when they heard we were going to Shiphay and we had a constant stream of visitors, but they were very understanding and helped us with food. We also from time to time had students from Lund University in Sweden as paying guests.

One incident the children have never let me forget – I wish they would. We were out for the day, walking in the country, and we passed a small shop selling sweets. Would I buy them some? I emerged with a single Mars bar. I cut it into five and we shared it between us!

At 3 p.m. on Saturday, April 21st, 1956 came the Laying of the Foundation Stone of the new church. The afternoon was fine and many diocesan dignitaries were present. The stone was to be laid by the Bishop, and Marjorie entertained him in the sitting-room while the rest gathered in my study. Before being consecrated, Robert Mortimer had held only one pastoral office – his first curacy. He was a great scholar and since then all his appointments had been academic. He was much loved as a bishop and was a first-class administrator – write to him and he replied by return of post. But he had no small talk. 'How I wish I was like Wilfred,' he once said to me. Wilfred Westall, his suffragan and Bishop of Crediton, could chat up anyone.

About 15 minutes before the service was due to begin, I ventured to say to him, 'Bishop, don't you think you should join the others?'

'Who's there?' he asked.

'The Archdeacon,' I replied, 'the diocesan treasurer, the Rural Dean, Mr Narracott, Fr Vokes-Dudgeon, Mr Gundry, the four churchwardens.'

The Bishop thought for a moment. 'I'll stay where I am.' And that was final.

Narracott's worked quickly and well and the church was consecrated on December 20th. In the following February I was Instituted and Inducted as Perpetual Curate of the benefice of St John the Baptist, Shiphay Collaton.

That was in 1957. The following year was our last full year in Shiphay and notable for two events: the long-planned

Parish Mission and a stewardship campaign.

Brother Kenneth had continued to visit Shiphay regularly in preparation for the former and on Monday February 3rd he and his team arrived. With him were two friars from Cerne Abbas, two sisters from Malvern Link and two lay-missioners. They were commissioned on the following evening by the Lord Bishop and the usual social functions and house parties took up the rest of the week. The Mission opened on the Sunday. I have no records concerning it but I remember our new church was comfortably filled each evening and packed for the closing service on Sunday the sixteenth.

One surprising result was how, during it, the hearts of the people of Shiphay warmed to the Malvern sisters. At first they were very nervous. Franciscan friars, yes. They had grown used to them and had found they were human. But nuns? I had some difficulty in finding accommodation for them. 'What do nuns eat?' was one of the extraordinary questions fired at me. By the end of the Mission both were loved.

More Confirmations followed and, in all, I presented 60 adults and 121 children for Confirmation during my seven years in Shiphay.

The Mission was followed in May by a stewardship campaign. In June 1956 Canon Leslie Walker of the Brotherhood of the Good Shepherd, Australia, had been in England and had paid me a visit. He had told me then how the Wells Fund-raising Organisation, which used American big-business marketing methods and which specialised in helping churches to increase their direct giving, had established itself in Sydney and had transformed church giving in Australia. When, then, I read in the *Church Times* early in 1958 that they were coming to England. I at once contacted them and their representative came to see me.

Before signing the contract of engagement I learned that they required a deposit of £500. They assured me, however, that such was their reputation that any bank would be prepared to advance it. Maybe, but that was only the beginning. They also required a percentage of the increased giving in the parish as a result of their services. I explained to him that we had no wealthy parishioners, that we were only just beginning as a parish, and that there was not the slightest chance of my PCC agreeing to a contract. What did he, advise?

'Well,' he replied, 'you could always run a campaign yourselves. You would not do as well as if we ran it for you, but you could do very well indeed.'

And so it was agreed and he could not have been more helpful. He even left me a full set of the brochures they employed. I later met clergy who were critical of Wells. I cannot be grateful enough to them.

We followed all the Wells guidelines at Shiphay – as I have in stewardship campaigns ever since – and on May 8th more than 250 sat down to the Stewardship Supper. Earlier we had decided on a division of labour: the ladies would be hostesses, responsible for the supper itself and for bringing a party of guests to it; the men would be responsible for visiting their guests afterwards and obtaining their pledges. The men were not so forthcoming as the ladies, but we gathered some 30 together and I put to them the challenge, their part in the plan, and answered their questions. But when I asked for names, not one responded.

Then Jim Cloke, a painter and decorator and a member of the PCC, spoke up. 'Come on, chaps,' he said. 'Let's have a bash at it.' Not, maybe, the words I would have used myself but they all liked Jim and the day was saved. Exactly 20 volunteered. We held three training sessions for them. One included role-plays and was hilarious.

The campaign was an unqualified success and 193 pledges were obtained. The emphasis throughout was on sacrificial giving and an excellent talk on Tithing by Josephine Hilton, broadcast at the beginning of the year, was reprinted with the permission of the BBC and enclosed with the campaign brochure distributed at the supper.

In the course of my ministry at Shiphay we had accepted at God's hand ever-increasing responsibilities, among them the mortgage on the Vicarage and the repayment of the Building Bonds on the new Hall. Nevertheless, at the end of 1958 our treasurer was able to announce that for the first time since he took office we had managed to balance our budget.

Early in 1959 I had what Marjorie is pleased to call 'itching feet'. I had been trained by SPG to work in foreign parts and I had kept up all my overseas links while in Shiphay. In seven astonishing years God had transformed Shiphay from a district of St Marychurch into a flourishing independent parish. But my heart was still overseas – it still is – and the time was opportune, so it seemed to me, to take steps to see if I could still be of service to my old society. So I again contacted them. They asked the age of my children. Peter was 15, Christopher 13 and Antony 10. When USPG heard, they replied that if I went overseas it would needs-be to a country in which the three of them could be educated, and, generally speaking, in their opinion such countries were not as short of clergy as was the north of England.

In my early years, 'Go north, my boy, and earn your fortune', was a popular saying. This, in a different context, was what USPG was saying to me now.

When Marjorie trained at Selly Oak John Ramsbotham was chaplain at her college. He was now Bishop of Wakefield, so she wrote to him and he asked us to come to see him. We went on April 6th. A friend, Mrs Saunders of the Melanesia Mission, agreed to have the children and, to stop tongues wagging, we let it be known in the parish that we were going to see my parents in London – as we were. We stayed that night with the bishop and his wife, and next day he took us to see the parish of Cumberworth with Denby Dale. They were two small villages 12 miles from Wakefield, 10 miles from Huddersfield and 9 miles from Barnsley. We had pictured being sent to a grim industrial parish in the centre of a town. This was not at all what we had expected and the Rectory was old and vast. I asked the Bishop if he had anything else to offer. He said he had but this was the parish he most wanted filled. So we said yes, and the

Induction was fixed for August 6th. Then we returned to London to my parents.

The next step was to inform the Bishop and the parish. I saw the Bishop on April 24th and broke the news to the parish three days later. The latter was on the spur of the moment. With three or four parishioners I was attending the annual Deanery Conference at Paignton. Just before the Conference was due to begin, the Rural Dean mentioned to me that he had to announce that one of his clergy was leaving. 'You can include my name too,' I said. And I told him that I was moving to Yorkshire in August.

I realised later it was a mistake. As soon as the meeting closed my parishioners came rushing up to me. 'Why, why, are you leaving us?'; 'Why didn't you let the PCC know first?'; 'It was a dreadful shock. I felt quite ill.' Yes, I had blundered badly, and I quickly called a meeting of the PCC and apologised.

The churchwardens of Cumberworth and Denby Dale had stressed that if I accepted the rectorship I would need a car. On our return to Shiphay we therefore set about acquiring one. We chose a 1952 Ford Anglia on sale for £200 and, having no money, we wrote to Pa for help. He replied that he could not easily help personally but that if his bank manager was prepared to loan me the £200, he would willingly guarantee it. I accordingly visited the manager. In 1927 Pa had been heavily in debt and haunted by the fear of bankruptcy. Of his current finances I knew nothing. When then I made my request to the bank, I enquired casually to the manager, 'I suppose my father is good for £200?'

The manager raised his eyebrows. 'Oh, I think so,' he replied, and the deal was done.

Marjorie and I left Shiphay on July 18th, our three sons having left earlier; Peter to holiday in Scotland and Christopher and Antony to stay with Billy and Dorothy James, Marjorie's sister and brother-in-law, now living in Orpington. We were not due in Yorkshire till August and so, having

172

a car, we decided to spend eight days relaxing at Lee Abbey, the Christian Holiday and Conference Centre near Lynton, North Devon. I had been there earlier on a diocesan conference and had immediately fallen in love with both place and people.

Lee Abbey has never been an abbey in the true sense. It was built by a wealthy Victorian. His friends having built mock castles, he built a mock abbey. In its time it had been put to many different uses: a private residence, a hotel, a school, and lastly the home of a Christian Community representing most Christian denominations and many countries. It is set, in the most beautiful position imaginable, on the North Devon coast. It has two miles of coastline, 170 acres of woodland to explore and its own private beach. Apart from a late-night service of Compline, all services, talks and group discussions are voluntary and the food (!) and the fellowship are wonderful.

Up to 120 guests are cared for by some 50 Community members, the great majority being youngsters in their early twenties who come to Lee Abbey from all over the world to share for a year or two in its fellowship of giving and receiving, the boys mostly working on the estate and the girls in the house.

Today, in addition to Lee Abbey itself, the governing body runs the prestigious Lee Abbey International Students Club in South Kensington – a tremendous enterprise – and three small cells in Aston (Birmingham), in Knowle West (Bristol) and in Walsall. The 7,000 Lee Abbey Friends throughout the world support it with prayers and gifts. I supply brochures of its activities to all my friends.

Our eight days there in transition from South Devon to Yorkshire was just what Marjorie and I needed.

Pickford's were moving us, and before July 17th we had packed all our breakables in tea-chests they had provided. These and the rest of our furniture we arranged for them to collect on Saturday, July 25th and the church treasurer – good old 'Robbie' – undertook to see them safely loaded.

173

At the same time as Pickford's left Shiphay, Marjorie and I left Lee Abbey. We spent the Saturday night at a bed and breakfast near Godalming and the Sunday night at Billy and Dorothy's, where we collected Christopher and Antony. We spent Monday night at Hugglescote near Coalville with the Vicar and his wife – John and Mildred Bishop, the friends of Cambridge Mission days I wrote about in Chapter 7.

Rising early on the Tuesday, we reached Cumberworth Rectory at noon, an hour before Pickford's were due to arrive. To our relief and joy, promptly at 1 p.m. Pickford's pantechnicon came lumbering up our drive.

A new chapter in my ministry had opened.

15

In the Yorkshire Dales

The parish to which I was instituted on the Feast of the Transfiguration, August 6th 1959, consisted of three small villages, Upper Cumberworth, Lower Cumberworth and Birds Edge, and a rather larger industrial village, Denby Dale; all little more than one mile apart. Upper Cumberworth had 302 voters on the County Register of Electors, Lower Cumberworth 271, Birds Edge 237 and Denby Dale 1,192.

Birds Edge was on the A629, the main road from Huddersfield to Sheffield, and its chief interest to me was that behind it stretched the Pennine Range and on its boundary the parish rose to 1,000 feet. It had no link with the rest of the parish but, just to show its handful of practising Anglicans that they were not entirely forgotten, I began a monthly weekday Holy Communion in the local, The Birds Edge Arms. Five or six attended.

The situation in regard to Lower Cumberworth was different. Upper and Lower Cumberworth were closely integrated, but as St Nicholas dominated the life of the former, so did the Methodist Chapel that of the latter. Indeed, as the Queen when in Scotland becomes a Pres-byterian, so Anglicans in Lower Cumberworth became Methodist and vice versa. However, I introduced a monthly weekday morning service of Holy Communion in Lower Cumberworth as in Birds Edge, and, for the same reason, in a public house. The day of shared churches had not yet dawned and the local was the most convenient common meeting-place. I was not a patron. I do not drink.

I remember being asked once in an officers' mess on the Frontier, 'Do you drink, Padre?'

'Yes,' I replied, 'like a fish.' Which completely nonplussed them until I added with a smile, 'Fishes only drink water.' Nonetheless, the landladies both at Birds Edge and Lower Cumberworth were most co-operative. Thank you, ladies.

Upper and Lower Cumberworth and Birds Edge were truly rural. Denby Dale was entirely different. It had grown up through industry. It had three wool mills and two clay works, and many from the village worked in Park Mill Colliery at Claydon West, two miles to the east. Originally, Denby Dale had been part of the parish of Upper Denby, one mile to the south, but around 1870 its vicar disowned Denby Dale and Denby Dale was linked with Cumberworth. They have as long memories in Yorkshire as in Northern Ireland and in 1965 their shotgun marriage to Upper Cumberworth still rankled. They would have no truck with Cumberworth. They would tell you in Cumberworth, 'We are dalesmen, we are.' I never heard that said in Denby Dale. A further difference was that though they were only a mile apart, Denby Dale was 200 feet lower and it made a surprising difference. Spring came a fortnight earlier in Denby Dale than in Cumberworth.

The Anglican Church in Denby Dale began in a tin hut, but in 1937 the foundation stone of the very attractive church of Holy Trinity was laid and the tin hut became the church room.

Yorkshire people are, dare I say it? a race apart, and I took longer to feel at home in Yorkshire than in any other place in my ministry. One had always to tread warily. 'We will be led but not driven,' they would say to you. To which I was tempted to reply, 'Yes, providing you are being led in the way you wish to go.'

A priest friend of mine, newly inducted, was paying his first visits in a Yorkshire parish. He called on a staunch member of his congregation and found her at home and her husband, a miner, with her. She introduced my friend: 'This is the new Vicar, George. We're glad to have him, aren't we?'

176

George looked up and considered. 'We don't know yet,' was his verdict.

They were blunt to a degree. I remember a PCC meeting in Shiphay. One of my churchwardens, a nice little man, made a suggestion. 'No one but a fool would say a thing like that,' came floating over the air. General horror. The interjector, as you have guessed, was a Yorkshireman.

A Cumberworth churchwarden tore a strip off me one evening. Who did I think, I was etc. etc? By chance, I met him out for a walk next morning. All smiles, he could not have been nicer. The previous night's outburst was completely forgotten.

In Cumberworth were many very lovable characters. I think of Luther Benson, the village joiner. He had sung in St Nicholas's choir since a boy but when one of my predecessors had sought to robe them, Luther had objected. Black cassocks in his eyes smacked of popery and he flatly refused to wear one. The choir duly appeared robed in cassocks and surplices. Luther appeared in a surplice only; and so it still was on my arrival.

I also made, in Luther's eyes, an unacceptable innovation. I suggested that on entering in procession the choir should turn east and bow to the altar, and once again Luther was odd man out. I went to see him and his good honest face was almost in tears. 'I can't do it,' he said. 'I can't do it. It's against the Bible. It's bowing down to wood and stone.' I suggested that he should just turn and face the altar; he need not bow. But Luther would have none of it. 'I would look like a fool,' he said. I thought of him processing in with the choir, wearing what looked like a nightshirt, but said nothing. In the end we compromised. He took a seat in the choir in his 'nightshirt' before the choir came in.

In his workshop, Luther had all the latest equipment and was always in demand. But he was no use if you wanted something done quickly. You would wait weeks for an estimate, months before he started work and then months again before you could get his bill. His son Brian worked with him, and when he heard one day that we were planning

177

to ask his father for an estimate, he came to me by night, like Nicodemus, and begged me not to. 'Please, please, don't ask Father. He never refuses work and we've already more work than we can cope with, enough to keep us busy for a year.'

And then there was old Mr Stott, our milkman, who had a farm bordering the Rectory and sold milk locally. We always kept a private milk book and, however many pints it showed, Mr Stott always agreed. One Friday morning we had slipped up in our recording and so we asked him what we owed. 'Well,' he replied, 'if you don't know how many pints it is, how should I?'

And again, there was Arthur and Doris Garrett who lived in Eunice Lane. Doris was a very large lady and a regular communicant. Arthur only appeared when Doris brought him. At his first appearance after my induction they knelt together at the communion rail and I gave Arthur the sacrament. As I gave it him he looked up.

'Thank'ee, surr,' he said.

'Arthur, keep quiet,' said Doris.

'No, woman,' replied Arthur. 'I know my manners.' And as I handed him the Cup, again he said, 'Thank'ee, surr.'

Friend Firth, who also lived in Eunice Lane, was blind and spoke such unbelievably broad Yorkshire that I could hardly understand him. Perhaps I should have written 'Such unbelievably broad Cumberworth', for every village had its own accent and every village its own local words. Holmfirth – famous for being the scene of *Last of the Summer Wine* on BBC1 – bordered the parish on the west; Skelmanthorpe on the north. 'That's not a Cumberworth word,' people would protest, 'that's what they say at Holmfirth,' or, 'That's what they say in Skelmanthorpe.' Skelmanthorpe, as its name suggest, began as a Danish settlement and the red hair of the Vikings still abounded in the parish.

Halfway through my Cumberworth ministry the diocese ran a Clergy Refresher Course at the Horbury Sisters' Convent near Wakefield, which I attended. One evening was set aside for parochial church councils and how to chair them, and the session concluded with a role-play. I was asked to be chairman. Ten others were chosen as PCC members and given roles to play. All hush-hush. The subject was how a bequest of £500 to the church should be used.

At the close, the director condoled with me. 'Of course,' he said, 'that was larger than life. You wouldn't get anything like that in a real meeting.'

'Larger than life?' I responded. 'That was child's play to some that I have to chair.'

One could never foretell before a meeting how it would go. I recall being left speechless at one PCC meeting at Cumberworth. The subject was the redecoration of St Nicholas Church and under discussion was the diocesan architect's suggestions. St Nicholas was a small sandstone-grit church of the last century, remarkable in only one respect. It was unceiled and its roof rafters were painted a vivid red, white and blue. 'They were', wrote the architect, 'completely out of character with the rest of the church,' and he recommended the removal of the paint and treating the timbers with a dark oak stain.

I expressed my own agreement and then put the recommendation to the meeting for comment. A complete silence followed. 'Are there no questions at all?' I asked. Still complete silence. 'Well,' I said, 'would someone like to propose that the recommendation be accepted?' Still no one spoke. I was baffled. 'Well then,' I said, 'I will put the motion from the chair: Those in favour?' Not a hand stirred. 'Those against?' Every hand was raised. And so, bless them, when the church was redecorated their beloved rafters were simply repainted and became more vivid still.

However, I did have my way with another similar body, the Day School Governors, on a kindred matter.

Two years before my arrival the small C of E aided school in Upper Cumberworth all but closed. Its schoolmistress of many years had moved to Penistone and depended on a chancy train service to bring her to Denby Dale Station, from whence she walked. She had been due to retire in 1957. It was all that she hung on for, and the enrolment went down and down. With a saddening frequency children arriving in the morning would find a notice pinned on the school door: 'No school today. Teacher cannot come.'

The county waited, not very patiently, for her retirement. She had, however, taught for them for many years and been a good teacher in her day, and they were loath to dismiss her. When finally she retired, the enrolment had fallen to eight – seven boys and one girl – and that was the enrolment when I arrived. However, a new and gifted teacher whose husband worked in the County Education Office had been appointed to the vacancy, and under Marjorie Lawton the school never looked back. Before I left enrolments had increased to 30.

Mr and Mrs Lawton had their own cottage in the village, and the old schoolhouse continued to be occupied by the school caretaker, Mrs Rollinson, whose husband also helped, but it was in a deplorable condition. 'We have no money,' insisted the Governors, 'so what can we do?' That they had no money was not surprising since Mrs Rollinson refused to pay more than five shillings a week rent. It was, she said, all that the house was worth – but she cheerfully paid seven shillings and sixpence a week rental for her television set!

The house had no indoor sanitation and the Government were offering grants, plus a loan if necessary, for such properties to be modernised. In those days the older dalesmen had a horror of falling into debt. Mortgages and hire-purchase were anathema to them. Nevertheless, I persuaded the Governors to accept both grant and loan. The house was modernised, Walter Lockwood and Ken Smith doing a splendid job. A new caretaker, Mrs Ken Wood, her husband and family moved in, and the increased rent of a pound a week more than repaid the annual loan interest.

Ken Wood was a textile worker with two children when he married Edna, a widow, also with two children; and they had a baby of their own. Textile workers were poorly paid, and after Ken arrived in Cumberworth he left textiles, signed

180

on at Park Mill Colliery and became a most enthusiastic miner: 'The comradeship underground is marvellous!' Each miner was given a daily quota of coal to excavate, Ken explained, but should a miner have an off day and fail to make his quota, as often as not his mates would make it up for him so that his pay was not docked. Real camaraderie!

But coalmining is dangerous work. On one visit to a miner's home in Denby Dale, I was surprised to find that he had returned home early. 'He had a nasty shock at the pit today,' explained Mrs Fisher to me. 'He was shovelling coal from a truck and he found a severed human arm among it.' One pit accident that never found its way into the papers.

Coalmining is not only dangerous; it is also tough. One Christmas at Cumberworth, friends from Shiphay, a Mr and Mrs Low and family, came to stay with us. Alan wanted to go down a pit – so did I – and I was able to arrange it with the Park Mill manager. We entered the cage with the liftman and he let it fall free, i.e. at breakneck speed, till near the bottom when he applied the brakes and brought it under control. On emerging we transferred to a small pit railcar, which clanged its way along a sizable tunnel to its journey's end. But not ours. We simply transferred to a second train, taking us on another mile or so till its track also ended. 'And now,' said our guide, 'we have to crawl.' And crawl we did, along a tunnel no more than four feet high. A painful business. Our guide had leather knee-pads on; we hadn't! Finally we reached the coalface then being worked, and there was a gang of miners lying on their backs, shovelling on to trucks the coal that had been loosened by an earlier shift.

Back in the pit office, the manager traced our journey on a map. 'At that point,' he said, 'you were just about under Cumberworth Rectory.' Four or five seams, all at different levels, were being worked.

Most of the miners I knew left home in the dark armed only with cold tea in a bottle and a wedge of sandwiches, leaving the rest of the household sleeping. They ate nothing more till their return, when they sat down to a colossal slice of bacon.

Some pits had showers but not all. I was visiting in a cottage in Cumberworth when Keith, a lad still in his teens, came home from the pit. 'You don't mind, do you,' said his widowed mother 'if Keith has a bath before eating?'

'Of course not,' I replied.

But then she produced a tin bath and filled it with steaming water and Keith had his bath in front of us both on the floor of the living-room.

Brother Kenneth and the Society of St Francis had helped so much by their three missions in Shiphay that I suggested their help also to the PCCs of Denby Dale and Cumberworth. Denby Dale said No, they knew all about missions. They had already had one. Surprised, I enquired further and found that they had had a Church Army Teaching Week, some 20 years earlier, and enough was enough. Cumberworth, however, had not then been included and they welcomed the opportunity of having a mission of their own. So I wrote to Brother Kenneth and we began preparing. The mission-to-be was codenamed 'Look-up Week' and on Sunday June 4th 1961 Brother Kenneth and a helper, Reginald Robson, Vicar of St Herbert's, Carlisle, were commissioned by Bishop John Ramsbotham.

Hymn-singing preceded the service each night and some good discussions followed in the 'Any Questions?' sessions in the day school. The theme was the new life given us by Christ through the sacraments.

A large drain-pipe, loaned by Naylor's of Denby Dale, stood in the centre aisle, and in the Notices Brother Kenneth invited those present 'to throw their money down the drain' to help meet the expenses of the mission.

Look-up Week had hardly closed in Cumberworth when, quite independently, no small stir occurred in Denby Dale in regard to its Sunday mid-morning service.

Before I arrived there had been Sung Matins at 10.30 a.m. on the first and third Sundays of the month, and a Sung Eucharist, also at 10.30 a.m. on the other Sundays. Following

182

a PCC meeting in March 1960 we had introduced in addition a Parish Communion at 9 a.m. each Sunday, hoping to attract therewith young marrieds with their families. It had failed to do so, and had only succeeded in dividing the never very large 10.30 a.m. congregation into two. A PCC meeting in the summer of 1961 had accordingly voted by 14 votes to 1 to revert to a single mid-morning Sunday service, and it was decided that this should be the Eucharist – at 10.30 a.m. in the summer and 10 a.m. in the winter. I left with my family for our summer holidays in August believing all was well.

It was not. Since 1948 Sung Matins had been conducted in Holy Trinity Church on the second and fourth Sundays by a young bank clerk, Alex Peace, whose family were mainstays of the church. He was not a licensed Lay Reader so was not allowed to preach, but for 12 years Sunday by Sunday, Alex sang the Office and said the prayers. Now we on the PCC had overnight insensitively deprived him of his ministry. His congregation rose in support.

This was not the ordinary Matins versus Eucharist syndrome. Denby Dale was the more catholic of my two congregations. I wore surplice and stole at St Nicholas, coloured vestments at Holy Trinity, but, as I now discovered, churchgoers in Denby Dale were as divided as were the Christians in Corinth in Paul's day.

While still on holiday, I received a long letter from Mrs Mabel Green, one of Alex's congregation. She had, she wrote, collected the names of 45 church members in Denby Dale opposed to the changes. She enclosed a list of their names and said that they had petitioned the Bishop to rule that Matins should continue at Holy Trinity. Much lengthy correspondence followed.

The September *Church News* giving particulars of the new order of Sunday services to begin that month was already at press, and the PCC and the Bishop were solidly behind me. I wrote and explained this to Mrs Green and said how sorry I was at the distress our decision had caused but, having made it, we had to go on with it.

On my return from holiday I visited all the dissidents and

most accepted, grudgingly, the new arrangments. A combined St Nicholas and Holy Trinity Stewardship Campaign the following year directed heart-searchings into more positive directions, but some scars remained unhealed and still remained unhealed, alas, when I left the parish.

Have I given the impression that dalesmen are a difficult lot? Maybe they are. But I was genuinely fond of them, and they could rise on occasion to great heights of co-operation and achievement; also of imagination and resource. In witness thereof: Denby Dale's tradition of baking mammoth pies.

The first, large enough to feed the whole village, was in 1788 to celebrate King George the Third's return to sanity – albeit only temporarily. The second was in 1815 to celebrate Napoleon's defeat at Waterloo. The pies got progressively larger and the third pie, baked in 1846 to celebrate the Repeal of the Corn Laws, was baked in a circular dish 21½ feet in circumference and 22 inches deep. It was not very successful and the fourth pie, baked to celebrate Queen Victoria's Golden Jubilee in 1887, was a complete disaster. But the resourcefulness of those responsible for these gigantic pies is breathtaking.

The Committee responsible for the Golden Jubilee Pie had appealed for gifts of livestock to be baked in it. There was an overwhelming response, and the cooks, supervised by a professional from Huddersfield, put into the pie whatever was offered them. They refused nothing and, we are told, when the baking was complete the pie contained 934 lb of beef, 160 lb of veal, 309 lb of pork, 142 lb of lamb, 45 rabbits, 3 hares, 44 fowls, 6 brace of grouse, 8 ducks, 1 turkey, 6 geese, more than 102 small birds and 580 lb of potatoes, the whole covered by a crust weighing more than 15 cwt.

Alas. It was worse than the rhyme of *Four and Twenty Blackbirds*. When the pie was opened it was found that the contents had decomposed and were quite uneatable. Such was the stench, says an eyewitness, that the unruly crowd clammering round the dish for a portion backed aghast in disorder.

Not to be outdone, the committee, on the spot, made a

public announcement. The contents of the pie, they declared, would be fittingly buried and a Solemn Funeral Procession would leave the field on Sunday for burial in the nearby Toby Woods. They even had funeral cards printed. These were sold to defray expenses.

But there was a further sequel. The specially built pie oven was still available, so was the pie dish, and the committee, moved by shame at the disaster, immediately made crash plans for a repeat performance. This time they played safe and instead of employing professional bakers they relied on the skill and know-how of a few women of Denby Dale and the surrounding hamlets to decide the contents and how they should be baked. This pie, though much smaller, was a complete success and was made and eaten within a week of the burying of the 'pie which went high'.

The pie tradition continued. The sixth pie, the Corn Law Jubilee Pie was baked in 1896 and the Infirmary Pie, organised to endow a cot in Huddersfield Royal Infirmary, was made in 1928. The plan for an eighth pie to commemorate the coronation of Queen Elizabeth II in 1953 had to be abandoned because of food-rationing restrictions. The eighth pie eventually materialised in 1964, and I was present to bless it.

It was the largest pie of all and was the dream-child of Mrs N Kitson, a former resident of Denby Dale living in retirement in Almondsbury, near Huddersfield. Denby Dale had two church halls but no community centre, and Mrs Kitson dreamed of building such a centre for the old people of Denby Dale from money raised by yet another pie.

The idea was enthusiastically taken up, a steering committee was formed and the date for the eating of the pie was fixed for September 5th 1964. Thereafter the pie took over.

Funds were needed, and in the next 18 months the Entertainment Committee ran a fashion show attended by 400 people, a bonfire and barbecue, two motor rallies, two motor cycle scrambles, a tractor-engine rally, four dances, a mammoth children's party and much else. Tiny Denby Dale became a recreation venue for miles around.

185

Other committees were equally active. The Publicity Committee went to town. The pie dish, 18 feet by 6 feet by 18 inches was made at Otley and the Publicity Committee decided to fit it out as a launch complete with bathing belles and float it down to Huddersfield on the Mirfield Canal. In point of fact the pie dish proved unnavigable and the attempt was abandoned but not before it had attracted the attention of the press – 73 newspapermen turned up for the launching. The proposed Denby Dale Pie was now national news and a 15-minute television documentary, shown in November 1964, was so popular that it was repeated on Boxing Day, the highlight of the film being the commentary by Fyfe Robertson. The pie was to contain $2^1/_2$ tons of boneless beef, $1^1/_2$ tons of potatoes, 10 cwt of gravy, and 3 cwt of a 'secret ingredient', a special sauce selected by a distinguished tasting panel presided over by Philip Harben.

Overwhelmed by enquiries not only from England but worldwide, the harassed Publicity Committee handed over to a firm of public relations experts to help with the concluding stages.

Problems multiplied. Between 100,000 and 150,000 people were expected. Car parks and coach parks had to be provided; so had toilets; the police and health authorities had to be satisfied; and the 10 cwt of gravy had to be persuaded not to slop over as the pie, on a Pickford trailer pulled by 'Marshal Foch', a prize-winning tractor, came down a steep hill from the pie bakehouse to the pie field. And the pie had to be kept hot. To ensure this, steel rods heated by dynamos were inserted during the journey, and on the pie field itself the pie was plugged in to an electric cable.

Before the day, hitches had occurred. Also a tragedy. On November 30th four members of the committee were returning on a foggy night from a television interview in London when the car they were travelling in ploughed into the rear of an articulated lorry. All died. Their families, however, were unanimous that Pie Day must go ahead as planned.

I personally had little to do with these preparations, but I

186

was called upon to bless the pie on Pie Day, and I can let you into a secret. In order to bake the piecrust and to support it, six-foot metal plates had been constructed. But the pie must not only be blessed, its crust must also be ceremoniously cut. How was Mr Jonas Kenyon, Village Council Chairman, to insert his three-foot carving-knife into it? The bakers had been forewarned and had found the solution. Between two metal plates halfway along the length of the pie they had left a half-inch gap covered over with ornamental pastrywork. Into this pastrywork Mr Kenyon inserted his knife, and the deed was done. Then 33,000 portions at half a crown a portion were served, and I can testify that the pie was excellent.

The pie had arrived on the field at 2.30 p.m. Serving began at 3 p.m. and continued for 90 minutes, the crowd meanwhile being entertained by bands and displays. Hardly, however, had the last portion of pie been served than down came the rain and the crowds, estimated at 60,000, started to melt away. Some hundred volunteers descend on the field to clear away the litter and in two hours the field was tidy.

Five years later the Denby Dale Pie Community Centre, built from the Pie Day proceeds, was officially opened.

There is an interesting postscript. The photo in the plate section showing me blessing the pie appeared in many Yorkshire papers, and in the following week I received a letter enquiring was I the Padre Lovejoy who accompanied the convoy to Datta Khel in 1942 soon after its relief? I was. On that visit I remarked to a Tochi Scout that I was surprised that, in view of its vulnerable position, a more permanent concrete fort had not been built there. He replied that mud forts were superior. 'Mud being soft stuff, shells hitting mud walls are less likely to explode.' I said nothing but privately thought, What utter nonsense! Now the writer of this letter gave the true explanation. After referring to the siege, he went on, 'Poor old tribies! Before they hurled their plundered hand-grenades at the walls they hadn't the know-how to release the safety catches!'

I cannot conclude these notes without mention of a boys' small private secondary school in Denby Dale which played a large part in our lives. In Shiphay, our second son Christopher, despite special coaching, had failed to pass his eleven plus and we were told he was not an academic and that it would be cruel to try to make him so. Nevertheless, during our last year at Shiphay we paid for him to attend, as a day boy, The Beacon School at Teignmouth. Poor Christopher! He hated it. His classmates were a brainy lot and he was soon completely outclassed. Nor could he derive any comfort from success in other fields. One day he returned modestly happy. He had beaten, he said, another boy in one of the races. Translated, this meant that instead of being last, he had been last but one!

He had to go by train to Teignmouth, changing at Newton Abbot, leaving early and returning late. But he never complained and eventually derived a certain satisfaction from his travelling.

One week Mrs Howard at the off-licence took Marjorie aside. 'I think I should tell you,' she said, 'that your Christopher is making a habit of coming in here with empty beer bottles and collecting the refund.' It was before the time of canned drinks and Christopher would occupy his time on the GWR walking along the corridors, picking up discarded beer bottles and stuffing them into his satchel.

When we arrived in Yorkshire, we discussed schools with the Bishop. Peter was immediately accepted at reduced fees at Wakefield Grammar School, and although under age, so was Antony. But what about Christopher?

'A boys' boarding school has recently opened up in Denby Dale,' said John Ramsbotham. 'I don't know that I can recommend it. You can try.'

We did. Christopher was accepted as a pupil and Marjorie joined the staff as an assistant teacher. Academic standards at the school were abysmal and it transformed Christopher. He regained his confidence, worked hard and did so well in his O levels, that he was accepted at Penistone Grammar

School and never looked back. He became a chartered accountant and, after 18 months doing voluntary service overseas at a Roman Catholic college of further education at Mwanza on the shores of Lake Victoria, became first a lecturer and then a senior lecturer at Birmingham Polytechnic. Currently he is living with his wife and two children at Beverley Minster and lecturing at Hull University. You never know! He was simply a late developer.

After two years at Wakefield Grammar School, Peter won a scholarship to Pembroke College, Oxford. He also became a chartered accountant and worked for many years with British American Tobacco. In 1991 he took early retirement and is now lecturing in accountancy at Nottingham Trent University.

Antony began by wanting to be a probation officer but was too young to be accepted when he left school. Marjorie and I accordingly persuaded him to go to St Luke's College, Exeter, for teacher training. A good preparation. While there, he became involved with the partially hearing children at the Exeter School for the Deaf and found there his vocation, going on to Manchester for specialised training. He now lives with his wife and two children in a large and delightful fourteenth century cottage in Geddington near Kettering, and works with partially hearing children and their teachers and parents for Northampton County Council.

Throughout our stay in Yorkshire Marjorie taught full-time at Christopher's School, and thinking of her, I think of the perfect wife conjured up by King Lemuel:

> She riseth early while it is yet night and giveth meat to her
> household....Her candle goeth not out by night. She
> openeth her mouth in wisdom and on her tongue is the
> law of kindness. Her children rise up and call her blessed;
> her husband also and he praiseth her.
>
> *Proverbs 31: 15-18, 26-28*

From early morning till late at night she never seemed to stop. And yet she found time to entertain Christopher's friends and even (when appealed to by the headmaster) to take in boarders. Each morning, having seen off Peter and Antony travelling on the 7.30 a.m. bus to Wakefield, she would gather up her schoolwork and trudge off, sometimes in blinding snow, to teach. And she still played a full part in parish life! How she got through it all, I do not know.

And then a dark shadow descended upon the school. Its headmaster and owner 'SH', was an Anglican priest and he and I worked well together. He helped me with my services and I helped him in return by taking religious instruction on two or three mornings a week. There were some 60 boarders, most of whose parents were overseas. One morning I received a cautiously worded letter from a parent in Kuwait. His son had been home for the summer vacation and while in Kuwait had confided to his father that SH had been making advances to him. When I told the Bishop, he was not particularly surprised. This, I learnt, had happened before. The upshot was that SH agreed to attend the clinic of Mr Smith, a priest-psychiatrist, in Huddersfield.

But there was no improvement. Indeed, matters went from bad to worse. SH believed in corporal punishment, and I am told that on one occasion when he was administering a public caning, an older boy in the class shouted out 'Bloody homo!' and that SH flushed but said nothing.

There was, however, no real evidence until one night a teacher and a sixth-former returning late at night found the lights on in the Head's study and the curtains drawn and saw the Head having sex with one of his boys.

Next morning teacher and sixth-former appealed to me: I must do something. I promised to, and two days later the police arrived at the school to question the pupils. After a few weeks the case was heard in Huddersfield Court. Thankfully, I was not called to give evidence but I attended the hearing, and the sight of SH when he appeared shocked me. He looked a broken man. He pleaded guilty to the lesser of two charges, was found guilty, and disappeared with his wife and children.

Meanwhile the school had been sold to David and Freni

190

Divall. Some children left but most continued. One teacher, a Mr P in charge of the younger children, also left. He occupied a cottage at the school-drive entance, and after the police had left, was found to have taken an overdose. He was a kindly person but quite ineffectual, and, taken to a hospital, recovered.

I only mention it because of an almost unbelievable coincidence. Staying with us in the Rectory at the time was Hope Symonds, Marjorie's college friend of whom I have written in Chapter 9. When we spoke of Mr P, it emerged that she knew him! Some 20 years earlier, 6,000 miles away in the remote prairies of Canada, Father P had been her parish priest. He had been found guilty of an affair with a boy and defrocked. His wife had divorced him and he had not been heard of since. And now here he was on our doorstep!

David Divall was likeable, immensely likeable, but irresponsible. He just seemed incapable of sticking at anything. Although a trained teacher, before coming to Denby Dale he had been, among other things, a market huckster. On taking over the school he threw himself back into teaching with infectious enthusiasm. He was a gifted teacher and genuinely cared for his pupils. Under his predecessor they were always hungry. David fed them like turkeycocks and won their hearts.

Then after 12 months his enthusiasm for teaching died. Once again he gave it up and busied himself managing the school and being odd-job man.

A few weeks after his taking over, he was holding a staff meeting when the telephone rang. Putting down the phone, he turned to the staff. 'That's funny,' he remarked. 'That was the police. They wanted to know if I had SH's address. What would the police want with SH?'

The staff looked one at another. Then one volunteered, didn't he know? Hadn't he heard of the court case?

And David's reaction? 'Poor fellow. When I asked him why he was selling St Aidan's, he replied that he had an incurable disease. I had assumed it was cancer.' No recrimination whatever.

One incident in conclusion. David was not a tidy person. Neither did he worry overmuch about cleanliness or hygiene. One morning he summoned the school together. 'Boys,' he said, 'I have just had a phone call from the Education Office. An inspector will be here at 10 a.m. We have just 35 minutes to see what we can do. It's a challenge. See to it.'

It was a challenge the school responded to. They all liked David. Floors were swept, desks and classrooms tidied, toilets flushed, basins washed. At the close David surveyed the scene with satisfaction. 'They've no idea at headquarters,' he chuckled, 'what we can do in half an hour!'

After we left Yorkshire, the school closed yet again, this time finally – with only 60 to 80 boarders it was not a viable proposition. And when we next visited them, Freni and David were living in a cottage at Icklesham in Kent. Freni had gone back to nursing, and David was a caller at a bingo hall and hating it.

16

Development in Rural Bucks

In 1964 Peter was at Oxford studying history, Christopher was articled to accountants in London, and Yorkshire was too distant for them to visit us easily. Marjorie longed to see more of them and suggested I should try to find a parish nearer London. My brother Jim was then Home Secretary of the Conference of British Missionary Societies (Edinburgh House) and living in Ewell. He volunteered to recommend me to his Diocesan, the Rt Revd Mervyn Stockwood, who arranged for me to meet Dr John Robinson of *Honest to God* fame, his Suffragan. This was in November. My visit proved unfruitful. The Bishop was charming but when he heard my age – I was 57 – he explained that the diocese's need was for younger priests; that they had difficulty in finding suitable parishes for their own older men.

I then phoned Christie Willatts (Dr E C Willatts, MBE.), a family friend from childhood and a leading layman in the diocese of Oxford. He phoned me back on January 28th. He had had lunch that day with the Venerable John Francis Pratt, Archdeacon of Buckingham. There was a vacant parish, Gayhurst with Stoke Goldington, in North Bucks, which the Archdeacon was anxious to fill. On Friday, February 19th, Marjorie and I met him and the four churchwardens in Lady Carlile's cottage in Gayhurst. Elizabeth Carlile was the widow of Sir Walter Carlile of Gayhurst House and a churchwarden. Sir Walter had stood as Conservative Member of Parliament for North Bucks from 1895 to 1906 and was the first Member of Parliament to arrive at the House of Commons in a motor car.

The Archdeacon's anxiety to fill the parish was quickly apparent. It had been vacant for some six years! When the last incumbent, the Revd Jock Woods, had retired, the patrons had tried for more than two years to fill the vacancy. The problem was the Rectory in Stoke Goldington. It was old and large without central heating with a huge garden. All who viewed it said No. The Vicar of the neighbouring parish of Ravenstone was then approached. Would he be prepared to take Gayhurst and Stoke Goldington over? It raised a storm of protest from Gayhurst and Stoke. Stoke had a population of around 950, Ravenstone only 110. They wanted the incumbent to live in Stoke.

By this time the patronage had passed to the Crown Commissioners, who agreed to the only sensible solution – the old rectory should be sold and a new rectory built on adjacent glebe-land. Two more years passed and then Dr Starkie, a chest consultant at Northampton Hospital, bought the old rectory and the contract to build the new rectory was signed. It was completed in 1963 and for 12 months had stood empty. Even with a new rectory no priest seemed to want the parish, nor was it very evident that the parish wanted a priest. At the beginning of the interregnum the parish had been reasonably well served by a priest-teacher living in Newport Pagnell, five miles away. Then he moved, and for the past three years the parish had just jogged along with one service a Sunday taken by a layman. From time to time the churchwardens would consult the registers. 'George,' Audrey Lane would say, 'it's six weeks since we had a Communion Service. We ought to have one.'

At the end of the meeting the Archdeacon took Marjorie and me aside for consultation and I put the question to him. He assured us that, whether the parish wanted the vacancy filled or not, the diocese certainly did. So we said Yes.

After the meeting, Audrey Lane, the Stoke churchwarden, drove us to Bedford railway station. From Bedford I was returning to Cumberworth and Marjorie was journeying to London to visit her family. En route for Bedford Audrey

194

assured me, 'The one thing we don't want any truck with is this stewardship business. All stewardship wants is your money.' I kept my counsel.

The spelling of Gayhurst has varied over the years. In the *Domesday Book* it is 'Gatehurst', less than a century later it was 'Gahurst', by 1290 it had become 'Gothurst' and in 1581 Queen Elizabeth conferred on Sir Francis Drake 'the Manor of Gothurste, otherwise Gayhurste, and Stoke-goldington'. The following day Sir Francis sold this reversion to the resident tenant, William Mulsoe, whose daughter Mary married Sir Everard Digby, later to become deeply implicated in the Gunpowder Plot of 1606.

The Plot, as is well known, was to hire a cellar beneath the Houses of Parliament, fill it with barrels of gunpowder and fire the train when King James arrived to open Parliament on November 5th. The conspirators argued that Lords, Commons, princes and king would perish in the common disaster and planned a Catholic uprising and a Spanish invasion in the confusion that would follow. Sir Everard, like Guy Fawkes, was a Roman convert, and it is said that when the plot was first disclosed to him he was horrified and refused to participate. Alas, he was later won over and promised to provide money for the purchase of the gunpowder. It is even believed that all the conspirators met together in Gayhurst House to discuss their plans. A mere chance saved king and Parliament – a cryptic note sent to a Catholic peer warning him against attending on November 5th. The cellars were searched on the night of November 4th and Guy Fawkes was found lurking in one of them, waiting to fire the train, and though the conspirators took arms on hearing of his arrest, they were quickly hunted down and slain. Sir Everard was captured and, according to the brutal custom of the day, both he and Guy Fawkes were first tortured and then hung, drawn and quartered. There is, however, one redeeming sign of grace in the story. According to the law of the land, a traitor's lands and possessions were forfeited to the Crown. However, before he died Everard pleaded to the king on behalf of his wife. He swore on oath that she knew nothing of the plot and that Gayhurst House was her family home, not his. Surprisingly, for it was an avaricious age, his request was granted and Lady Everard was allowed to continue to live in peace in Gayhurst House. She died in 1653 and was buried at Gayhurst. Her son, Sir Kenelm Digby, born at Gayhurst in the year of his father's death, succeeded to the property. Earlier, Sir Kenelm had distinguished himself in the Navy and he became a well-known courtier and astrologer.

George Wrighte, son of Sir Nathan Wrighte, Keeper of the Great Seal of England to Queen Anne, bought Gayhurst in 1704, and it was he who built the present Sir Peter's Church in 1728, one hundred or so yards east of the house. Few rural churches were built in the first half of the eighteenth century, and Gayhurst is acknowledged to be one of the finest examples. It is fortunate in that the building and its furnishings are virtually in the same state as on the day on which it was completed. An organ has been added and the clerk's desk has been removed from what was originally a three-decker pulpit; otherwise all is the same.

There are two attractive peculiarities in the church. The first is the double negative in the first commandment in the left-hand panel on the east wall: 'Thou shalt not have none other Gods but me.' The year after my arrival extensive repairs to the church were found to be necessary, and the PCC embarked on a substantial programme of restoration. The cleansing of the two panels was a problem, but John Piper, the British artist who designed the 'Christ in Glory' east window in Coventry Cathedral, came to our rescue. He loved Gayhurst church and offered to restore the panels free of charge if we would bring them to him at his studio in Marlow. This I was privileged to do.

The outstanding feature of the interior of St Peter's is a huge, exquisitely carved white marble monument on the eastern wall of the nave, depicting, it is believed, a father and son, probably George Wrighte and his father. The

196

second peculiarity is that the large black marble slab beneath the monument is completely blank. In his will George Wrighte left two hundred pounds for the monument's erection. It is suggested that his executors used the whole sum and more to pay for the monument and refused to find the extra money for the inscription. Likewise his son.

As part of the restoration work the supports of the oak floor had to be examined, and this entailed the opening of the vaults beneath the nave, left undisturbed for more than a century. Descending was a eerie business. In them we found the brass-studded coffins of members of the Wrighte family covered in decomposing red velvet, and in a corner the tiny skeleton of a new-born babe. Who had put it there and when? Could it speak, what story would it tell? We left it undisturbed.

The cost of the restoration, originally estimated at £2,000, rose to £9,000. Appeals were made to the general public on the BBC and to various trusts. There was a generous response and eventually the whole £9,000 was found – a tremendous sum in those days for a tiny parish with less than 40 voters on the Parliamentary Voting List.

Gayhurst House itself had a chequered history. During World War Two the Admiralty requisitioned part of it, and two hundred Wrens lived and worked there. Next, a boys' preparatory school shared the house with Sir Walter and Lady Carlile. Then it became a depository for the Swiss Bank Corporation and finally, a year before I arrived, Rodbourne College from near Bristol moved in. The College was a private boys' boarding-school, owned and excellently run by the Revd Leslie Martin and his wife, assisted by their son Ian and daughter Angela. I taught scripture at the school every Wednesday morning in term-time, and Mr Martin assisted me in the parish.

The college held many efforts in aid of the church's restoration and one f[?]te I especially remember. At the previous PCC Mr Martin had announced that if we liked, the boys would be happy to run the sideshows. We were indeed happy for them to do so, and they went to town. There were go-carts provided by a parent, coconut shies, tip the bucket, hoopla, slides, competitions, raffles, the lot. The boys excelled themselves, their highlight being a tour of the dungeons. Beneath Gayhurst House lay a network of tunnels – one, now blocked up, was a half-mile secret escape route to the River Ouse. For the 'tour' we descended into these tunnels, led by a guide with a torch. From time to time there were floodlit scenes of horror, and one I vividly remember: a wretched boy was tied to a scaffold and on each side of him were two torturers armed with whips. 'They gave him ten lashes at the stroke of each hour,' explained our guide. 'His cries are terrible!'

It is time to leave Gayhurst and to travel one mile down the A50 to Stoke Goldington. Like most English villages, Stoke Goldington has a long history, its turning-point being the great plague of 1348-49, known as the Black Death. Before then, St Peter's Church stood in the centre of the village; afterwards the cottagers built their homes where they still stand today, nearly a mile to the south, where building materials were plentiful. All the original church cottages fell into decay; only Church Farm remains, keeping guard over St Peter's. Dag Lane, leading to St Peter's, is part of the ancient road meandering between Newport Pagnell and Northampton. It is now a bridle path, its borders a botanist's paradise. Honeysuckle flowers and wild hop-fruits bedeck its hedges, and for one harvest festival David Armstrong, our organist, festooned the pillars of St Peter's with wild hop tendrils. By the Sunday, when St Peter's warmly welcomed its visitors, it smelt more like a pub than a church.

Harvest Festivals were and are great occasions in rural areas, and before I left Stoke the whole of October was dedicated to them: Stoke on the first Sunday, Gayhurst on the third, Ravenstone on the second and Weston Underwood on the fourth – Ravenstone and Weston, because when their parish fell vacant in 1967 I became their Priest-in-Charge. Thereafter on three Sundays out of four I was at Stoke Goldington for Holy Communion at 8.30 a.m., and at Ravenstone and Weston for Parish Eucharists at 9.30 a.m. and 10.45 a.m. I was at Gayhurst at 4 p.m. and back at Stoke for Evensong at 6 p.m. The other Sunday, the first in the month, was an exception; I had a rest. 'For three Sundays each month,' I explained to my four PCCs, 'I tear round your churches like a scalded cat. On the first Sunday each month, would you agree that there should be just one service in the united parishes – a Parish Communion at 9.30 a.m. at Stoke Goldington? – and would you agree to come to it?' All four councils agreed, and the 9.30 a.m. service at Stoke Goldington each first Sunday became the main service each month, a bus collecting those from Ravenstone, Weston and Gayhurst who were without cars or who did not wish to use them. Bob and Bill Wesley of Stoke Goldington provided the bus, and I drove it.

After the First World War Bob and Bill and their sister Hilda bought a Model T Ford, converted it into a coach and Wesley Bros. Coaches Ltd was born. Year by year they added to their fleet, and by 1967 they owned some 15 coaches. Besides a daily service between Newport Pagnell and Northampton, they ran British and Continental tours and were awarded numerous school contracts. They had trained my predecessor, the Revd Jock Woods, as a stand-in driver for their school commitments and, on my appointment to Stoke, approached me: could I likewise help them? I had driven cars, on and off, since 1927 and did not imagine driving a coach would be that much different. I quickly found it was and it was some months before 'John', Wesley's foreman, considered me ready for a test. When he did he took bets with his fellow-drivers that I would pass first time.

Tests were held in Northampton. There was a set route. John knew it by heart and took me over it a few days before my test was due. On it he pointed out to me a quiet T junction. 'If they want to test you backing round a corner, take a good look, that's it.' I devoutly hoped they wouldn't

– backing a 42-seater round a corner is no picnic – and as we approached the corner on the crucial day I held my breath. I was never asked. I received my certificate and John his winnings.

Wesley Coaches only called upon me in emergencies, rarely more than twice a month, and I received no wages – that would have caused union complications – but I was given a coach free to take our Sunday school children on their annual outing, once to Whipsnade Zoo, twice to Wicksteed Park in Kettering, and also to collect worshippers from Ravenstone, Weston and Gayhurst for the first Sunday in the month's united service in Stoke Goldington. In addition, once a month I collected senior citizens from Stoke, Weston and Gayhurst for the SRW Club, which met monthly in Ravenstone Village Hall. The club had been started in 1968 by Jean Amberg and Jean Topsom (the two Jeans) and myself. It fulfilled a real need and never ceased growing. For this trip Wesley Bros. charged us one pound towards the cost of petrol!

Their coaches range from 29-seaters to 52-seaters and one never knew in advance what size coach one was being given. Each size needed slightly different handling. Also, I was a beginner. Whenever, therefore, I climbed into the driving-seat I said a silent prayer for safe travelling. But I enjoyed driving. One towered above smaller traffic on the road. They all made way for you, and all too easily you could imagine you were God Almighty. However, I learned by experience that these magnificent monsters which glided along motorways so smoothly could be like helpless babes if they left the Tarmac.

One year I drove our Stoke congregation along to Gayhurst to swell their numbers at their harvest festival and parked with visiting cars on level grass in a field near the church entrance. During the service, there was a sprinkling of rain, and when afterwards I tried to reach the gravel roadway, the wheels refused to grip. They simply spun. Pushing proved useless and finally Francis Whiting, one of Gayhurst's churchwardens, had to drive back to his farm and bring along his tractor.

I also learned by experience never to take advice from strangers. The Sunday run involved much backing and turning. 'Come on. Come on,' they would advise, watching only the rear, oblivious of the need to allow for the swing of the front. Even dear old Frank Cole, a retired bus-conductor, once let me down. I was backing towards a low bank outside Stoke Goldington Church and it was again 'Come on. Come on.' I obeyed, and suddenly there was a horrid crunching sound. The tail of the coach had cleared the top of the bank with ease but beneath the tail were the exhaust pipe and silencer. They were ruined.

One Sunday I had Rosamund Essex as a passenger. She was in Stoke on the first Sunday in the month to speak on Christian Aid. She stayed with us on the Saturday night and in the morning expressed the wish to do the Sunday trip with me. That morning a 52-seater monster had been allotted to me, and when she saw it, words failed her. She thought it would be a minibus! Afterwards she wrote a charming and witty letter thanking me. Alas, I have lost it.

Rosamund Essex was a one-off passenger, but on most of my Sunday runs I was accompanied by two small children who have since made a name for themselves. Currently, they are watched by ten million viewers three times a week in *EastEnders* on BBC 1 – Letitia Dean as Sharon and her brother Peter Dean as Pete.

They came with their parents to Stoke Goldington not long after ourselves. Their father was in the rag trade, with a factory in Northampton, and supplied us generously with novelties from his workshops for our sales of work. They lived in a large modernised cottage adjoining Wesley's coach station and the recreation ground. Peter and Letitia attended Marjorie's Sunday school and could have caught the monthly coach from their doorstep, had they wished. But no, they liked to do the whole run, just for the ride.

One morning Letitia arrived alone. 'Peter's been naughty,' she said. 'He's being kept in.' It transpired, however, that he had not been 'naughty', simply overzealous to help. The family had arrived home the evening before to find they were without keys and the house was locked. 'I'll have to break a back window,' remarked Peter's father, having in mind a small pane in the back-door window.

Suddenly there was a resounding crash and a delighted Peter, beaming with joy, came round from the back. 'I've done it, Daddy,' he shouted, 'I've smashed the window.' He had! Not the tiny pane but one of the large casements of the sitting-room.

Letitia was about four years old when we left Stoke. She came round, hand in hand with her mother, to present Marjorie with a bunch of flowers.

Marjorie ran a very lively Sunday school in the Rectory. On one occasion she had told the Parable of the Lost Sheep, and she was choosing children to play-act it. One little boy put his hand up. 'Please, please,' he begged, 'could I be the lost sheep. Mummy says I'm very naughty.'

The prize story comes, however, from the day school. The children were asked to write a poem about Christmas. These were posted up for Parents' Day. Imagine the surprise of my churchwarden and his wife to read the following effort by one of their offspring:

> Christmas is near,
> Christmas is near.
> Mummy likes gin
> But Daddy likes beer.
>
> *David Gates*, aged 5

Stella Gates did not like gin but, maybe, David had heard of poetic licence.

My four parochial church councils were all special in their own way and I quickly discovered one great difference between Ravenstone and Weston Underwood – their understanding of punctuality. Both were timed to start at 8 p.m. One month I arrived at Ravenstone Village Hall at 7.55 p.m.

The first to arrive was one of the churchwardens, Barry Topsom. He arrived at 8 p.m., looked round, said 'I'll come back later,' and left. At Weston Underwood, arriving dead on time, I would find the whole council seated and looking at their watches.

Barry Topsom was a sales manager for a paper company and an enthusiastic member of a local sailing club. Ravenstone's one Sunday service was at 9.30 a.m., and in winter Barry was regularly there. In summer, however, his attendance record was dismal, sailing duties taking precedence over worship. So we asked him, would he like to help by reading the epistle on certain Sundays? 'Of course.' The Sunday arrived and Barry was there. He read the epistle as arranged, closed the Bible and departed. The sailing club was calling.

I do not recall a dull PCC meeting. Three I remember clearly. The first was at Stoke Goldington a year after my arrival, called, *pace* Mrs Lane, to consider running a stewardship campaign. It was essential. Direct giving in Stoke hardly existed. You only gave when you went to church, and even then 'Hear the pennies dropping' expressed traditional practice.

Since the first Shiphay Collaton campaign, stewardship had taken on nationwise, and Oxford diocese had its own stewardship adviser. He had already met members of the council informally and explained what stewardship involved. Now, at an Extraordinary Meeting of the council, the vote was to be taken. There were 12 present, and it was agreed that the vote should be secret. Six voted for it (including Marjorie and myself). Six voted against. I therefore claimed my right as chairman to a casting vote. The motion was carried and the meeting closed. Afterwards Mr Harland, the diocesan adviser, said to me, 'You'll never go forward.'

'Why not?' I asked.

In the event, several objectors changed sides, Gayhurst joined in, and we had a successful campaign. Results could have been better but it provided the needed breakthrough in direct giving.

The second PCC meeting I clearly remember was also an Extraordinary Meeting, this time at Ravenstone, soon after my appointment as Priest-in-Charge, and the point at issue was the future of the Ravenstone Vicarage. The diocese wished to sell it. The parish objected. They still hoped one day to have a vicar of their own, and saw that if the Vicarage went, this hope went too. One of the churchwardens at their daughter church at Weston Underwood was Lord Denham, then Conservative Whip in the House of Lords. He argued Ravenstone's case persuasively and the diocesan representative, Christopher Pepys, Suffragan Bishop of Buckingham, listened quietly.

When Lord Denham sat down, the Bishop spoke. 'We have,' he said, 'fulfilled the legal requirements. You have been consulted. In due course you will be informed of the diocese's decision.' It was the expected one: the Vicarage was to be sold. The whole consultation had been a legal charade. Nevertheless, one concession was made: the Vicarage would not be sold for five years.

Its only tenants were a Mr and Mrs Holmes and their daughter. The husband had a brain disorder and his wife managed all their affairs. She was a strong character. One had to respect her. They were constantly behind with their rent, and once when they were more than three months behind, I tried very gently to remonstrate. She turned on me like a wounded tigress: 'Here am I with a sick husband on my hands and you, a priest of God, try to bully me, a poor weak woman!' If she was a poor weak woman, I would hate to meet a wealthy strong one!

My third memorable PCC meeting was also at Ravenstone. The *Book of Common Prayer* was in process of revision and Series I and Series II had been issued for experimental use. While open to criticism, they were clearly a move in the right direction. After much private discussion the matter came before the Ravenstone PCC for discussion. However, I had hardly begun to put the case in favour when Claud Leetham, an ex-churchwarden, interrupted. 'We've heard all this before,' he snapped. 'We've discussed it, all of us, among ourselves. I propose we waste no more time. I propose the motion be put.' Claud was a die-hard conservative, as were most of the PCC and I groaned inwardly. However, Claud's proposal was passed, the vote had to be taken and I called for someone to propose the motion. (Would I have to propose it from the chair? Memories of Cumberworth.)

To my astonishment, Claud was the one to speak: 'I propose the motion,' and it was passed unanimously! I am pleased to add that the three other PCCs also voted in favour.

Paul in 2 Corinthians Chapter 11 speaks of his sufferings on behalf of Christ and of the many dangers he encountered on his missionary journeys:

> Of the Jews five times received I forty stripes save one,
> Thrice was I beaten with rods, once was I stoned. Thrice
> I suffered shipwreck, a night and a day have I been in the
> deep.

and he concludes his catalogue of woes with: 'Beside those things that are without, that which cometh upon me daily, the care of all the churches.'

He is thinking of his scattered congregations. For the modern incumbent, however, 'the care of all the churches' embraces in addition the care of the fabric of the buildings in which his congregations gather.

Of the history and restoration of St Peter's, Gayhurst, I have already spoken. St Peter's, Gayhurst, was built in the eighteenth century. My other three churches all dated back to the twelfth century and each had its problems: St Laurence's, Weston Underwood, the crumbling mullions in its nave and chancel windows; All Saints', Ravenstone, its lack of a damp course and its leaking lead roof; St Peter's, Stoke Goldington, again its lead roof, which one night was stripped by thieves, and the crumbling coping-stones of its tower.

St Peter's, Stoke Goldington, was my village church in which I said my daily offices and it had, in consequence, a special place in my heart. The diocesan surveyor, Mr Laurence King, also loved it. It was a simple village church and quite unpretentious. It never found its way into books on English church architecture but it had two unusual features: the Norman masons marked out the stones of the narrow chancel arch for dog-tooth carving but never carved them; and the chancel, instead of being aligned to the nave, tilted slightly to the south. The tilt occurs in other churches also and some have suggested that it represents Christ's head tilted to one side on the Cross, an idea pooh-poohed by Laurence King.

All Anglican churches in England have to submit to a quinquennial inspection, the reports of which are sent to the diocese and the local PCC. Recommendations are divided into three: repairs needing to be undertaken immediately; repairs to be completed within the next five years; and, finally, repairs to be undertaken when funds allow. The first item in Mr Laurence King's category of 'those to be undertaken when funds allow' was a new stopper in the font!

Not only buildings, but also their contents come under the modern interpretation of 'the care of all the churches', and we had at Ravenstone a fifteenth-century chalice used every Sunday and reputed to be valuable. In a misguided moment we sent it to be valued. It was valued at more than a thousand pounds and our troubles began. Our insurers decreed that it could no longer be kept in the church safe; it must be put into safekeeping with the bank and used only on special occasions. They also decreed that the key of the church safe must no longer be kept in an unlocked drawer but must be concealed. We concealed it so successfully that one week we could not find it. Happily, our treasurer came to our rescue. He worked at the local Diplomatic Wireless Station, and they had on their staff – for occasional diplomatic service overseas! – a reformed ex-convict capable of cracking any safe in Europe. Those were the bad old days! Ravenstone Church safe was child's-play to him; the safe was opened and all was well.

Almost as soon as I arrived in Stoke Goldington a member of the congregation, Owen Warren, said to me, 'What we really need in this village is a village hall.' I soon realised that this was true. The only room in which public meetings and village activities could be held was the larger classroom, itself not very large, in the church school at the north end of the village opposite the recreation ground.

It was quite a small school – never more than 30 pupils – but admirably run by Roy Kitchener, a young and dedicated Christian, ably assisted by Mrs P Clark in charge of infants, and Mrs Kemp, the dinner lady, who, on limited resources, provided quite outstanding lunches – never a complaint! Roy was fantastic. He fooled with the children and they loved him. Visiting a parent one December, I learned that they had had the school Christmas lunch that morning. What did they have? I asked. Her little girl replied: 'We had turkey and Christmas pudding and every one of us had a sixpence in the pudding.' (You see what I mean about Mrs Kemp.) 'All of us except Mr Kitchener. He didn't get one. He did cry!'

On the other hand, he was a strict disciplinarian. Going into his classroom one lunch-time, I was surprised to see a small seven-year-old still there, busily doing sums. 'You're a good lad,' I said to him. 'Still working hard?'

He scowled at me. 'Mr Kitchener says I'm to stay here till I have finished them.'

When the field next to the Rectory, known as 'Garden Wells', was bought by developers, Maltings Close was built and executives from Milton Keynes, now taking shape six miles away, began to occupy the houses. Roy was optimistic: 'Some new blood is just what we need.' He was soon disillusioned. Not only were most of their children more backward than the village children, they were also more unruly. One morning he showed me where one of the little darlings had bitten him!

His classroom was quite inadequate for public meetings. The desks had to be moved into the infants' room, or, for smaller meetings, pushed against the walls; or, for the weekly whist drives, sat upon.

Urged on by Owen, I began expressing the need for a village hall when visiting members of the parish council. All assured me it wasn't possible: where would I build it? Some even denied the need: it would be a white elephant – and where was the money coming from?

When I suggested the obvious site – on the recreation ground opposite the school, I was told it was not large enough: even now it was too small for a football pitch and in any case it wouldn't be allowed. They had already gone into it. The land had been given to the village by Sir Walter Carlile and the trust deed laid down that, apart from a shed to house a mower and tools, it was not to be built on.

These were weighty objections, but no other site was available and it was the obvious choice. Fortunately, in due course both objections were overcome.

The land at the bottom end of the 'rec' was farmed by William Needham, a newcomer from Scotland who had bought up Jack Whiting's farm. Mr Needham agreed to sell us a strip of his land at the going farming-land rate, which would not only compensate for the land required by the hall but also allow for a football pitch.

The question of the restriction in the title deeds was trickier. Fortunately, we had Lady Carlile, Sir Walter's widow, on our side. She wrote through Mr Henry Durbridge, her solicitor, to the Charity Commissioners, informing them that Sir Walter had discussed the trust deed with her before its execution and that they had included the 'no building' restriction solely to prevent the parish council from selling the land for development. She was sure that Sir Walter, had he been alive, would have supported the present project. So a second hurdle was overcome.

There remained the third: raising the money. Geoff Thompson, an architect and a newcomer to the village, generously agreed to help, and drew up plans to suit our requirements. His estimated cost was £10,000 and we set about raising the money. We wrote to all the likely charities recommended to us, but only the Bucks Playing Fields Association responded, and they only agreed to meet the cost of returfing the cricket pitch. It was up to us.

Now that the dream was taking shape, the village responded with a will, and regular efforts were organised, the most successful being a weekly village 'sweep'. Terry and Sheila Hands and Brenda Clark were responsible. Terry and Sheila lived in Mount Pleasant, a collection of some 15 cottages on the road to Ravenstone at the back of the Rectory. If I remember rightly, subscribers paid five shillings a week and half the proceeds were returned as prizes. First prize in the opening draw went to a resident of Mount Pleasant. So did the first prize of the second draw. The third week and I drew again. Not Mount Pleasant this time, please! It was!

Even more remarkable was a grand Christmas draw. Some 3,000 tickets were sold, near and far, and there were numerous prizes. When the draw was made, Marjorie won the eighth prize – the basket of fruit she herself had given – and Sylvia Warren of Mount Pleasant, a neighbour and Marjorie's close friend, won the tenth prize. It was a cake and she herself had baked it!

The proposed new town of Milton Keynes was still on the drawing-board when Marjorie and I arrived in Stoke Goldington. Then the plans were published and the usual public enquiries held. The people of Newport Pagnell protested. They did not wish to be included within the proposed new town's boundaries. They wished to remain as they were, a small market town on the banks of the River Ouse, which was once navigable as far as Newport and had been invaded by the Danes. Their plea was heard. Boundaries were adjusted and, though when I and my family left Stoke not a house had been built, a whole network of Tarmac roads together with public services had been completed,

When I had phoned Christie Willatts to thank him for his help in my appointment to Stoke, he had asked where Stoke was. 'In the extreme north-east corner of the county,' I had told him. 'The parish borders Northamptonshire.'

'Oh,' he had replied. 'Well, you know what they say about Bucks: that it is divided in two by the Chilterns, with one foot in London and one foot in the grave.'

That may have been true once but, thanks to Milton Keynes, that is true no longer.

1   Off to Southsea in 1917? (*see pages 6-7*)

2   Brotherhood of the Good Shepherd, Brotherhood House, Dubbo, 1938
(Front row: Leslie Crossman, Leslie Walker, Harry Kitley,
John Hudson, Principal [Later, Bishop of Carpentaria],
Bishop Arnold Wylde, Alan Wight, Jeff Tredwell, Author, Fred Dryden)

3   Mrs Meer Khan, Doris and Betty, with goats and chickens at Gongolgon
(see pages 48-49)

4   Church of the Good Shepherd, Goodooga, 1936 *(see page 42*

5   Jack Hawkins and Richard at Dalwallinu, 1940 *(see pages 54-55)*

'Just married'

6   Outside St James' Church, Delhi, 1942 (*see pages 57-58, 66*)

7   Marjorie outside 17 The Mall, Kohat

8 Living in the house and servants' quarters, 17 The Mall
(Karim Shah, 3rd on left holding child; Marjorie holding Peter;
behind Marjorie, Mr and Mrs Nicholson)

9 Outpost of Empire, Datta Khel Fort (*see page 73, 187*)

10 Audax planes at Kohat (*see pages 78-79*)

11   Wana Noticeboard, NWFP (*see page 78*)

12   Wilbert N'doro inspecting schoolchildren's handiwork at
Marisamuka, Zimbabwe (*see pages 127-129*)

13   Baptism in the Chipashu river, Zimbabwe (*see pages 130-133*)

14 Peter outside our house at St Mark's, Mhondoro, 1951

15 Marjorie crossing the Sivandazi River (*see page 146*)

16   Family Portrait, Shirehampton, 1952
(Back row: Author, 'Pa', Jim.
Front row: John, Peter, Marjorie holding Antony, Auntie Rose,
Doreen holding Elizabeth, Catharine, Christopher)

17   Shiphay Church-cum-School c.1940 (*see pages 158-159*)

18   Rebuilt Church of St John the Baptist, consecrated 20.12.56
(*see pages 161-162*)

19   Shunem Guest House, Shiphay Collaton. On the left the elm tree lopped by
the Australian lumberjack (*see pages 162-163*)

20   Mr Jonas Kenyon cutting the 1964 Denby Dale Pie (*see pages 184-187*)

21   Denby Dale Boarding School, staff and pupils
(David Divall and Freni in centre. Also in photo Marjorie and Christopher)
(*see pages 190-192*)

22   Gayhurst House and St Peter's Church (*see pages 195-198*)

23   Convalescing – Bishop Paul Burrough and Bess
outside Bishop's Mount, 1972 (*see page 224*)

24   Azariah in a rickshaw in a street in Khammam
(*see pages 239-243, 254-255*)

25   Stacklands Retreat House, West Kingsdown, Kent

26   The Shell of St Monica's Church, Seke.
St Francis Glenora visited in 1982 was a similar shell-church. (*see page 335*)

27   The Real Life Procession in Sevenoaks, 1986 (*see pages 288-289*)

PART III

AUTUMN FLOWERING

17

Once More on the Move

When we left Cumberworth for Stoke Goldington in 1965, we left Antony in Yorkshire. He was in the sixth form in Wakefield Grammar School and due to take his A levels in the following May, so we arranged for him to become a boarder for his final year. It was not a success. In those days to get to a university, candidates had to pass in three subjects at A level. Antony passed only in history.

He rejoined us in Stoke Goldington, linked up with a probation officer and decided this was the work he would like to do. However, at 17 he was far too young and so he spent a happy 12 months working for churchwarden Ted Adams on his farm at Gayhurst, and then we persuaded him to take up teacher-training. It would stand him in good stead, we assured him, if later he still wished to be a probation officer. Peter and Christopher, articled to be accountants, were unhelpful. 'Those who can, do; those who can't, teach.'

Nevertheless, in September 1968 Antony began a three-year course at St Luke's C of E Teacher Training College in Exeter. Which was why Marjorie and I decided to take a short break after Easter in 1971 to visit friends in Shiphay and Antony at St Luke's.

On our way up to Cumberworth in 1959 we had spent, as you heard, a night with John and Mildred Bishop at Hugglescote near Coalville. John was now Rector of Singleton near Chichester, and he invited Marjorie and me to spend a night with him and his wife on our way home. We stayed with them and that evening they showed us photos of a house in

Chichester which, they explained, they had recently bought for their retirement.

'But why the hurry?' we asked, for John was not due to retire for another three years.

'Because,' said John, 'if the price of house properties continues to rise at their present speed, in three years' time we shan't be able to afford one.'

This set us thinking.

In what proved to be a vain tax-avoidance exercise, Pa had just given Jim and me £10,000 each – and six years earlier I had asked the bank manager in Hounslow whether he was good for £200! No wonder he had smiled! We were therefore in a position to invest, like John and Mildred, in a house to retire to.

Ever since the time during the First World War when we had picnicked on Sundays at Newlands Corner, Hindhead and Frensham Ponds, I had loved that part of England. On our way home from Singleton we therefore visited estate agents in Goldalming and Guildford, seeking information. In consequence, in the weeks that followed almost every mail brought us particulars of some 'desirable property' in these areas. We had told them we could not go above £8,000, but this did not discourage them from sending us particulars of properties costing very much more. Nothing attracted us until on a Saturday in June we received details of a property for sale in Guildford which seemed just what we wanted. We phoned at once, saying we were interested, and made an appointment with them for 12.30 p.m. on the Monday. When we arrived they were apologetic. They had sold the property that morning.

We were due to take a fortnight's holiday in early July and Marjorie's sister Dorothy, who had moved with Billy from Orpington to Otford near Sevenoaks, once more came to our help. They invited us to spend a week with them in which to house-hunt. On Friday the ninth we scoured Guildford, Goldalming, Fleet and Farnham; on the tenth, Otford, Sevenoaks, East Peckham and Tonbridge; and on the

214

twelfth, Bromley, Orpington and Chislehurst, returning to Otford for tea.

Our choice was 11 Weald Close, Sevenoaks Weald, which a Mr and Mrs Dodd were offering for £8,450. He apologised for the price. He had, he said, paid only £4,500 for it four years earlier, but his estate agents assured him that £8,450 was its market value. We liked both him and his wife, clinched the deal, and agreed to see his agents next morning. They too greeted us apologetically. How apologetic people were! A previous bidder had offered £8,250. They had been in touch, she was now willing to pay £8,650, and they must, of course, advise Mr Dodd to accept the higher offer.

We left crestfallen, but Mr Dodd turned up trumps. 'No,' he said, 'she tried to beat me down. You didn't. You shall have it.' He was a clergyman's son. Perhaps he had a soft spot for the clergy.

Dad and 'Auntie' Rose, my stepmother, had been blitzed out of their home in East Sheen in the Second World War and they had taken refuge in one of his vacant properties, a terrace house, 448 London Road, Isleworth. It was meant to be a temporary move but they were still there in 1970 and when Marjorie and I, still in Stoke Goldington, paid them what we thought was a routine visit on February 11th, we were hardly inside the door when Auntie Rose calmly announced, 'We are coming back to stay with you. I'm tired of cooking. We've packed our bags.'

'Yes, and I'm tired of having sausage sandwiches for supper!' Dad chimed in.

So back with us they came.

Pa was 92, Auntie Rose 82. They stayed six months with us. My brother was now Vicar of Westleton in Suffolk and in April 1971, as arranged, Dad and Auntie Rose went to stay with him and Doreen. They were to stay with us turn and turn about. However, they did not like Westleton and after a few weeks moved to a nearby nursing home at Scole near Diss which Jim had found for them. Here they settled happily.

That summer Marjorie and I were again involved in family affairs. Three years earlier Antony had worked in a youth volunteer camp in Holland. It brought together young people from all over the world to work and play. They worked in the morning on community projects; in the afternoon tours were arranged and they learnt about Holland; in the evening they relaxed. Antony returned, his heart aflame for a girl called Blasna from Czechoslovakia. All he wanted to talk about was Blasna. Did she speak English? we asked.

'Very little,' he admitted.

'Then how did you communicate? How did you get to know each other?'

'We used to wash up together!'

A true kitchen-sink romance.

As soon as he got home, Antony was off to Northampton. He returned with *How to Speak Czech,* studied it assiduously and in due course ventured to write a letter in Czech to Blasna. The result was disappointing: 'Dear Antony. Thank you for your letter. I do not speak Czech; I speak Slovak....' Off again went Antony to Northampton. Unable to find a *How to Speak Slovak* there, he found what he wanted in Foyles in London.

The romance burgeoned and in 1970 he spent a fortnight in a Czechoslovakian labour camp for young people. He described it as a slave camp; they were made to toil morning, noon and night. However, at its close he spent a weekend with Blasna and her family in Bratislava. They were devout Roman Catholics and Antony went with them to the Mass at the cathedral on the Sunday. Although in those days Czechoslavakia was a communist state under the watchful eye of Russia, Antony was greatly impressed, especially when Blasna told him that theirs was but one of many Masses held on a Sunday and the cathedral was always packed.

Czechoslavakia only allowed her citizens to leave the country on holiday once in three years. Blasna and her sister Louise were both due to receive their visas to travel the following year, and Antony invited them to visit England

and Stoke Goldington. They arrived at Heathrow airport on August 7th. Antony was there to meet them and I picked the three of them up at Wolverton that afternoon. Two blissful weeks followed for Antony. But they weren't entirely blissful.

Christopher invited them to stay five days in his London flat and to see the sights of London. Antony drew up a quite ambitious programme: the Houses of Parliament, the Tower of London, the art galleries, the British and the Kensington Museums, Kew Gardens, and so forth.

On their return we asked Antony privately how many they had seen. 'Not many,' he answered wearily.

'Well, what did you see?'

'Shops – shops, shops, shops. After the empty shop-windows and empty shelves of Bratislava, it was their only interest. It bored me.'

Marjorie and I had the same experience when, at the end of their stay, we drove them to catch the Continental ferry at Harwich. We stopped at Colchester for lunch and I imagined they would like to see its very interesting Roman castle. Not at all. Shops were their only interest.

It was a tearful farewell, and back at Stoke Goldington Antony waited for a letter. 'You will write, won't you?' he had said. But he waited and waited and no letter came. I think it was deliberate. Blasna realised Antony had no desire to live in Czechoslavakia. She on her part had no desire to say goodbye to her family and country. And even if she had been prepared to make the complete break it involved, would she have been allowed to settle in England? The kindest thing was to forget. Antony consoled himself by strumming on the ukelele, over and over again, hour after hour, *Jesu, Joy of Man's desiring*.

It is now a romance of the past, its one tangible reminder a colourful linen tablecloth Blasna and Louise gave us on leaving. We use it constantly. It is beautiful and appears to be everlasting.

Christopher Pepys, Suffragan Bishop of Buckingham, had

been given pastoral responsibility for the county by his Diocesan, and a little bird had whispered in his ear that the clergy in his care were beginning to resent what they considered his incessant prying into how they ran their parishes. He resolved to remedy this by a series of purely social visits. And the reaction at a clergy gathering? 'Has the bishop been to see you lately? He called on me yesterday, asked how I was, asked all about the family. Never asked a word about the parish. What a bishop! I don't think he was interested.' Poor Christopher! Who would be a bishop?

That was in 1970, the same year that Blasna and Louise visited us. By then I had been five years in Stoke Goldington. I was eligible to retire on full pension in 1972, but I did not have to and did not want to. It occurred to me, however, that if I wished for a change I should start things moving. Another move would be another challenge. I put this to Bishop Christopher when he made his 'social call'. He was not remarkable for tact and his reply was in character: 'My dear old chap, who do you think would want you at your age?'

In 1971 I learnt that the Vicar of South Hinksey on the outskirts of Oxford was looking for an experienced priest to take over a daughter-church. We went to see him. He was an attractive young priest and I felt that we would be able to work well together, but he said No. He did not doubt, he said, that I would fit in but he doubted himself. Would he feel comfortable in working with someone so much more experienced than he? I wondered if the Bishop was right.

I turned, as so often before, to USPG. Had they anything to offer? I journeyed to Tufton Street in October and saw their Overseas Secretary, Canon Sydenham, at USPG House. He was optimistic. The English Church in Saigon (now Ho Chi Minh City) had written asking if they could supply a chaplain who would be responsible for the spiritual needs of the English, Australian and American embassies there. 'You should be just right,' said the Overseas Secretary. 'You're English, you've worked in Australia, and the American Embassy is undemanding. And your age, you know, is

218

almost an advantage – the Communists are advancing on Saigon. It's very touch-and-go, and as against a younger man you would be, if I may say so, more dispensable.' His eyes were twinkling and we both laughed.

It was to be a two-year tour and the church authorities in Saigon would find my expenses. On November 24th I had my medical, and passed. The next step was to be my inoculations.

But it was not to be. On December 31st USPG informed me with regret that the proposed tour was off. The chaplain to the Australian forces in Vietnam had completed his term of service and was due to return to Australia. He had applied for the Embassy chaplaincy and had been accepted. Not unnaturally. He was there on the spot and people liked him.

It was probably all for the best, but when Bishop Christopher heard, he was worried. He had my successor at Stoke Goldington lined up – the Revd A K Pring, Priest-in-Charge of Radnage, West Wycombe – and Kerry and his wife had already been to see us. The Bishop wanted to know if I would now be leaving. I assured him that we would. Soon afterwards the Venerable Arthur Lewis, Rector of Rusape and Archdeacon of Inyanga, advertised in the *Church Times* for a locum while he was on furlough in England. I offered and was accepted.

On March 6th in Stoke Goldington school, Stoke, Gayhurst, Ravenstone and Weston Underwood bade us farewell. They presented us with a cheque and showered gifts upon us; a lawnmower, a tea trolley, a camera, a cut-glass jug and glasses, a briefcase, and much else. They were wonderful people. Marjorie and I still receive their monthly magazine, sent to us for 20 years by Sylvia Warren, and when the village hall was eventually built, I was invited back to open it.

The invitation was a great surprise, for at one stage after we left it seemed that it was never going to happen. We had been given to understand its cost would be around £10,000. We had £3,400 in hand, and just before we moved, the committee had invited a recommended local firm to tender. They estimated £23,000. Money would also be needed to furnish the hall. The task seemed impossible and the whole project would have collapsed had not a public-spirited 'comer-in', Geoff Marriner taken the scheme under his wing. He knew all the right people and obtained their support. So much so that when in 1975 the village had raised £8,000 and estimates were again called, although the recommended estimate was a staggering £30,000, it could be accepted because Geoff had obtained a likewise staggering £21,000 in grants from various sources. They were in business again and Derek George, also on the committee and also a 'comer-in', did a magnificent job delving into local history, arousing village pride and rallying everyone for a supreme and final effort. Thus it was that on January 31st 1976 at 3.30 p.m., I was able to declare the hall, built and fully furnished, officially open. Since then the hall has gone from strength to strength, the pride and joy of the village and, apart from an interest-free loan of £1,000 at the start, soon repaid, the accounts have never gone into the red.

There are some well-known words of Sir Francis Drake that have been made into a prayer:

> O Lord God, when thou givest to thy servants to endeavour
> any great matter, grant us to know that it is not the
> beginning, but the continuing of the same unto the end,
> until it is thoroughly finished, which yieldeth the true glory.

When people were singing my praises at the opening, I remembered that prayer and thought of Geoff Marriner, Derek George, John Gates, the Hall Committee and the warm-hearted villagers of Stoke Goldington. They were the ones future generations should thank – and God who gave the increase.

> I planted, Apollos watered; but God gave the increase.
> *I Corinthians 3: 6–7*

18

Retracing the Past in Rhodesia

On March 8th 1972 we moved from Stoke Goldington to 11 Weald Close, Sevenoaks Weald, and on the 28th, Tuesday in Holy Week, my niece Margaret Taylor drove me to Heathrow Airport. What awaited me in Rhodesia? All those by whom I had felt myself betrayed 20 years before had either died or left the diocese, and I was looking forward to my six-month locum. I also looked forward to meeting Bishop Paul Burrough and Bess, his wife, who had invited me to stay with them in Bishops Mount over Easter. I also found that they had arranged for me to take Easter Day services in the parish of Banket, which was vacant. I gave Easter Communion at Raffindora at 7.15 a.m. and in Banket at 9 a.m., and felt once more integrated into the diocese. All was well.

On Easter Monday, April 3rd, I travelled by train to Rusape. Arthur and Gladys Lewis and their children were not leaving until the tenth, and on the evening of the third Arthur had arranged a cheese and wine for me to meet the PCC. On the sixth he took me to Inyanga to meet the churchpeople there. Anything the PCC agreed to do was OK by him, he said, but there was one thing I mustn't do – I must not lose Viola!

Arthur owned a holiday cottage in Inyanga and Viola looked after it. She was an attractive, cheerful local girl who lived in a hut in the compound with her boyfriend and many children.

Inyanga was the *par-excellence* holiday centre of Rhodesia. I took services in Inyanga township, 65 miles east-north-east of Rusape, and at St Catherine's, ten miles further into the mountains. The scenery was incredibly beautiful and I was *required* to spend the second weekend each month amidst it – as if I needed any 'requiring'! And I quickly discovered why Viola was, in her own way, a VIP. The cottage was always clean and warm when I arrived, with logs burning in the hearth and a hot meal prepared.

Besides St Bartholomew's, Rusape, and St Catherine's, there were two other churches in the parish: at Headlands, 35 miles to the north; and at Inyazura, 18 miles to the south. Except when in Inyanga, I had Holy Communion in St Bartholomew's at 8 a.m. each Sunday, and Holy Communion at 11 a.m. each third Sunday of the month at Headlands, and each fourth Sunday in Inyazura. In addition, the parish also had a service centre at the Lonhro Copper Mine at Inyati, far out into the *bundu*, which I visited monthly. I stayed with Mr and Mrs Borradale, who were always most welcoming.

On the third Sunday in April I not only celebrated at Inyazura, I also took a Baptism. Four children of a railway family had never been 'christened' and I was asked to baptise them. Little Lisa, aged four, was a pet. Her mother later told me that that night when she put her to bed she confided to her: 'Father Geoffrey put water on my head, Mummy, but he didn't use any soap!'

My close friend and helper in Rusape Township was Phyllis Matthews, churchwarden and widow of a previous rector. They had had no children of their own but had adopted two boys, Tim and Terry. In 1972 Tim was 23 and Terry a few years younger. Tim was married and in England. Both Tim and Eugenia, his Mashona wife, were outstanding. He was Director of the African Educational Trust in London. Eugenia worked in the Zimbabwean Embassy. Alas, in 1988 Tim died in London after gradually becoming helpless with creeping paralysis. Phyl wrote: 'Eugenia and their three boys, $14^{1}/_{2}$, 9 and $5^{1}/_{2}$ years, were wonderful... Tim was buried at Warren Hills, the national burial place in Harare, and hundreds of people of all nationalities, races and colour, came to pay their respects.' (Warren Hills was then the 'Westminster Abbey' of Rhodesia.)

Terry was a complete contrast. He was a thorough, yet likeable, scallywag,

The parish office was a small brick building on the further side of the compound from the church and rectory. One morning it was discovered that a window had been smashed and a typewriter stolen. Terry offered to repair the window if the wardens would supply the glass. His offer was accepted and the window repaired. Then came the first surprise: Terry sent in a bill for labour! The second surprise was two days later when the police arrived. The typewriter had been traced and Terry had stolen it! He received a six-month prison sentence in Umtali jail.

But the story ends happily. Terry had a displaced shoulder. There was no NHI in Rhodesia at the time and Phyl had not the money to pay for its correction. While serving his sentence, the repair was effected at the Government's expense. Ian Smith's Government may have been racist but it had a human face.

It was less human and less successful with its African protégés. The African population-explosion was one of its problems. In 20 years it had grown from 1¼ millions to an estimated 7 millions, half of whom were under 16. In consequence a vigorous family-planning campaign was initiated. Street hoardings and clinic notice-boards depicted an African husband and wife and two children, cheerful and opulent; and in contrast, another haggard and impoverished husband and wife surrounded by half a dozen sad and ragged children. Beneath was the slogan 'Use Family Planning'.

On May 21st I was travelling to Salisbury to attend a clergy meeting when, just beyond Marandellas (Marondera) I stopped to give help to a young African sitting by the roadside seeking a lift. As we journeyed he asked me about my work and family. I asked him about his:

Was he married? He was.

Had he any children? He had.

How many? Four.

How old? Five, four, three, two. No luck last year. Better luck this year.

I thought of all the Government's efforts on behalf of family planning. 'No luck last year. Better luck this year.' Poor Ian Smith's Government!

About 40 miles west of Rusape was the church of the Holy Name, Matsika. I had no responsibilities in regard to it, but when a Confirmation was to be held there on Sunday, August 6th, it was arranged that I should drive the Bishop's wife there. She would arrive in Rusape by train on the Saturday night. The Bishop, meanwhile, was to arrive at Matsika on his Honda cycle after visiting and taking Confirmations in the Mondhoro Reserve.

The service was due to start at 2 p.m. but there was no sign of Bishop Paul. We waited and waited, and then at 5.15 p.m. he appeared, dishevelled and dragging his left foot beside him. On the last lap of his journey the Honda had skidded in a patch of loose sand. He tidied himself and the Confirmation started. Some 500 candidates, gathered in from throughout the district, awaited him. After 90 minutes the Bishop began to show signs of strain. 'How many more?' he asked. Another 180, he was told. 'All right,' he replied, 'I think I can manage it.'

At the end of the service, he was rushed to Rusape Hospital, where he was given a pain-killer and then sent in an ambulance to Salisbury, where an X-ray revealed he had a broken leg. He never once complained. His only remark was, 'I couldn't let them down.' It was in character: 26 years earlier he had been made an MBE (Military) for bravery in the Second World War.

I was, of course, anxious to visit the Mhondoro myself, and especially St Mark's. The opportunity came at the end of August. I left on the 25th and spent seven happy days travelling round the Reserve with its African priest, Baba

Alban Machiha of Zimhindo. Some of our schools had fallen back, most had gone forward. A new school at St Catharine's, Chimatira, particularly impressed me. There had always been a strong Anglican congregation there but they had never had a school, the school of another mission being within three miles. A few years earlier that school had closed and before it could be re-opened the St Catherine's congregation had built the long-desired school of their own and obtained 'recognition' for it. The headmaster, a young Dutch Reformed Church teacher, was a devout Christian and had worked wonders.

Not far away was St Saviour's, Marisamuka, and there, to my joy, I found Wilbert Ndoro, retired from teaching but still doing the work of an evangelist and making full proof of his ministry. We prayed together in his small house.

We were in the vicinity of the paramount chief, and Baba Machiha took me to him that I might pay my respects. He was an old man and spoke little English but was shrewd and dignified. After the opening greeting, I enquired, as politeness demands, of his family, and this is the substance of the intriguing dialogue which followed:

'How many children have you?'

'Eleven sons; 18 daughters.'

'How many wives?'

'Five.' Then sadly, after a pause, 'Two not working!'

I told the story at our fortieth wedding anniversary.

The highlight of the trip was revisiting St Mark's. I found much had happened in my absence. After five years St Mark's had become a diocesan primary boarding-school under the care of a Fr Amos Matendi. Buildings had both multiplied and disappeared. Of the house that Marjorie and I planned and occupied, only the outside PK remained! The church built by Ronald was falling down and the robes and vestments he had laboriously collected had been eaten by the ants. But the school itself was flourishing and had a long waiting-list. I spoke to teachers and pupils at the morning assembly. 'There would have been no St Mark's,' I told them, 'had not "Paraffin" persuaded the local headmen to inspect the site at the first crucial meeting with the Native Commissioner.'

Our tour concluded in Salisbury on September 1st, when we attended the Diocesan Synod. There I renewed acquaintances with Tony Grain of the Cambridge Fruit-Picking Campaign of 1930. Ordained and in Rhodesia, he had phoned me up in Rusape Rectory a few weeks earlier. 'I believe you are Geoffrey Lovejoy. Are you the same Geoffrey Lovejoy I sold my motor cycle to in 1930?' On being assured that I was: 'Are you attending Synod on September 1st? I will meet you then.' We met and he entertained me in style.

Before I arrived in Rhodesia, a possible settlement to give Africans a greater say in government had been worked out by negotiators. Africans owning property above a certain value, or Africans with the required educational qualifications, were to be allowed to vote and, like the traditional paramount chiefs, to be represented in parliament. A condition was that the settlement should be found acceptable to the majority of both black and white; and the Pierce Commission, out from England, was already in the country to sound out white and black opinion when I arrived.

While we were in Salisbury for Synod at the beginning of September, their report was published: A majority of whites were in favour; a majority of blacks were against. And the blacks were delighted – unquestionably. They cheered as they read the result in the evening papers. They didn't want the settlement – it didn't go far enough – and they had viewed the Commission with suspicion – it was a white commission; it would find for the whites. When it found for them, their delight knew no bounds.

'Thank God for the Pierce Commission', I wrote two days later in the October issue of the *Rusape Church News*, and I gave my reasons.

'You can't say that,' said Anne, the Parish Secretary, when I gave her the script to type. 'Parishioners will be furious.'

'But,' I protested, 'it's true.'

What Anne had said was also true, and my words made front-page headlines in the English press: ANGLICAN PRIEST SAYS "THANK GOD FOR THE PIERCE COMMISSION".' Thereafter I was a marked man, and when I returned ten years later, I found that the Smith Government had compiled a thick dossier on my activities. By then, however, Rhodesia had become Zimbabwe and the dossier, inherited by Robert Mugabe's Government, was all in my favour.

Arthur and Gladys Lewis arrived back on Wednesday, October 11th and on the thirteenth parishioners had a bottle party for me – perhaps they thought I was not so bad after all. I took my last services in the parish on the Sunday and that night travelled by train to Salisbury.

Throughout 1972 my second son, Christopher, was engaged in Voluntary Service Overseas and teaching accountancy at a Roman Catholic college of further education near Mwanza on the southern shore of Lake Victoria. Before leaving Africa, I resolved to visit him and to fly home from Nairobi. It entailed a journey of 2,450 miles by bus and hitch-hike. Quite a journey! I could write pages about it but will describe just one incident.

I travelled by bus from Salisbury to Sinoia (Chinhoyi) and spent the night with Gordon and Mrs Kirk in the Sinoia Rectory. My destination was 'Ndola on the Copper Belt, and, as there were no buses to Zambia on Tuesdays, around 8 a.m. I seated myself by the roadside to thumb a lift. An hour later I got a lift to Karoi and after 20 minutes another lift to just inside Zambia. My third lift was obtained soon after 2 p.m. with an Austrian doctor returning overland to Vienna in a Dormobile.

Our ways parted at Kapiri-Moshi, which in those days was simply the fork where the road north to the western side of the Red Sea diverged from the road to the Copper Belt. No habitation of any kind existed. I sat myself by the Copper Belt road and waited. Four hours went by and only five cars passed. One stopped but was unable to help, the others took no notice. Night falls quickly in the tropics and suddenly it was dark. My plight was getting desperate when a car stopped. Two large Africans were in it. They were bound, they said, for Kitwe but could take me as far as the 'Ndola turn-off. I thankfully joined them. It transpired that they were Jehovah's Witnesses and had been expelled from Malawi. I was wearing my clerical collar and they knew I was a priest – in their eyes a 'child of Satan'. (They also probably associated the Christian Church with the persecution they were suffering in Malawi.) Notwithstanding, when we reached the 'Ndola turn-off, without my saying anything they turned down it and left me at an all-night café on the outskirts of the city. They had gone 12 miles out of their way to help me. Can you wonder that ever since I have had a soft spot for Jehovah's Witnesses? They may be mistaken but one can very much admire them.

This return visit to Rhodesia had been in part a mission of reinstatement. I had left Rhodesia in 1952 under a cloud. In 1972 that cloud was lifted.

This record of my six months in Rhodesia following my retirement would not be complete without the mention of two losses I sustained during them, the first of Auntie Rose, my stepmother. She died suddenly the day I flew to Rhodesia, a letter from my brother reached me eight days later. The second was of my father. I returned from Inyanga on September 11th to find two cables awaiting me. The first, sent on September 7th told me Pa was seriously ill; the second, sent on September 9th, told me he had died and that the funeral was to be on the thirteenth. I learnt that he had missed 'his Rose', and had seemed lost without her.

I am a strange, cold fish. My father's death moved me as little as my mother's. And yet I want to be loved and when people are kind to me, as almost always they are, I am reduced to tears. I do not know what God must make of me!

228

19

Assistant Stipendiary Curate in Sevenoaks

After returning from my locum in Rusape in Rhodesia in October 1972, I offered my services to the Bishop of Rochester, and in January 1973 he asked me to help the Revd Stephen Crookshank, Vicar of the parish of Seal, near Sevenoaks. Stephen was a sick man. Not only had he had a series of dangerous operations, he had also lost all confidence in his ability to take services, calling at the last moment on the help of others. Little was done in the parish. I was to relieve him of parochial duties and to take any services he asked me to take. The arrangement worked well and after six months Stephen took early retirement.

I shall never forget his Farewell Service. He insisted on taking the whole of it himself, and afterwards in the packed village hall he was the life and soul of the party. I went round to the Vicarage the following morning, expecting to find him absolutely whacked. Not a bit! The Pension Board and the Diocese had combined to provide him and his wife with the house of their choice in the area of their choice – they chose Orpington – on very generous terms. I found him on 'the morning after' busily packing and nailing down crates for removal, as happy as a sandboy. He died in 1995.

I remained in charge of St Peter and St Paul until six months later, when the Revd Canon John Barnard was inducted as Vicar.

After John's Induction I was given permission to officiate as a priest in the Rochester Diocese and on May 18th 1974 was made a Curate of St John's Church, Sevenoaks.

The legal document ran:

> To our beloved in Christ GEOFFREY WILLIAM
> LOVEJOY, Clerk, M.A., L.Th., Greeting. We do
> by these Presents give and grant unto you Our
> Licence and Authority to perform the office of
> Assistant Stipendiary Curate in the Parish Church
> of St John Sevenoaks within our diocese and
> Jurisdiction.... And We do by these Presents
> assign unto you the yearly stipend of £5.00 to be
> paid quarterly.... And We do direct that you reside
> in the Parish.

As I was already receiving £14.08 weekly from National
Health Insurance and £66.67 monthly from the Pensions Board,
my £5 a year from St John's was only a nominal payment; but
how generous to stipulate that it be paid quarterly! The
direction 'that I reside in the parish' was fulfilled 18 months
later on my return from India, as you shall hear.

Until 1878 the present parish of St John's was the northern
half of the ancient parish of St Nicholas, Sevenoaks, whose
most famous rector was John Donne, the metaphysical poet
born in 1573 who afterwards became Dean of St Paul's. Its
daughter-church, St John's, to which I was licensed, was built
in Kentish ragstone in 1858 and in 1876 was enlarged by the
addition of a new north aisle, chancel and vestry. At first it
had been hoped to construct these, like the nave, in ragstone,
but for reasons of economy red brick was used, as in later
additions. The result is that externally the church today looks
an incongruous mixture of stone and brick. Internally the
effect is far otherwise.

In 1878 St John's was made a separate ecclesiastical
parish, and due to the energy of its seventh Vicar, Martin
Heal (1962–71) and the skill of his architect, Laurence King,
FRIBA, of whom I wrote in Chapter 16, in 1964–65 its east
end was completely transformed. The high altar was removed
from the traditional position against the east wall and set

upon steps in the western half of the chancel, thus enabling the celebrant, as in ancient days, to face his congregation. Over it was erected a magnificent gold and white baldachin with the Holy Dove hovering in bas-relief on its blue ceiling. Suspended above the entrance to the chancel is a huge figure of Christ reigning from the Cross, highly formalised, but evoking devotion. One treads softly in St John's. 'Surely the Lord is in this place.... This is none other than the house of God, and this is the gate of heaven.' *Genesis 28: 16–17.*

Although listed in 1901 as an artisan parish with some five thousand parishioners, for staunch Anglo-Catholics it is today the one truly Anglican Catholic church in the district. They are drawn to St John's as by a magnet, and now, except in one respect, its congregations provide a wide spectrum of England's 40 million inhabitants: rich and poor, professional and artisan, young and old, sitting side by side – Lord Sackville of Knole at one end of the spectrum, 'John Blogg' of the Hillingdon Estate at the other. 'Except in one respect', because although England today is multiracial, Sevenoaks remains one of its 'White Highlands', and on most Sundays the St John's congregation is completely white. Those born and bred in the parish and 'comers-in' are roughly half and half, and I remember all with affection.

Many were delightful characters, and I think especially of the late Mrs Moore of Swaffield Road.

In 1972 she was a widow of fourscore years, living alone; and on Sundays and Thursdays, Marjorie and I would collect her to take her to church. On returning from church on Thursdays her words as we helped her out of the car were always: 'Come inside and have a nice hot cup of coffee', and inside Mrs Girton, her friend and neighbour, had always prepared it.

Each Friday Mrs Moore toddled down with her trolley to collect her pension and do her shopping. She loved a little flutter and once a week would totter across the zebra crossing at the Bat and Ball to put tenpence on the horse of her fancy. I never heard of her winning.

She died peacefully in a Tonbridge nursing home a few years later, and Father Michael at her funeral service in St John's declared it to be a miracle that she had never been knocked down and killed by a motorist. It was. She was deaf and nearly blind and she never looked where she was going. Coming to the zebra crossing at the Bat and Ball on her weekly betting excursion, she made no attempt to look before stepping on to it, pushing her trolley before her. Halfway across she would stop, fumble in her pocket and leisurely blow her nose, quite oblivious of the hooting queue of indignant motorists unable to proceed. Her life was charmed.

When she was unable to attend the services in church, I used to give her her Communion each week in her sitting-room in Swaffield Road. The service over, she normally opened her eyes and invited me to stay for coffee. On one occasion, however, she remained with eyes closed, wrapped in thought. Then with her eyes still closed, she smiled and her lips began to move. I bent forward to hear what God had been saying to her. Her words surprised me. 'I think,' she said, and paused before continuing, 'I think I will have a nice pork chop for my dinner!'

When Marjorie and I joined the St John's congregation in 1972, Fr Martin Heal had been made Vicar of St Mary Magdalen, Munster Square, and Fr Crichton had succeeded him at St John's. Harry Crichton was in his own way as remarkable a priest as Martin Heal and as much a character as Mrs Moore. His talents were manifold. He was a skilled woodcarver and the oak communion rails in St John's are his workmanship; he had a printing press in the clergy house by means of which he published the occasional parish handbill and leaflet; he played the organ and when Rite A first made its appearance, not liking any of its musical settings, he wrote his own setting, still sung in St John's; and, I discovered later, he served as a Church Army officer prior to ordination and, as described in Chapter 15, had led a Church Army teaching mission in Denby Dale.

Above all, Harry was a master of improvisation. One bitterly cold winter morning the congregations arrived to find the church freezing. (He had forgotten to switch on the heating overnight.) Before the services began he apologised to the congregations: 'My dears, I am so sorry the church is cold – the heating has failed to go on. But I have cheering news for you. It costs £20 a Sunday to heat this church. I have consulted the churchwardens and they have agreed that we shall give the £20 saved to the Church Army for coal to give to poor people in London to heat their homes. That warms your hearts, doesn't it?'

He worked hard in the parish but never really liked it and left after five years to become Rector of Lavenham in Suffolk – a world-famous village with a world-famous church. More than two thousand tourists visited the church annually and Harry was in his element.

He was succeeded at St John's by the present incumbent, Fr Michael Shields, who has gifts but of a very different kind. Harry had been exuberant; Michael is quiet, a wise counsellor and remarkable for his clarity of thought and expression. He has been Rural Dean of Sevenoaks since 1984 and a help to many. After what will have been a 19 year incumbency, he is due to retire in 1995. In 1994 he was made a Canon of Rochester.

Fr Michael had hardly established himself before Barry Griffiths and his family moved into the parish. Barry was then Leader of the Royal Philharmonic Orchestra in London and his whole family were or became gifted musicians – Angela, his talented and attractive wife, Clare (12), Francis (11), Katie (9), Peter (7), Cecilia (5) and baby Dominic. Antonia was born in 1984 and Susanah in 1987. And the wonderful thing was that the whole family were in church every Sunday for the Parish Mass and behaved perfectly. I congratulated Angela on it one Sunday. She smiled, 'Ah,' she said, 'you don't know what I say to them before they

233

come in!' Together they created new standards in the church's musical tradition – and very much more.

Dominic proved especially attractive. As a small boy his loud 'Amen' resounded round the church at the close of every prayer, and on one Mothering Sunday he brought the house down in laughter. The speaker, possibly Jim Cheeseman, was extolling the virtue of love: 'Because we love God, we obey him. We obey those we love and so, children, when our mothers ask us to do something, why do we do it? Hands up.'

Several little hands went up and he chose Dominic's. 'Yes, Dominic.' Tiny Dominic stood up. 'Yes, Dominic.'

'She's bigger then me!' Dominic said ruefully.

How we teased Angela!

I have written of the Griffiths family and Mrs Moore. Would that there was space to speak of the many others – I think of Ed and Alice Shirras, of Michael and Annie O'Donoghue, of Douglas and Marigold Seal, of Dorothy Shotter, Cecil Miller, Gertrude Sparrow, Miss Styan, Miss Bennett, of Timothy Lipscomb and of a succession of curates who enriched our life at St John's – but there is not. Nor is there space to speak of Marjorie's work with the crèche and Mothers' Union, or of Thelma Kellaway's work with the knitting circle. I must, however, find space to mention my work with *About St John's* and the Overseas Committee, for they occupied much of my time.

(i) Like most parochial church councils the St John's PCC had many subcommittees. One of these, the Outreach Committee, led by a churchwarden, David Ashenden, was very alive, and on January 16th 1986 it reported to the PCC that in its opinion the first priority of the parish should be to set up a working party to produce a news-sheet in May to be distributed to every home in the parish, and thereafter to publish a similar news-sheet regularly, if this proved feasible. The second priority in their opinion was, they declared, to improve and expand the present weekly bulletin put in the pews each Sunday. The PCC appointed me to chair the working party.

The purpose of the bulletin was to provide church news

to churchpeople; the purpose of the news-sheet was to reach out into the parish and, while keeping parishioners informed of church events, to interest and befriend readers having no church links.

The working party decided on *About St John's* for the name of the news-sheet and its committee was blessed with a large and enthusiastic band of distributors. They had to do more than push the news-sheet through the letter-box; they had also to get to know the subscribers – hence the nominal annual subscription of one pound, payable half-yearly – and to befriend them. Twice a year we also had a well-publicised canvas in selected roads in the parish. In all these ways the distributors became the spearhead of evangelism in the parish.

We obtained the names of 80 would-be subscribers as a result of our first promotional issue. By December 31st this had increased to 180; by March 1987 to 245 and by June to 307. The circulation finally evened out at around 400.

(ii) The PCC elected me to its Overseas Committee soon after Marjorie and I joined the congregation and later made me its chairman. My links with Delhi and Zimbabwe were a great help, and by means of various functions we were able to increase St John's' giving overseas considerably. One memorable effort was an Indian Evening put on in the parish hall, by two loyal friends of St John's, Mary and Richard Chamberlin. The hall was transformed for the occasion. One could have been in India. Even joss-sticks were employed to give the authentic smell, and the meal was superb.

A similar occasion, but on a lower key, was a Zimbabwean Evening when we welcomed Julius and Flora Murumbedzi, who were in England attending courses at the College of the Ascension. Flora, I remember, made a hit by telling the meeting her surprise at her first encounter with snow. 'I never thought,' she said, 'that it came down in flakes. I thought it came down in little balls!'

St John's also supported the diocese of Guyana, where the link was with Bishop Randolph and with two members of the Company of Mission Priests to which Fr Michael belongs and who were working at a training-centre for Amerindian priests far in the interior.

In addition, St John's has a link today with a Russian Orthodox priest in Moscow, Fr Martirii, through Tony Bishop, a member of the PCC who is in the Diplomatic Service and fluent in Russian. When John Major and other cabinet ministers visit Russia, Tony invariably accompanies them as interpreter. A Russian Evening in the parish hall last November was a huge success. When Fr Michael asked Fr Martirii what he thought about the current problems of the Church of England – he was thinking of the ordination of women and finance – Fr Martirii replied, 'Compared with the problems of the Church in Russia, they are very small indeed!'

20

Two Holidays in India

I have already described how my first act on retirement was to revisit Rhodesia in the spring of 1972, and this was followed by my second and third visits in 1982 and 1988 described in Chapter 26. In this Chapter I record return visits to India in 1976 and 1985.

Marjorie and I had left India in 1945, and on my first return visit I flew to Delhi by the Ariana–Afghan Air Line, my plan being to return via Kabul. I had hoped to stay again in Brotherhood House, but all its guest-rooms had been booked for a conference and the Brotherhood had arranged for me to stay instead with the St Stephen's Community in 4 Rajpur Road.

I arrived in Delhi on Monday afternoon, February 23rd, and Dr Ruth Roseveare and Phyllis Challenger of the Community were there to greet me. Room 4, they told me, had been made ready for me, and I wondered whether it was the same room which Marjorie had occupied 30 years earlier and in which I had proposed to her! At any rate, when I asked if there was a spare cycle I could borrow, they presented me with her old faithful, which was rusting away in a godown. It proved a useful acquisition and played a part later in a minor mystery-comedy drama.

The population of Delhi had multiplied tenfold in the previous two decades and was now over four million, but all the historic sites and monuments remained, as lovingly cared for as ever, and I spent eight happy days revisiting them. At the Red Fort built by Shah Jahan in the seventeenth century,

I saw its history retold in a fascinating *son et lumière*; and in the parade of shops, or should I say 'surgeries'?, under the shadow of the main entrance to the great Jumma Masjid Mosque opposite the Fort, I saw a wooden name-board which raised a smile. Under the doctor's name was painted *'Specialist in Female and Child Deceases'*. True or false? At the Qutb Minar, the stupendous vertical tower of victory built eight miles to the south of the city to celebrate the foundation of Muslim power in India, many parties of schoolchildren were enjoying an educational visit, well-behaved and delightful.

There were also hallowed modern monuments to see: the ashram where Mahatma Gandhi was assasinated by a Hindu extremist on January 30th 1948; the site of his cremation by the banks of the Jumna; the huge Lakshmi Narayan Temple built in 1938 by the Hindu industrialist Seth Raja Birla, and so on. Also, of course, the Delhi Mission buildings: Brotherhood House, St James' Church, St Stephen's Hospital, St Stephen's College, St Mary's School, etc.

The new St Stephen's Hospital was the biggest surprise. Across the road from the 150-bed hospital where Peter was born had risen a new multi-storeyed 220-bed building complete with operating-theatres, lecture halls, clinics and much else. The Medical Superintendent of the original St Stephen's, Doctor Lucy Oomen, a South Indian Christian appointed in 1961, had appealed in 1968 to the Protestant Central Agency for Development Aid in Germany for help in its building. They had responded magnificently – several million rupees! The work had begun and the building was officially opened by Indira Gandhi, Prime Minister of India, 11 days after my arrival in India. The previous year the combined hospitals had performed 2,020 major operations, 4,329 minor operations, admitted 15,832 patients and delivered 5,538 babies!

Dr Ruth Roseveare was on the hospital staff, and on March 2nd Ruth, I and two others were sitting in the *kothi* having lunch when an SOS came for Ruth. 'There's a woman in childbirth across at the hospital,' she said. 'There are complications. I am wanted immediately. I'll put my kedgeree in the

238

hot-case till I return.' She returned within the half-hour while we were still finishing our meal. Ruth collected her kedgeree from the hot-case and returned to the table. A few minutes later she said, apropos of nothing, 'These Indian women! They ought to be taught to slim. I had to cut through two inches of fat before I could get to the baby.' Then she fell silent again and resumed her kedgeree.

I was due to leave for Khammam on March 3rd. The day before I cycled through the Kashmiri Gate to Delhi's main railway station to buy a ticket and parked my cycle on the station verandah. Emerging with my ticket an hour later – nothing is done quickly in India – I found both cycle tyres flat and on examination discovered that someone had stolen the inner-tube valves – nothing removable is safe on a cycle in India! I appealed to a small boy squatting nearby and he advised: 'See station policeman.' I found him, and pointed to my tyres. To my utter astonishment he was carrying two cycle valves in his pocket – the things they carry! – and handed them to me. Then the mystery was solved. He pointed to a notice in English at the platform entrance: *'No cycles must be parked on railway premises'*. The valves were my own! He recognised my white cassock and smiled as he waved goodbye.

'Now why would you want to go to Khammam?' the ticket clerk had asked when I bought my ticket. The answer was to spend a weekend with Azariah. Azariah is a South Indian evangelist whom Marjorie and I first met when he was a mature student studying theology at Ridley Hall, Cambridge. He stayed with us at Stoke Goldington in January 1966 and showed films about his work. Since then we have kept in touch and have met whenever he has been in England.

Azariah was born in July 1931. His mother was a Christian, a Lutheran 'Bible Woman' who married a high-caste Hindu, and when her first child was six years old she dedicated him to God. He was baptised Azariah but his father called him by his Indian name of Raja Sekhar and sent him to a Hindu

239

school, where he studied Sanskrit and learned the Hindu scriptures. The turning-point came when, at college, he was introduced by a friend to Father Devadas, a saintly Christian, 90 years old and blind. Under him he studied the Bible and found his vocation, and when, in 1952, he left college, he spent his next two years working under Fr Devadas. Later, he and Mary Seethamma, another of Dr Devadas' converts, settled in Khamman in Andhra Pradesh, where there was a Church Missionary Society school and hospital, and they linked up with the missionaries there.

Today Azariah is the inspiration and driving force of Christ For All in Andhra Pradesh, the registered charity which he established in 1984 to consolidate their work. Andhra Pradesh is one of the 22 States of India. In its population of over 60 millions 85 per cent are Hindu, 10 per cent Muslim and 5 per cent Christian. The language spoken is Telegu.

I left Delhi on the night of March 3rd, travelling second-class in a carriage shared with 70 others, and in it spent Wednesday night and all Thursday, arriving in Khammam at 6.10 a.m. on the Friday, a journey of 995 miles costing Rs.60.50 (£3.32 in 1976!) Before leaving England I had promised Marjorie that I would not travel third-class on the railways. She was pleased to hear that I was not doing so. What I did not divulge until I returned home was that third-class no longer existed on Indian railways. It had been renamed second!

Azariah was there to meet me when I arrived in Khammam, and he drove me to the Polio Unit attached to St Mary's, the CMS Hospital adjoining Azariah's house. I was to stay with the Unit's Director and physiotherapist, Clare Heaton, a native of Warwick in Queensland, a wonderful girl with whom I found much in common.

My weekend with Azariah was a revelation. At 7 a.m. on the Saturday I spoke to the St Mary's staff in their chapel and at 4 p.m. left with Azariah, Mary, and three others in the Mission Jeep, bound for Jammalapuram, 60 miles south-east of Khammam, where the Bishop of Dornakal was due to baptise and confirm on the following morning. Although

240

we started at 4 p.m., we did not reach Jammalapuram until just before midnight – not because of any breakdowns but because of constant stops to visit Christians on the way – a long stop at 6 p.m., another at 8 p.m., another at 9 p.m. That, surely, is the last, I said to myself, but no. Around 10 p.m. Azariah remarked, 'They will be having a prayer-meeting in a village over there' – he pointed to the left – they always have one on Saturday nights. We must pay them a visit', and so we did.

It was being held in a convert's house and perhaps 20 people were squatting on the ground in a single room lit only by a flickering oil-lamp. Azariah introduced me, read a passage from scripture and gave an address. Numberless extempore prayers in Telegu followed, the climax coming when one of the congregation started speaking in tongues. I had heard speaking in tongues in England. This was the first time in India, and my chief impression was how little the congregation seemed affected; some indeed seemed bored. Was this, perhaps, a set performance and they had heard it all before? He went on and on and I thought how wise was Paul's ruling that if anyone wished to speak in a tongue in church it must only be if there was someone present to interpret. There was no such person present on this occasion.

Jammalapuram was sleeping when we arrived but came to life early next morning. The Bishop was due at 9 a.m. and arrived in the diocesan minibus not very much later. The service started at 10 a.m. in the church compound. It began with the Baptism of 13 adults, followed by 7 infants. Then came the Confirmation, when the 13 adults just baptised were joined by 24 others from neighbouring pastorates. Finally, the Bishop celebrated and gave Communion to all the confirmed Christians present – some 60 out of a congregation of over 200. Wine wasn't used. Andhra Pradesh was a dry state and alcohol was forbidden. A sweet red syrup was used instead, and I was interested to find that the chalices never touched our lips. In true Brahmin fashion the syrup was poured into our open lips from a distance.

After the service was the feast – vegetarian and served on plantain (banana) leaves. The Bishop did not stay. He had another engagement 60 miles away. I also had an engagement – a siesta offered me by Mary Saragini, the local church leader. Mary was a caste-Hindu who had been married when six and widowed three years later. She had been converted to Christianity by Mary Seethamma in 1956. She had been left some money by her husband's people and in 1965, when the need of a Christian house of prayer in Jamal had become urgent, she offered one-fourth of this money for its building. Azariah was in England studying at Ridley Hall, but the two Marys got together, and when Azariah returned to India in 1967 he found the new centre ready for dedication. I spoke no Telegu, my hostess spoke no English, but she showed me her family photos and her treasures, and in a mysterious way we had fellowship together.

Our second engagement that Sunday was in the village of Ithavaram, 35 miles east. We left Jammalapuram as the sun was setting. The first Christian in Ithavaram had been baptised only five years earlier and it was, I believe, the first time Bishop Solomon had visited the village, so it was a very great occasion. Five more Christians, one man and four women, all converts from Hinduism, were to be baptised. To greet the Bishop and to witness the Baptisms a great crowd of between two and three hundred squatted on the ground outside the tiny church. It was a cool night and the whole area was floodlit.

The Bishop arrived, had a meal, and soon after 10 p.m. the proceedings opened – but not with the Baptisms. The newly appointed head of the government school was a Christian and so was his wife, and each day after school she held an English-speaking class for those anxious to improve their English and not averse to doing so by reading the Christian scriptures. With their parents' approval some 30 children attended. All 30 were Hindus and were present that evening to demonstrate their knowledge and mastery of English.

The teacher gave them a passage of scripture to read and

then questioned them on it and, in some cases, how Christianity came to Ithavaram. One question surprised me. 'Who,' she asked one boy, 'was the first Christian to be baptised in this village?' The child named him. He had been a devout and highly respected Hindu and had been converted by reading a gospel given him at a mission hospital. We will call him 'Eliazer'. 'Is Eliazer present?' asked the teacher, and an elderly bearded South Indian put up his hand. 'Will you stand and show yourself, Eliazer?' asked the teacher. Eliazer stood; and to my amazement all the Hindus present, instead of hissing (as they would have done in North India) clapped. Christianity is not regarded as a foreign religion in the South. It is accepted and respected.

But what I chiefly recall about this children's demonstration came later. Among the passages selected to be read was the parable of Dives and Lazarus. A small boy was called forward to read, which he did clearly and well. Then came the questions. I remember only one. 'And who, Ramesh,' asked the teacher 'would you like to be, Dives or Lazarus?' Ramesh considered the question. The other children had answered the questions so well and so promptly that I judged them to have been carefully rehearsed. Clearly not so Ramesh. He seemed uncertain. 'Come, Ramesh,' said the teacher the second time. 'Who would you like to be, Dives or Lazarus?'

Ramesh still seemed uncertain. Finally, he volunteered, 'I would like to be like Dives in this life but like Lazarus in the next!'

'But that,' exclaimed the embarassed teacher 'is not possible.'

But isn't that, if we are honest, what we would all like to be? Like Dives, have all the good things of this world in this life yet still have, after death, all the good things of the life to come.

We arrived back at Khammam at 1 a.m. I slept on till noon and spent the rest of the day quietly. Next day I travelled to Dornakal and revisited the cathedral, and on the Wednesday I prepared to leave Khammam. I was out with Azariah and Mary at 8 a.m. to visit the mission's paddy-fields, and at 10.30 a.m. caught the train to Vijayawada (Bezawada) bound for Calcutta, which I had always wanted to see. My train reached Calcutta's Howrah Station at 4.45 p.m. the following day and I was met by a student from Bishop's college, where I was to stay for a week as the guest of Michael Westall, the Vice-Principal. Fr Westall was kindness itself and took me with him on quite a few pastoral engagements, sometimes on the pillion of his motor-cycle!

Calcutta has been called 'A city of palaces and slums'. I saw little of the former, much of the latter, and, remarkably, there was so much life and hope in the people, they didn't depress me in the way I expected. Nearly all the international charities are at work in Calcutta. I saw their work and admired it, but what most impressed me was the Social and Relief Services of Calcutta's Anglican Cathedral. Founded and led by Canon S K Biswas, they not only organised relief work of their own but also closely interlinked with much of the other charity work being carried on in the city. For example, when at the first light of morning, the CASA milk van arrived at Bishop's College, it was the CSS which organised its distribution. The children who gathered in the compound to receive their daily ration had all been vetted and enrolled by CSS. They were given one cardboard cupful each, which had to be drunk before leaving. If they took it away, as one of them tried to do on the morning when I was present, the chances are that it would be sold for pice on the black market.

As darkness fell there was 'Operation Twilight', run entirely by CSS, which reached out to the most destitute of the city's pavement-dwellers. A Jeep left the cathedral each evening with a driver, social worker and volunteer, who sought out the most needy of these unfortunates – those sleeping apart – either, I was told, newcomers to the city or sleepers for some reason ostracised by their fellows. Food and clothing were given out; medical and mental cases were hospitalised and followed up. Our most fruitful harvest was in the forecourt of the railway station. One boy offered food said No, he had enough, and for proof showed us his food-bag.

Again, there were the Mobile Medical Units. I accompanied one led by a Dr Chawri. It was bound for a leprosy treatment centre at Dhapa. Normally it is held in a schoolroom but on this occasion it was held outside as the weather was favourable. A trestle-table was brought out and the unit sister set up her dispensary. The 36-odd patients attending all lived at home, for theirs was a 'safe', i.e. non-infectious, variety. Many, nonetheless, were terribly disfigured. Dr Chawri examined them one by one, prescribing as he did so the pills or ointment needed. These, I noticed, were dispensed by the sister on small squares of newspaper! Costs must be kept to a minimum!

Dhapa, on the outskirts of the city, was the site of its refuse tips – huge mountains of garbage by which the inhabitants of Dhapa, some housed, some living in makeshift camps, earned their livelihood; scavenging for filthy bits of rags, which they washed, for bits of metal and for stale bread and offal on which to feed their pigs. Pigs wallowing in gay abandon in the mud were everywhere. Dhapa is no tourist attraction and it was a relief to return to the city.

The previous Sunday morning I had preached at St James', Calcutta, where Canon Basil Manuel was Vicar. Basil was the son of the Canon Manuel with whom I had stayed in South India in 1934 on my way to Australia, and he entertained me and showed me much brotherly love.

That Sunday evening I sat with Fr Westall in St Paul's Cathedral to hear a recital of church music by a combined choir of the Anglican and Roman Catholic Cathedrals of Bristol, England, which was touring India. The recital was held in the chancel as were all church services for a special reason.

In 1971 as a consequence of East Pakistan's War of Independence, wave after wave of refugees from the new self-proclaimed state of Bangladesh had come flooding into West Bengal. To help meet their needs Canon Biswas then founded the sister society of CSS: CRS (Cathedral Relief Service). Against tremendous odds it worked amongst thousands of refugees in two camps and built another three camps itself. The nave of the cathedral was turned into a warehouse, and day and night trucks and volunteers left for distant places. 'We saw clearly,' writes Canon Biswas, 'that what was involved was not simply the alleviation of a suffering which numbed the imagination, but a fight for human dignity and justice against impossible odds.' On December 11th CRS became the first relief agency to cross into Bangladesh. In 1976 the nave of the cathedral was still being used as a warehouse.

The following Wednesday I travelled by bus to Behala (5 miles for 20p) and met there the Brothers of the Oxford Mission and the Sisters of the Epiphany. The latter baked not only the Communion wafers which were despatched all over India but also the soya bean biscuits for distribution by CASA and in Operation Twilight.

In the introduction to a pamphlet on St Paul's Cathedral, Canon Biswas writes:

> Calcutta fascinates. Visitors come from every part of India and of the world to pass judgement. Many come to see a city in the throes of death. They come to be shocked, to revel emotionally in stark poverty, to have their heart-strings plucked, to pity. Calcutta has the strength to bear with them to chide them gently and to send them silently away.
>
> But there are other visitors, sensitive and mature, who come on a pilgrimage to meet their brothers in struggle. To them Calcutta reveals a strange face of beauty. But it is a beauty which only those who have learnt to love their brother see.

I had come to Calcutta like the first-named, expecting to be shocked. I left on March 19th *en route* for Delhi, the North-

West Frontier, Kabul and home, completely captivated by the hope and courage of its government and people.

Delhi was simply a three-day stopover to say goodbye and thank my friends, and on March 23rd I began the first stage of my journey home. In the days of the British Raj, to journey from Delhi to Peshawar was simplicity itself – one caught the *Frontier Mail* in Delhi and some 12 hours later disembarked in Peshawar. In 1976 it was simple no longer. Since the creation of Pakistan in 1947 the *Delhi Frontier Mail* terminated at Amritsar, and it was necessary to travel from railway station to bus station, and from there to travel to the border. From there one had to carry one's luggage on foot across a no man's land, satisfy the Pakistani immigration officials, catch another bus into Lahore and then, and only then, to board the *Kyber Mail* to Peshawar. I had enquired of information offices in Delhi, could they tell me the times of the *Kyber Mail*? They could not. Could I phone Lahore? No, I must go myself. In 1976 India had no dealings with Pakistan. In the event I spent five hours at Lahore Station, and having left Delhi at 9 pm on Tuesday only reached Peshawar at 5.30 a.m. on the Thursday.

During my wait in Lahore I had a meal in the all-male station restaurant. While having it the Muslim *Muezzin* called to prayer. Immediately all those present took a prayer-mat from the counter, prostrated themselves and prayed towards Mecca. 'Great is Allah and Mohammed is his prophet.' I was much moved.

An incident some time later outside on the platform was moving in another sense. I had bought some bananas from a fruit-vendor and, having eaten one, wondered how I should dispose of the skin. Fellow-passengers were throwing theirs on to the railway track. This I couldn't force myself to do. 'Keep Britain tidy! Take your litter home with you!' And then I saw a railway-coolie sweeping the platform. I salved my conscience and gave him the skin. It was not a success. He continued sweeping the platform for a few more yards then swept all the garbage he had collected, not into a litterbin, but on to the railway line! 'Keep India tidy!' Not 'Arf!

From Peshawar I took a bus to Kohat. Little seemed to have changed. The gunsmiths were still making rifles from pilfered railway lines at an illegal gun-factory at Dira in Tribal Territory just outside Kohat, and their rifles were still openly displayed in the local bazaars. Pakistani soldiers had replaced their British counterparts in the Cantonment but, as in the past, scouts, militia, road guards, bribes and subsidies were still the main instruments of law and order.

I paid a courtesy call on the owner of 14 The Mall, once the Chaplain's bungalow. He was a Mr Asaf, a middle-aged Muslim advocate, and he outdid me in courtesy, entertaining me with cakes and sweets which he had hastily despatched his servant to obtain for me in the bazaar. The temporary Anglican Church just opposite the bungalow and in which I had ministered was still there and was still, I was told, occasionally used. However, the main Christian witness was now a flourishing Roman Catholic mission which had opened in the Mall and had a Fr Kapitan, a Dutch priest, as its director. He proudly showed me round.

I enquired about Karim Shah, my church bearer. He had vanished without trace. Of all whom I had known in Kohat 30 years earlier, not one remained. I wondered whether the two cemeteries were still maintained, but had no time to visit them before catching the last bus back to Peshawar, where I was to be the guest of Dr and Mrs Edmonds at Edwardes College. The college, run by the Church Missionary Society, was the oldest and most respected college in Pakistan. Most of the Government were ex-Edwardes boys, and Dr Edmonds, its Principal for over 20 years, was on friendly terms with the President. Hence it had escaped the fate of other foreign institutions, had kept its freedom and was flourishing. It had, I was told, 800 students and a long waiting-list. We stayed up late into the night talking, and early next morning Dr and Mrs Edmonds drove me to the bus station.

At the bus station one encounter made a lasting impression

248

on me. I was sitting by a window, waiting for the bus to fill, when a leper, his face horribly disfigured, begged for alms. I felt immense pity but hardened myself. I believed begging was degrading. I would give to charities but not to individuals. I said No, and he moved on. I sat and thought of our Lord, I thought of St Francis and I changed my mind. I moved to the other side of the bus where the beggar was now pleading and called him. Then I drew out of my wallet a five-rupee note and handed it him. It was extravagantly generous. There were 16 annas to a rupee and he was expecting two annas at the most. But I shall never forget the look of sheer joy which transfigured the poor mangled face which stared up at me, and I am confident he shared his windfall with his friends. I have been wrong. I have been wrong, I said to myself, begging does not degrade in the East. When an affliction is genuine, begging satisfies and fulfils. And I thought of Mother Teresa of Calcutta, who encourages the beggars she befriends to continue begging – but they must beg, she insists, not for herself or for her Sisters of Charity, but only for themselves and their families.

I spent Friday and Saturday nights in Kabul, on the Saturday watching *Buskashi* (Afghani polo) in the stadium, and on the Sunday I flew back to Heathrow, arriving at 5 p.m. (BST). I had been away only five weeks, but how much I had seen and learned in them.

Next morning at breakfast Marjorie broke some news to me.

For some months we had been considering the possibility of moving into Sevenoaks to be nearer to St John's Church, and before I left for India Marjorie had said that she would want something to do in my absence. Would I mind if she looked at some houses? It would be only 'looking'. It transpired that she had not been idle. She had found a maisonette for sale in the Dartford Road within walking distance of St John's Church; she felt it might well be suitable; and it had got a stage beyond only looking.

'I hope you won't mind, dear,' she said to me. 'It seemed so right that I've put down £100 on it, but it's my money and they will refund it if you don't agree.'

This seemed to me a good moment to confess to her that I too had gone a little beyond my promise. And I explained to her about third-class and second-class travel in India.

As regards the maisonette, having seen it I liked it, and we moved into 73 Dartford Road on Monday, August 9th. We sold 11 Weald Close for £16,800 and paid £16,250 for 73 Dartford Road and never regretted it.

*   *   *

I returned again to India nine years later, leaving Heathrow at 2.30 p.m. (GMT) on March 21st 1985, and arriving at Delhi Airport by KLM at 2 a.m. (GMT) the following day – 6.30 a.m. Delhi time. I took a bus to Connaught Circus in New Delhi and then a motor scooter to Brotherhood House in the Civil Lines, where I was to stay. The scooter-driver asked Rs.12 but I beat him down to Rs.5, only to learn from Christopher Robinson that the real charge was Rs.2. The same old India, I reflected.

I noticed, however, that one thing had changed. As I passed a cinema at the Kashmiri Gate, I discovered that while the hold of the cinema over the general public continued – they would queue for hours to gain admission – the character of the films was changing. On my last visit the Indian films I had seen had all been simple, sentimental and innocuous. Judging from the posters, Indian films were so no longer. They had become violent, bloodthirsty and sexy. The title of one film luridly portrayed on the poster was '*I love Paris! It Tells All!*' Imported James Bond films were also being shown. Has Mary Whitehouse no Indian counterpart?

Living in Brotherhood House were five of the Brotherhood's six members: Ian Weathrall, Christopher Robinson, James Stuart, Kenneth Sharpe and Collin Theodore; and five guests, including Canon David Marriott.

On March 24th (Passion Sunday) I attended a Confirmation in St James' in the morning and the final of the Diocesan

250

Youth Cricket Competition in the afternoon. Next day being a Monday (and also Lady Day) the 6.45 a.m. Lord's Supper in the Brotherhood Chapel was sung. For it we all sat in a circle on the sanctuary floor around a lighted centrepiece, flanked by candles and joss-sticks. Ian celebrated sitting before a low table at the eastern end of the circle. I and the other priests present, robed in white cassocks concelebrated with him, i.e. said the words of consecration in unison. It was all very Indian and impressive.

The following day, Christopher took me in a taxi to New Delhi where I cashed some traveller's cheques. In passing we called at the Bishop's House, but as we were entering the gate, Jane, the Bishop's English wife, an ex-CMS missionary, came cycling out. She told us her husband was out. She was young, unaffected and charming – as was Bishop Caleb Maqbul, her husband.

On Palm Sunday I preached at St James', and having made my Communion watched from my stall the congregation filing up to the altar. To my amazement Bishop Caleb walked past. As Lord Bishop of the Diocese he could have been pontificating. Instead he chose to sit quietly in the congregation.

The Sikh taxi-driver was one of Christopher's new-found friends. Eight months earlier, following Indira Gandhi's assassination by two Sikhs in her bodyguard, the streets had run with blood as mobs of Hindus had run riot shouting, 'Kill them! Kill them!' It was to the Christian church that the terrified Sikhs had run for shelter. The taxi-driver was one of those who had run to Brotherhood House for sanctuary and whom Christopher had received. Now, eight months later, tempers had cooled and Sikhs were again accepted citizens.

On another trip, Christopher took me to visit Ione Browne (née Biswas) in the Christian Colony of Karol Bagh in the Old City. She had been a member of St James' congregation in 1940–42 and we had kept in touch. Since my last visit in 1976, her son David had been killed in a scooter accident, her daughter had disappeared and her husband, a funeral director, had lost his contract with the Delhi Council and was unemployed. Her brother Cedric no longer had contact with her, and tenants living in their house would neither pay rent or leave – litigation concerning the tenancy was in its eighth year! Nonetheless, Ione continued hopeful. She attended either St Thomas' or the cathedral in New Delhi every Sunday, and on Easter Day took me to a spellbinding presentation of *The Mighty Acts of God* by New Delhi YMCA. Creation and Christ's birth, life, death and resurrection were depicted through sound, light and tableaux in the courtyard of the YMCA Tourist Hostel in Jai Singh Road, New Delhi.

The sixth member of the Brotherhood, whom I had still to meet, was Amos Rajamoney from South India, who was resident in the Brotherhood's recently opened Second House. The land had been acquired in 1982 in Shahidnagar, a large new squatters' camp on the further side of the Yuhuma River, and the Delhi Brotherhood Society had begun building on it in the following year. Progress was rapid. By 1985 the Second House had been opened; also a school and library, carpentry and leatherware workshops, and a clinic visited weekly by a doctor from St Stephen's Hospital. A school had also been established at Seemapuri and work had begun in leprosy centres at Anandgram and Amar Jothi. Seemapuri, about two miles away, is a resettlement colony, to which about 15,000 slum dwellers were removed from the centre of Delhi in 1968.

On March 27th David Marriot and I visited Shahidnagar. David was the Vicar of the parish of Wye with Brook in Kent and the founder of the Wye-Brook Trust which raises money to provide personal gifts to India's needy. A parishioner had given him the money to buy a sewing-machine in India. He had done so; it had just arrived at Shahidnagar and we watched it being assembled and handed over into the care of a delighted trainee. When qualified, he would take the machine with him and begin business on his own. Shahidnagar was a squalid place, some 20,000 people living in small houses and mud huts with few amenities. But here was hope.

A week later I returned to Shahidnagar on my own. I had tea with Fr Amos Rajamoney, and Mr Thomas, an Indian Christian worker, took me on the pillion of his motor cycle to Anandgram, about two miles away, a colony of some 200 leprosy and ex-leprosy patients sponsored by the Delhi Brotherhood Society. The families there had taken over the management and were working for rehabilitation and self-support. Two hand-looms were producing 200 cotton blankets per month, and the poultry project housed in a modern shed, built with help from the Netherlands Embassy, was producing 1,000 birds every three months and finding a ready market. There were also piggeries and a small herd of buffalo. There were a few Indian Christians in the colony and they had their own place of worship, St Francis Chapel. After being vandalised the previous year, it was now renovated. Fr Amos had acted as peacemaker, as in other disputes.

My previous visit to India had been in three stages: Delhi, Khammam and Calcutta. My programme in 1985 also divided neatly into three: Delhi (11 days), Khammam (7 days) and Simla (3 days). Three other days were spent flying to and from India, and the rest in travel in India. These were full of adventure, adventure which began the moment I arrived on New Delhi Station at 5.30 p.m. on Easter Monday bound for Khammam.

All seats on trunk trains in India had to be reserved in advance, no matter in what class you were travelling. My first duty, then, on arriving in New Delhi Station was to find from what platform my train was leaving, and the next to discover the carriage and seat that had been allotted me. Swarms of passengers were milling round the reservation boards and I was looking on helplessly when a railway official took pity on me. He asked where I was going and I showed him my ticket. 'Don't worry,' he said, 'I am the guard on the train. I will find your seat for you.' He was as good as his word, showed me to my seat and was most solicitous for my comfort. Would I need blankets? What about meals on the train? Had I booked my return journey? My answer in each case was No. I had my bedding with me and also food. It was a 28-hour journey of nearly 1,000 miles now costing Rs.116 (£8.12), and on it, as on all my Indian train journeys, I lived on dry muesli, fresh fruit from platform vendors, and tea (*char*) from the char wallahs. Not being sure when I bought my outward ticket of how long I should be staying in Khammam, I had not booked my return. This the guard assured me was a great mistake – I might have great difficulty in obtaining a return ticket in Khammam. So he persuaded me to give him cash to purchase one. At 6.10 p.m. the train left. Nearing Agra the real train guard arrived in the carriage and asked to see my ticket. He was wearing a uniform identical with that my bogus guard had donned and was sympathetic. I had been conned out of £10.50.

The train arrived at Khammam at 10.20 p.m. and, as in 1976, Azariah, my host, was on the platform to greet me. Azariah was the same as ever, as God-directed a person as I have ever met.

In his book *Something Small for God*, Dr David Rowe of Plymouth, New Hampshire, USA, describes Azariah's ministry as one of 'See a Need, Meet a Need' and he describes an incident at Khammam railway station when he, his daughter and Azariah were waiting to take a train to Madras. David, while surrounded by a group of inquisitive young Indian students, saw out of the corner of his eye Azariah striking up a conversation with a poor elderly woman, which finished with him giving her a note, handing her some money and calling a rickshaw-driver, whom he instructed: 'Take this woman to my house for the night. Tomorrow she is to be transferred to my Faith Home for the Aged', all this taking place in a matter of minutes. Dr Rowe, anxious to learn more of Azariah's spiritual insight – had he some prescription for discernment? – proceeded to question Azariah:

'How did you know she was in need?'

'I asked her,' Azariah answered.

'Why did you go to her?' asked Dr Rowe.

'She was there,' said Azariah.

'That', writes Dr Rowe, 'is a simple prescription for ministry. See a need, meet a need. Open your eyes, look around, ask questions, get to know, offer help.' It was Azariah's method.

On the day following my arrival, I accompanied Azariah first to the Habitat Village – where many more houses were being built – and then to a nearby village where Christ For All in Andhra Pradesh had opened a nursery school. Small children the world over are much the same and I caused much delight teaching them:

> Round and round the garden
> With my teddy bear.
> One step, two steps.
> Tickle him (her) under there!

At the Polio Unit I met Wendy Aubrey from Christchurch, Dorset, standing in for Clare Heaton, who had left the week before to visit her parents in Australia. Wendy, a nice girl, was writing a thesis on Indian Village Agriculture for her BA at an agricultural college in Shropshire.

Next day, Wednesday, April 12th, Azariah left to attend a conference in Hyderabad, a fine city and the capital of Andhra Pradesh, and on the Thursday John Mark and I joined him. We returned to Khammam on the Friday.

I was due back in Delhi on the Wednesday and I had still to obtain a reservation on a mail train. Khammam station said they had nothing to offer. 'My best plan,' they said, 'was to go to the railway headquarters in Vijayawada in person.' Accordingly John Mark and I arranged to catch the first train there, a local, the following morning. It was scheduled to reach Khammam at 7.15 a.m. But 7.15 came and went, so did 8 a.m., 9 a.m., 10 a.m. Finally it arrived at 10.40 a.m., belching out huge clouds of blackest smoke and bearing in front under the funnel a large hand-made placard: *The Rocket*!

Vijayawada was 50 miles from Khammam, and an hour later we had only completed ten miles. The Vijayawada ticket officed closed at 4.30 p.m. We would never make it! And then came the breakthrough. It was a single-line track and we were halted at a wayside station to allow the Secundarabad–Madras mail train to go through. For some reason it halted immediately opposite us, and an Indian fellow-traveller hurriedly collected his baggage and transferred to it. 'Come on,' I shouted to Mark, 'follow him.'

'We can't,' said law-abiding Mark. 'It's illegal.'

'It's a necessity,' I shouted back. We scrambled aboard the express just in time and reached Vijayawada at 2 p.m. But with no success. Reservations were only available in the Pullman-class carriages and I had insufficient money with me to purchase a ticket.

Dispirited, we returned to Khammam by bus, but better news awaited us: a second-class reservation was available on the Andhra Pradesh – New Delhi Mail stopping at Secundarabad at 9.20 a.m. on the Tuesday. Azariah had a 'brother' living on the outskirts of Secundarabad. He phoned him to make the reservation on my behalf. I breathed again.

But it was not all plain sailing. Secundarabad was three hours by train from Khammam, and when John Mark and I arrived by rickshaw at St Thomas' Church Presbytery, Kisapah, where Azariah's kinsman lived, we found he had been called away in an emergency and his house was locked. I have no note of what happened next but the upshot was that I slept free in the guest-room of an empty house near to the station. The guest-chamber was on the housetop, reached by outside steps. I laid out my bedding on a string-bed – the room was furnished – and there I slept. Inevitably, I thought of the Upper Room in Jerusalem, furnished and prepared, where Jesus kept the Passover with his disciples. Having seen that I was comfortably settled in, John Mark returned to Khammam. Once again I was grateful for his help.

The journey back to Delhi was straightfoward with but

one complication. When I found my seat on the train, I found it occupied by a burly Indian. I politely showed him my ticket and reservation. He as politely showed me his. The seat had been double-booked! The guard, however, was helpful and I was found a seat in another compartment.

We arrived punctually at New Delhi at 7.30 a.m. and I was in Brotherhood House in time for a late breakfast. That morning I walked to the bus terminus in Kashmiri Gate and booked a seat in a bus to Simla leaving at 7.30 p.m. that evening. I then contacted the dhobi living with his family in the servants' quarters at Brotherhood House. I asked him if he could wash my clothes and let me have them back by 7 p.m. He could and did. He was a very superior dhobi – he possessed a colour television which was more than Brotherhood House possessed. A TV set was a great status symbol. However, it really belonged to his son who had earned money as a contract labourer in one of the Gulf States. In the afternoon I slept – whacked.

It was still dark when the coach arrived in Simla in the early hours of Thursday morning. I was staying for two nights at Prospect Lodge, the holiday 'cottage' of the St Stephen's Community, and although I engaged a coolie we found it hard to find. When we did I was welcomed by Shree Jhampa Ram, the courteous Miss-Norris-trained caretaker and warden, who quickly prepared breakfast for me. Looking through the Visitor's Book I discovered that I was the first guest in 1985 and that there had been only 12 guests in 1984, staying a total of 28 days. Why was this?

Simla, renamed Shimla, had not changed greatly in 40 years, the main difference being that whereas in 1945 it was Europeans who strolled along the Mall and whose children, riding on ponies, chattered away excitedly in Punjabi to their pony-men, now hardly a European was to be seen. It was Tibetans who had fled from their homeland on its invasion by China who thronged the streets and bazaars.

I spent the day quietly and booked a seat for a sightseeing

tour to Narkanda on the Friday. Narkanda, said the brochure, was a quaint, sleepy hamlet with breathtaking views of the snow-clad Himalayas; the charge was Rs.40 per seat on a luxury coach.

However, on arriving at the Tourist Office at 10 a.m. that morning, I was told that the coach would not run as only four seats had been booked. The other would-be tourists, a Bombay businessman and his wife and two children, were present and the operator said he could offer us a car for Rs.250.

'Yes, certainly,' said the businessman; and then, turning to me he said, 'We will go fifty-fifty.'

'Not on your life,' I replied. 'You will be occupying four seats, I only one. You will pay Rs.200 and I will pay Rs.50.'

We finally compromised on Rs.187 and Rs.63 and we started off.

The scenery *en route* was, as promised, superb. Equally, as promised, Narkanda was sleepy. There was nothing to do there and the 'snow-clad Himalayas' were shrouded in mist. After 30 minutes we started for home, my fellow tourists grumbling continually; cherry orchards at Matinia had been advertised – why hadn't we seen them? A potato-marketing centre at Theog had been advertised – why hadn't we visited it? etc. etc. The last straw was when we arrived back in Shimla and the Tourist Office claimed an extra Rs.20 because we had arrived back late.

'We will go outside,' said the businessman, 'and discuss it privately.' Outside he said to me, 'Give me Rs.10 and I will settle with him.' Now too exhausted to argue, I handed him the Rs.10. A transformation followed. He fell on his knees and said, 'Father, give me your blessing.' And when I had done so – 'and now a blessing for my wife; and now a blessing for my two children.'

When I told the story at Brotherhood House on my return to Delhi, they were much amused. 'You should have said 'Rs.10 for yourself; Rs.10 for your wife; Rs.10 for your two children,' said Christopher.

They were, however, not amused but very concerned when

I mentioned that, on the way home, the coach had stopped at a wayside village opposite a well fitted with a pump, and admitted that I had joined in drinking from it. I protested that the pump had drawn the water straight out of the well. Christopher was still worried. 'But how do you know what was at the bottom of the well?'

And so I told him what had happened once in the Australian bush when I was sharing the Brewarrina Rectory with Leyland Bird. The Rectory had two sources of piped water. One tap in the kitchen gave water straight from the Barwon River, often muddy and undrinkable, which we used for washing; the other, drinking water, rainwater from the roof collected in a galvanised iron tank at the side of the Rectory. One day we noticed a strange acrid taste in the drinking water. We went outside to investigate and removed the safety cap from the top of the tank. Inside, floating in the water were the decomposing bodies of several frogs! 'We switched over to drinking the Barwon water,' I told the Delhi brothers, 'and came to no harm.' They were reassured.

It was a Saturday, April 20th. Next day, Easter II, I preached at the 8 a.m. Sung Eucharist in the New Delhi Cathedral on 'The Christian Hope' and next morning at 1.45 a.m. (Delhi time) embarked on a KLM flight to Amsterdam. Soon after 10 a.m. (British Summer Time) I was excitedly greeting Marjorie on the steps of 73 Dartford Road.

21

Sunday Duty and Hospital Chaplaincies

While attached as a curate at St John's, I spent a good deal of my time beyond the parish boundaries, especially in doing Sunday duty in other churches during interregnums and in emergencies, for example, when ministers were sick or on holiday. On these visits I always tried to adapt myself and took great trouble to learn how congregations were accustomed to having their services taken. No one wondering 'What is he going to do next?' can properly worship.

Every church has its own customs; some congregations, for example, communicate left to right, some vice versa. At Holy Communion, the celebrant is also faced with the question of how much wine to consecrate. He is normally told at the offertory the number of those present expected to communicate, and consecrates the wine accordingly. Normally, too, a layman would assist me with the chalice. On my first visit to one particular church, when the assistant returned the chalice to me, having finished administrating, it was completely empty. (Usually there is some wine left over). On my second visit I remembered to be more generous in consecrating the wine, but again apparently insufficiently so. On my third visit I made, I thought, quite sure. Again there was none left over! I then discovered that in this particular church the custom was for the churchwarden to receive last of all and drink whatever was left!

Besides doing Sunday duties, I also served on a large number of Sevenoaks committees, drove for the Sevenoaks Council of Churches' Volunteer Transport Unit, which involved frequent trips to London hospitals and railway stations, and acted as Secretary of its Ministers Fraternal. This met monthly on Fridays from September to June and average attendances grew from 8 to 18. This growth over the years had little to do with me. It was largely due to the marvellous lunches provided by the wives of the clergy in whose rectories, vicarages, manses or church halls we met, and which preceded the meetings. Through it real fellowship developed among the clergy of the different churches of Sevenoaks and district and I made many useful contacts.

Most of my time outside the parish during my 15 years at St John's was, however, spent in hospital duties. Soon after we came to St John's, Fr Crichton, its then Vicar, asked me to take over from him the chaplaincy of Sevenoaks Hospital, which I much enjoyed. This finished when Fr Michael became Vicar in 1976 and decided to take over the chaplaincy himself.

However, that same year Stanley Hare, Chaplain of Orpington and Farnborough Hospitals, hearing I was free, asked me to become a stand-in for him for holidays and sickness. I gladly agreed, and bit by bit my duties increased until my chaplaincy at these two large London hospitals, ten miles from Sevenoaks, was keeping me busy 30 hours a week. It was an enriching experience and I am grateful to God for both chaplaincies.

As I look back, I think especially of some to whom I ministered. Attached to Sevenoaks Hospital, but some distance away, was the Emily Jackson wing for geriatric patients. Two confined to bed were characters – one, who against all orders smoked incessantly, had danced, she said, with Pavlova, and the other had been an Edith Cavell nurse in the First World War. 'And I can tell you,' she said to me, 'an incident never recorded in any biography of her I have read. We were sitting down to supper. It was at a long table lighted by candles, and one of the nurses, counting the candles said: "We are 13. It is unlucky!"

"No," Nurse Cavell replied, Not for you all. It is only

unlucky for the first one who leaves the table." '

It was a version of the superstition based on the story of the Last Supper recorded by St John I had not heard before.

'At the end of the meal,' said my informant, 'Edith Cavell as Matron and according to custom, rose and left the table first.'

Another patient, this time in Sevenoaks Hospital itself, was blind, and I asked him about his blindness. 'I was born blind,' he said, 'but three years ago a new operation completely restored my sight and for the first time I saw. I can never be grateful enough. Yes, I know I am blind again now but now I can understand. Before, people would talk about colour. I could never understand what colour was. Now I know. And though, before, I could feel things, I could never picture their shape. Now I can. I am so very grateful.'

And there were humorous incidents also. I was once being shown round the female medical ward in the same hospital by a Sister Mitchell, wife of an Anglican priest. As we approached one bed, a confused senile patient suddenly drew up her knees and threw off her bedclothes, exposing herself to all and sundry. Sister Mitchell hurried forward and replaced the blanket. 'You know what they say,' she said to me. 'If he is a gentleman, he won't look. And if he isn't, it doesn't matter.'

A similar incident which promised to be still more embarrassing concerned an elderly spinster from St John's who had gone to a local nursing home for a hysterectomy. I went to visit her. Nursing homes do not usually do major surgery – they send their patients to a hospital for it – and in the course of conversation I asked my spinster lady, 'And where did you have it?'

'Would you like to see, Father?' she asked, and started to remove the bedclothes!

In the course of 40 years I had done much hospital visiting as a parish priest. Only now was I actually a hospital chaplain responsible to the Department of Health and charged with ministering to both staff and patients. I felt at first much out of my depth and was very grateful for the lectures and residential conferences laid on by the Hospital Chaplains' Fellowship. Over 40 years, attitudes to prayer had changed. In the thirties, if you were an Anglican you knelt to pray, whether in church, hospital or home – only chapel people sat! When in the Holy Communion Service in the *Book of Common Prayer* the priest exhorted people to confess their sins, he was instructed to exhort them to do so 'meekly kneeling upon their knees'. ('On what else could you kneel?' Fr Crichton used to ask devotees of the BCP.) But with the coming of the *Alternative Service Book*, knees were out, and when praying with patients in hospital wards I simply sat and held the patient's hand – all much more natural and less embarrassing – but was I right? The training courses reassured me, and I would offer prayer according to the patient's custom – the 'Hail Mary' with Roman Catholics, and St Augustine's wonderful, all-comprehensive prayer:

O God, the light of the minds that know thee,
the life of the souls that love thee;
and the strength of wills that serve thee:
Help us so to know thee that we may truly love thee,
so to love thee that we may fully serve thee
whom to serve is perfect freedom.

with Jews, Muslims, Hindus and agnostics.

In ministering to the dying, I never 'pushed' the sacrament of unction. I only used it with those already instructed and normally used the commendatory Prayers of the 1928 Prayer Book, preceded by Bible texts and concluded by the words of Charlotte Elliott's well-known hymn which begins:

Just as I am, without one plea
But that thy blood was shed for me,
And that thou bidd'st me come to thee,
O Lamb of God, I come!

At Farnborough Hospital there was, and is, a psychiatric unit. I visited it every Friday and once a month held a Communion Service in the cafeteria and lounge, where there was a piano and which was carefully prepared for me by a helpful charge-nurse – I forget his name. The service was, of course, much simplified. Even so, one never really knew what to expect – but one thing was quite extraordinary. When it came to the Prayer of Consecration and the giving of Communion, clamour ceased. It was as though they sensed 'Here was mystery, here was a Presence, here was heaven.'

> Let all mortal flesh keep silence,
>> And with fear and trembling stand...
> Christ our God to earth descendeth,
>> Our full homage to demand.

With one patient I struck up a relationship which endured. David, who when not in Farnborough lived with his elderly parents in Otford, always came to speak with me when I visited his ward and always carried a Bible with him. Otford is only six miles from Sevenoaks, and I got to know his parents and on at least one occasion brought them over to see him. Frank and Elizabeth worked as gardener and housemaid to a Mr Cripps, who lived alone with Ruth, his unmarried daughter, in a large house in Brasted near Sevenoaks. David, their only child, was born in their old age. Ruth Cripps became his godmother and took him into her care. She worshipped regularly at the local church and saw that David was 'godily and Christianly' brought up and in due course confirmed. He was quite bright, and when he finished his schooling she apprenticed him to a plumber and he passed his City and Guilds. But he was becoming wayward and difficult, and after her father's death Ruth took him into her home and he became her chauffeur. They were happy days for David. When Ruth died in 1981 she left half of her considerable estate to him. He would never lack for money. But David continued to deteriorate and schizophrenia developed.

Our friendship has been a close one. Despite his unpredictability he is very lovable and fundamentally good. He has a childlike simplicity. His great aim in life is to please God, to get to heaven and to be like Jesus – and it explains much of his behaviour. For years he would roam the streets in the summer months, sleeping in bus-shelters and under hedges. He lived and looked like a tramp – did not Jesus? – and

264

when he could he would gather crowds around him: 'What does this mad fellow want?' (Compare John 9: 11, Mark 3: 21.) Then he would preach the gospel to them.

And, of course, he fell foul of authority. He caused disturbances and at times was violent. More than once, on a sudden impulse, he attacked both his father and his mother, and it was useless making a court order against him to report regularly to a probation officer – he never knew what day of the week it was. In consequence he was frequently in prison and in and out of psychiatric units. I was called in more than once when he was violent. On one occasion he phoned me himself: 'Come quickly. I've just banged Frank.' But he had always recovered before I arrived.

Two special memories to conclude. The first a night out at the London Palladium in June 1991 when he took me to see *Joseph and the amazing Technicolor Dreamcoat* with music by Andrew Lloyd Webber. It was a Charity preview in aid of Oxfam's Disaster Fund and David paid for two circle ticket, costing £120. David loved it.

The second was earlier, when he came to lunch with me one Sunday morning when Marjorie was away. He was at the time living with his parents in Otford and coming to church each Sunday at St John's. After the service I invited him back to lunch. He accepted but said he must go home first. In church he had worn an old anorak and jeans. When he arrived on my doorstep 30 minutes later, he was dressed to-the-nines. 'My, David!' I exclaimed. 'Why this?'

'I wouldn't come to lunch with a Vicar,' he replied, 'except properly dressed!'

He often refused medication – 'You don't need medication if you believe in Jesus'. He became violent and in 1990 the Sussex police picked him up wandering distraught on a highway. After some months in Hellingly Hospital he was 'sectioned' to Oakwood, the Psychiatric wing of Maidstone General Hospital as 'a danger to himself and the public' (which he wasn't).

When Oakwood closed in 1993 David was transferred to a new psychiatric unit at Pembury Hospital and is, I am told, very happy there and has made friends. But he refuses to let even his mother visit him and also rarely visits her at home – perhaps because it brings back memories of his now dead father. But he meets his mother from time to time in Sevenoaks and last month bought her an expensive Mother's Day present.

Small children can be very attached to a person and then suddenly drop them like a hot potato. So David has dropped me and no longer wants either to see me or know me. I still, however, remember him regularly in my prayers.

One day he upset his mother by declaring that Frank was not his real father. 'I can't make him out,' she told me.

I had to explain to her that David was only obeying Jesus literally: 'Call no man your father on earth, for you have one Father, who is in heaven.' (*Matthew 23:9.*) To that Father I commit him. To that Father I commit myself.

22

Once Again Down Under

I had revisited Zimbabwe in 1972 and India in 1976. In 1978 my thoughts turned to Australia, and on April 12th I wrote to John Beiers, the Superior of my old Brotherhood, and asked him if I could be of any use for a month or so in 1979 in my old parish of Brewarrina. He replied that the parish was now vacant and likely to remain so, and that he would be most grateful for my help. I also offered to help further north.

In 1957 the Brotherhood of the Good Shepherd had extended its work into the Northern Territory and by 1978 was well established. I was on the BGS London Committee and at a meeting in London in May 1978 we had as speaker a former Bush Brother, Kenneth Mason, then Bishop of the Territory. I told him of my correspondence with John Beiers and that I was hoping to be in Brewarrina for a few weeks in May. While in Australia, I asked, could I be of any use to him in the Territory? (It was a part I had always wished to visit.)

The Bishop jumped at my offer and eventually it was arranged that I should fly out to Darwin in mid-March, spend till April 18th at an Aborigine station and then assist in Darwin Cathedral till mid-May, since from April 18th both the Bishop and the Dean would be away. On their return I could travel down to help in Brewarrina. And so it happened.

I travelled from Heathrow to Darwin on March 14th, flying with Quantas, the now worldwide airline, which had its humble beginnings in the tiny Queensland and Northern Territory Air Service – hence its name.

We took off at 8.45 p.m. It was a comfortable journey and quite an experience, being my first time on a jumbo jet. What a size they are! There were three cinema screens and I was in front of the third. One of the films shown was *International Velvet*. All three screens showed the same film but I could see the second screen in the distance, and as it had started screening a few minutes before mine I could, when I wished, journey into the future! The jumbo was built to carry 550 passengers.

It was a 28-hour flight, but because we were flying west to east we had to keep putting our watches forward. In consequence it was pitch-dark and 3 a.m. on Friday, March 16th (Darwin Time) when we arrived there. Nonetheless, the Bishop was there to greet me.

I was his guest at Bishop's Lodge, and next day he showed me the new Christ Church Cathedral consecrated on March 13th two years before. It is circular and its sides are entirely of glass. Indeed, it could be used as a Kew Gardens' tropical tree house! The exterior is striking rather than beautiful but its sides can be opened to catch any breeze and, as I discovered later, it is the centre of a very lively parish and a real house of prayer.

That evening we discussed the future. The Aborigine station to which the Bishop wished to send me was Oenpelli, not far from Darwin – 150 miles east, as the crow flies. Bishop Ken was having, he told me, a barbeque in his garden that evening and Irwin and Marie Vines from Oenpelli would be present. He would introduce me. I was to stay in their house.

Next morning, the Third Sunday in Lent, the Bishop took me to the 8.30 a.m. Eucharist in St Peter's Parish Church in the suburb of Nightcliffe, where he celebrated and preached, and at 3 p.m. Ron Watts of the Mission Aviation Fellowship (MAF) flew us to Oenpelli. After celebrating and preaching, the Bishop returned next morning to Darwin.

Oenpelli was completely different from what I had supposed.

My only previous contact with an Aborigine station was while I was stationed at Brewarrina between 1934 and 1939. Ten miles out of the town was a settlement of some 30 adults who, with their children settled there in tin huts because, while there, they received free food rations from the government. A European manager ran the settlement with the help of an Aborigine, Jimmy Barker, who was his jack-of-all-trades. A Presbyterian minister from Bourke was officially responsible for the spiritual welfare of the camp, but I visited it on various occasions. Once I showed gospel slides. A conversation I had with an old gin on one such visit, I vividly remember. She told me she had eight children, and I congratulated her. 'Yes,' she replied, 'my ol' man says it's better than keeping sheep!' (They received five shillings a week for every child!)

I pictured Oenpelli as larger, maybe, but similar. It was completely different.

Oenpelli had an interesting history. In 1906 Paddy Cahill, one of the earliest pioneers of the NT, settled with his wife at Oenpelli, close to the East Alligator River. Paddy took out a government lease on what he described as 'the finest dairy country in the world' and established a profitable dairy herd, which produced butter for the population of Darwin. There were some 500 Aborigines living on the property and Paddy learned their language and won their complete confidence. He relinquished the property in 1924 and retired with his wife and son to the south.

The Commonwealth Government, which since 1911 had been responsible for administering the Territory, had no wish itself to take over the running of Oenpelli. Aboriginal settlements were, reported a commission it set up, 'much cheaper run by Missions who employed more dedicated staff.' It could have been John Major speaking. On its advice, Oenpelli and its reserve were offered to the various missionary societies at work in Northern Australia. The Bishop of Carpentaria, the Rt Revd S H Davies, immediately urged the Church Missionary Society of Australia and New Zealand (CMS) to accept the offer. In a letter to the Victoria CMS dated September 25th 1924 he wrote:

> There is a possibility of an offer being made to your society to take over the Aboriginal Reserve on East Alligator River in the North Territory.... The Oenpelli Reserve is 2,000 square miles in area, fertile and well-watered, and it is less than 48 hours' sail from Darwin.... A white couple have been living here for some time looking after the stock. The stock number about 1,200 cattle, 80 horses and 500 goats.
>
> The natives on the Reserve number about 500; it is for their benefit that I hope that you will consider this matter favourably. These natives are not hostile but are cannibals of the worst kind, their special feast is their own piccaninnies...
>
> The Government would expect you to suppress this cannibalism *peaceably* as soon as possible, for the Government, while wishing to suppress this cannibalism, realise that there are only two ways of doing it, by armed force or through Missions.

This was the Mission and these were the forebears of the Aborigines the Bishop sent me to minister to in 1979. The older members of the community, I reflected, would all in their earlier days have been, in the words of Bishop Davies, cannibals of the worst kind. He had, however, been ill-informed. 'Their own piccaninnies' were not eaten for pleasure, and only special parts were consumed. It was a funeral ritual.

When I was lodging with Mrs Wray in Colchester in 1927, there was once an argument regarding meat at supper-time. John, the elder of Mrs Wray's sons, said he liked lamb. The younger son said he liked beef. 'I want,' he said, 'to grow up strong like an ox; not to become like a silly sheep.' And this primitive belief, that we become like what we eat, is universal. It can be found in the Bible in the words of Jesus: 'As the living Father hath sent me, and I live by the Father:

270

so he that eateth me, even he shall live by me.' (*John 6: 57*)

When, more than 60 years ago, the Aborigines at Oenpelli, grieving over the deaths of their piccaninnies, ate their privy parts, it was that their souls might be reborn into the tribe in the next children born to their mothers.

In its official history by Keith Cole, published in 1975, Oenpelli is described as follows:

> Oenpelli today is a small town, managed largely by the Aborigines themselves, with the help of European advisers, most of whom have been recruited by the CMS. Mr Alf Wilson, who first came to Oenpelli in 1953, is the Superintendent, a role which is changing from being executive to that of being advisory. The population numbers 580, made up of 285 adults and 295 children.

On arrival on March 18th, Bishop Mason had introduced me to the Wilsons, Alf and his wife Helen – a grand couple – and the following morning Alf gave me a map and a list. The list set out the names of all the whites working on the station, together with the names of their wives and children. There were 34 white adults and 17 children – and I had expected two white adults at the most!

There was a newly rebuilt hospital with three trained nurses, a Government school with an enrolment of 183 children, a mission-run supermarket and an outdoor cinema, but not a single swimming-pool in the whole of Oenpelli. There was a reason for this: there was to be no apartheid in Oenpelli and any swimming-pool must be able to be shared by black and white. Syphilis was endemic among the Aborigines and the whites were not prepared to take risks. They enjoyed cold baths in the privacy of their homes and, for swimming, travelled to where there was running water. One such place was Little Falls, a delightful pool six miles away beneath a waterfall, where one shared the pool with shoals of 18-inch fish. Another was the nearby East Alligator River.

How did I spend my time? My first priority was to visit the

271

homes of all whites on the station and to get to know them. My second, was to minister to them and to all Oenpelli Christians, black and white. I taught in the school, led prayer-meetings and Bible study groups, and, of course, took Sunday services.

Large herds of wild buffalo roamed the fertile pastures of Oenpelli, descendants of domestic water-buffalo imported by Papuans in an earlier agricultural experiment and abandoned when, like so many experiments, it failed. Ed Kennedy was the licensed buffalo-shooter and also manager of the Gunbalanya Meat Supply Company, an Oenpelli-owned company formed in 1973. One morning Ed took me out on a shooting trip. We travelled in a Jeep plus trailer. Ed was a crack shot. Every time he fired, down went the beast, which was then machine-hoisted on to the trailer. As soon as four bleeding, still quivering, carcases had been loaded, we raced at breakneck speed (so it seemed to me) to the abattoirs in Oenpelli, the law requiring that their processing began within the hour. In due course 'prime buffalo meat from Oenpelli' found its way on to the refrigerated shelves of the Darwin supermarkets.

On another morning, Wednesday, April 4th, Alf Wilson flew me to an Oenpelli outstation, Table Hill. Soon after the CMS had taken over responsibility for Oenpelli, a commission had recommended the acquiring of an aeroplane, and the plane Alf was flying in 1979 was an almost new Cessna 207, dedicated by Bishop Mason in 1971. *En route* for Table Hill, we called in at Gumarderr, another small Aborigine camp with a one-teacher school with an enrolment of 24.

The airstrip at Table Hill was a mile and a half from the settlement. The villagers had been told earlier by pedal-radio of our coming, and were there in force to greet us. Moreover, the MAF plane from Oenpelli had arrived earlier that morning and unloaded a cargo of supermarket stores on the runway. Our first duty on arrival was their disposal. Diane, the Table Hill schoolmistress, was there to conduct the sale and received 10 per cent for doing so.

Normally, the Table Hill tractor would have been there also, to carry back the stores. Unfortunately, its starter was defunct and the object of Alf's visit was to bring and fit a new one. At the end of the sale the stores were therefore all stacked temporarily into a small unlocked shed on the airstrip.

'Will they be safe?' I asked Alf.

'Oh yes,' he replied. 'The people here are very honest.'

This was in 1979. I wonder if they still are!

Alf trundled the starter in a wheelbarrow to the village, the villagers all following but making no offer of help. However, on the way we met a boy of about 12 years old. Alf had had the very special honour of being made a member of an Aborigine family in Oenpelli, and this boy was one of his tribal 'sons'. 'I can ask him,' Alf explained.

While Alf was fitting the new starter, I was making contacts. Some 50 adults and 20 children were then occupying tin huts and other shelters, but the numbers can decrease or double overnight because, as in all such camps, families overnight can go *walkabout* and not return for many months, perhaps not for a year. While going *walkabout* they live on the land, fishing, digging for yams, eating grubs and berries. Each tribe has its traditional area. To this it keeps. To stray beyond would be dangerous.

Among those in camp were skilled bark-painters, and a lady flew in from Darwin once a fortnight to buy their best work for sale in Sydney. The bark is stripped from the trees, treated and flattened, and then decorated with natural clay or dye, generally black, white or brown. They are also usually X-ray paintings of living creatures. I call them 'X-ray' because they show not only the exteriors, but also the organs of their subjects.

The bark 'clothes' worn by the women on *walkabout* are also flatboards which they carry on their heads unless they spy a stranger. Then they hold the boards in front of them! The males wear nothing.

Of the same 'school' are the rock-paintings, often centuries old, to be found in caves throughout Australia. Oenpelli had its own rock-paintings in a ledge on a rocky ridge a mile beyond its billabong.

On my last Monday in Oenpelli, Joseph took me to see them. Joseph was a Christian (of sorts) and quite old. He told me that he was 70 and had just married a girl of 17 – presumably his first wife had died. However, had he not been baptised, the story would have been different. The girl might have been only nine or ten when the marriage was consummated and he would have been betrothed to her when she was born. Once the marriage was consummated, she belonged to him and he could use her as he wished. He could lend her to friends for intercourse at will, and when she had been properly 'taught', i.e. to know that her husband was her master and lord, he would pass her on as 'husband-trained' to a younger man.

This appears very wrong to us, but in the Aborigine way of life there was nothing secret or very special about sex. Children would watch their parents having sex from their earliest years and would look forward to the time when their own turn would come.

All this I learned from a standard textbook for missionaries: *The World of the First Australians* by Ronald and Catherine Bernot. Incidentally, the authors said that they had not found any evidence of homosexuality among Aborigines – 'Perhaps because the female was so accessible.'

My time at Oenpelli drew to a close, my last Sunday being Easter Day. It started very uncertainly. I went to the Church of Emmanuel at 9.15 a.m. but at 9.30, when the service was due to start, only a handful were present and I heard that the bus had broken down. Oenpellians, I am afraid, are a lazy lot, (or perhaps it is because they are not time-orientated) but they will go neither to clinic, school or church unless a bus calls to collect them. At 10 a.m. the bus arrived but without any passsengers. Trouble? However, Alf went and collected Hannah and her choir and the service began with *Jesus Christ is risen today*. After the Epistle I announced: 'The choir will now sing to us.' As there was no movement I added, 'I think,' at which the choir all rose and left! But it was only a walk-around. A few minutes later they entered by another door, mounted the dais and sang *There's an Old Rugged Cross* (which later I taped). Wendy Kennedy, Ed's wife read the gospel in English, Hannah in Gunwinggu. Hannah also gave a short address in the same language which I followed with an address in English on the importance of the Resurrection. Our second hymn was *Low in the grave he lay* and we closed with *Praise, my soul, the King of Heaven.*

That night, at the open-air cinema an excellent film, *He Lives*, was shown, and the day which had begun so shakily ended in triumph. I would add that Hannah and Rachel had made the church beautiful with frangipani and water lilies gathered from the billabong.

On the Monday, as already described, Joseph took me to see the rock-paintings, and on the Tuesday I gave Sick Communion to Nancy, suffering from leprosy, and to two others. I packed my belongings and that night Hannah and Rachel presented me with two bark-paintings of baramundi fish caught in the Gumadeer River, given by the Oenpelli Council, and I said my farewells. Next morning Ron Watts of the MAF flew me back to Darwin.

The Bishop was away and the Dean, Clyde Woods, met me at the airport and drove me to Bishop's Lodge, where I was to stay. With the Dean was Andrew Hawes, an ordinand from Westcott House, Oxford. In your second year at Westcott you are required to spend time getting parochial experience. Andrew was getting his in Darwin! He is now a vicar in Lincolnshire.

That afternoon the Bishop's Secretary, Mrs June Cameron, brought along a cycle for me to ride, and in the evening Mrs Brenda Wilson, the parish hospital visitor, called to introduce herself. I was made a temporary hospital chaplain and subsequently spent much of my time hospital visiting.

Brenda had been told that every time she visited a ward, she must visit every bed. It was a large hospital; it was an impossible instruction; and we were not, as in England, the 'established' church responsible for the spiritual welfare of every inhabitant. I advised her when visiting the hospital to ask Reception for the admission book giving the denomination of every patient, to list the names of all Anglicans in a ward and to make a point of seeing them, but only to 'Cheerio' the others unless they showed interest. It lifted a burden from Brenda's shoulders and she was immensely grateful. She has now moved with her family to South Australia but we still correspond.

One surprise. Looking down the admission book on Friday, April 27th, I came across: '*Nancy, Aborigine, from Oenpelli*'. It was the Nancy suffering from leprosy to whom I had given Communion on Easter Tuesday. She was now suffering from a further complication and very ill but her eyes lit up when I spoke to her. A fortnight later she was well enough once again to receive Communion. She was very brave.

Another memory. On Monday, April 30th at 8 p.m., Dr Rhys Jones began a course of lectures on 'The First Australians' in the Civic Centre. The opening lecture, 'Man on the Savannah', had been well-publicised, the room was packed and the audience enthralled. To get there I had to cycle and I had no cycle-lamp. I chanced my luck. The only real danger was the Darwin police station which I had to pass. I dismounted as I approached, walked past it, then breathed again and remounted.

A day or two later I was visiting an imposing house nearly opposite Bishop's Lodge. I was invited in, the conversation turned upon the lecture in the Civic Centre and I explained my difficulty in getting there: how I salved my conscience and showed respect for the law by walking past the police station. My host pursed his lips and seemed unamused. It was only the next day that I discovered that I had been speaking to the Chief Justice of the Northern Territory!

Bishop Ken returned late on Sunday, May 13th, my last Sunday in Darwin. I had booked to travel down to Alice Springs on the Tuesday by the daily Ansett coach, to fly from Alice Springs to Charleville, North Queensland, on the Sunday, and then to hitch-hike my way to Bourke, NSW, and Brewarrina. On its route to 'The Alice' the coach called at Katherine and Tennant Creek, at both of which were Anglican priests. Bishop Ken kindly phoned up Fr Jim Stacey at Katherine and Fr Bill Ginns at Tennant Creek and Fr Ben Wright at The Alice, and arranged for me to stay with them. The first two were ex-Bush Brothers, the third a priest on secondment from Western Australia.

The arrangments worked perfectly and I arrived at Alice Springs on May 18th, at Charleville on May 20th, at Bourke on May 23rd and at Brewarrina on May 24th. The most revealing phase of my travels was the flight from Alice Springs to Charleville; the most unpredictable, hitch-hiking from Charleville to Bourke.

We left Alice Springs at 7.25 a.m. and flew south-east across the Simpson Desert. Never have I see such aridity – the Sahara is a fertile plain in comparison. One could have been travelling over the barren surface of the moon! Just occasionally, a line of dead trees would indicate the dried-up bed of a stream, but of human existence there was no trace whatever until we were nearing our first port of call, Birdsville, on the Diamantina River and close to the Queensland-South Australian border. What a place! Perhaps a dozen houses, a store, a police station, a school, and a pub so close to the runway that passengers could leave the plane to slake their thirst at it. It was blazing hot. On a small tin shed (toilets?) a wag had scrawled '*Birdsville International Airport*'.

At Charleville I stayed with the Rector and his wife, Bruce and Rhyl Henzel, in their huge Rectory, once the headquarters of the defunct Charleville Bush Brotherhood. In the evening, after Rhyl had served supper and put their four lively youngsters to bed, Bruce and I watched television while Rhyl span wool on a spinning-wheel. She is given fleeces free, and washes, combs, spins and dyes them; then cords the wool and knits it into attractive pullovers. Cost: nil. Yet again the industrious wife and idly sitting husband and friends of Proverbs 31: 10–31.

Next morning Bruce took me just outside the township and after little more than an hour I was lucky enough to thumb a lift from a passing wool-buyer living in Cunnamulla, my next port of call, a distance of around 150 miles.

At Cunnamulla was Fr John Braun, a member of the Oratory of the Good Shepherd in Cambridge. Ken Mason, who was also a member of the OSG, had arranged for me to stay with Fr John. He had in his parish a remarkable retired missionary, Lil Best-Shaw, a relative of Sir John Best-Shaw of Boxley Manor, Maidstone. Lil, an expert photographer, was planning to go to Papua in the following month to make a filmstrip for the diocese.

I spent the next morning sightseeing in Cunnamulla, and in the evening Lil invited John, me and a friend to supper. We had a hilarious evening together.

Next day John Braun offered to drive me to Bourke, and I gladly accepted. I stayed the night at the Rectory with Philip and Denise Hanlin, and on the following morning, May 24th, Kevin Light, a haulage contractor from Brewarrina, who happened to be in Bourke on a weekly run, took me in his Servis, a huge articulated lorry, on the final leg of my journey. We reached Brewarrina, 'The Place of the Fish-ponds', at 1 p.m.

> We are proud to say that Brewarrina is a pleasant town. All its tree-lined streets are fully bitumented and kerbed. It boasts a modern hospital, excellent schools, and several well-tended parks. Sewerage and filtered water are also among the the facilities provided within the town...

Thus the Brewarrina Tourist Information leaflet of August 1975.

Surprisingly, it does not mention Christ Church, which is the oldest church, possibly the oldest building, on the Western Plains, its foundation stone having been laid on July 12th 1877, only 64 years after the Great Dividing Range which separates the coastal plains from the interior was first crossed.

When I arrived to join Brother Leyland Bird in Brewarrina in 1934, the church was in danger of falling down, great

278

cracks in the walls letting in the daylight, but in 1936 it was beautifully restored through the efforts of Brother Ley.

In those days we lived in a dilapidated rectory, made of sun-dried brick, close to the Barwon River, and took our midday meal at the Far West Boarding-House run by a Mr and Mrs Ted Frost. Ted was white and a churchwarden, his wife an Aborigine brought up on Milroy Station. She was a tower of strength both to Ted and in the town and parish, and was respected by everyone. They had no children and on their death left all they had to the church. Around 1969 the old rectory had collapsed and a new rectory in the church grounds had been built in their memory. It was built of weatherboard with a galvanised iron roof, as were nearly all the other houses in Brewarrina, but had been empty since the last Brother had fulfilled his time of service and left, and I spent my first days in making it habitable.

In 1979 there were no Brothers left in the Brotherhood. Single men prepared to spend five years in the spartan conditions of the bush were no longer forthcoming. The BGS remained in operation but only as a grant-making body. Services in Christ Church were supplied by an ex-Rector of Walgett, now managing a much-reduced Charlton Station. Goodooga remained in the Brewarrina parish but its other six bush churches had all been portioned off to other parishes, Angledool and Lightning Ridge to Collarinebri, Cumborah and Carinda to Walgett, St Mary's, Marra Creek, to Warren, and St Matthew's, West Bogan, to Nyngan.

On Sunday, May 27th, the first Sunday after my arrival, the Bishop of Bathurst, the Rt Revd Kenneth Leslie, was in Bourke, and on the following day he came over to Brewarrina to meet the PCC and discuss with them the future of the parish. They had not had a Rector of their own for over five years and they pleaded for one.

The crucial question was a financial one: were they able to support one? What support could they expect from the people of the bush? I was asked to discover, and it m   I had to have a car. No suitable second-hand car was obtainable in Brewarrina and the Bishop was asked to enquire on their behalf in Bourke. So the meeting closed.

The Bishop wasted no time and that evening phoned me up. There was nothing much in Bourke, but he was told that Sherman Motors in Dubbo were good friends of the Brotherhood. He advised me to try them.

The railway line from Brewarrina had been closed but a railway coach ran to Nyngan on Mondays, Wednesdays and Fridays, and a lorry on Tuesday, leaving at 5.30 a.m. This I caught and arrived in Nyngan around 8 a.m. The Bishop, I knew, would be passing through Nyngan later that morning, so I seated myself beside the road just beyond the level-crossing and prepared myself to wait.

However, before he arrived a driver in a large but shabby car drew up and asked if I wanted a lift. I did, so I got in beside him and very soon wished I hadn't. He was a shearer who had finished his round of sheds and was returning to his wife and family in Gulagong, the home town of Yvonne Gulagong, the young Aborigine girl who earlier had delighted the crowds at Wimbledon.

My 'Good Samaritan' told me he could take me as far as Narromine. 'I devoutly hope so,' I said to myself quietly, for he had been boozing up, and was careering along the highway at 70 mph, one hand on the steering-wheel and one on a bottle of neat whisky, to which he helped himself every few miles.

'Let me hold the bottle for you,' I said, and he handed it over, but next minute asked for it back again.

'Are you afraid to die?' he asked me a little later.

I said 'No' (not very confidently).

'Well, I am,' he replied. 'I guess if it's true what you preachers say, I'm due for that b— b— furnace,' and then he began to relate his life to me, and I took his point. We reached the Narromine Hotel without mishap and, clutching his empty bottle, he made his way to the public bar. He was so drunk he could hardly walk, and my heart went out to his poor wife and children. How would they welcome him?

A lorry-driver in the bar was due to deliver sheep in Bathurst. He offered me a lift and we arrived in Dubbo in the early afternoon. The Bishop had phoned Sherman Motors. They made me welcome, and I came away with what proved an excellent buy – a white Valiant VC Regal fitted with Kangaroo bars – which gave me no trouble whatsoever and which the parish later sold in Bourke at a profit.

I stayed the night with Bishop John Hudson, who had been head of the Brotherhood when I was first in Brewarrina. Now retired, he was caretaking Brotherhood House. It was good to meet again.

The following night I spent with Ella Hall in Nyngan. You may remember that on my way down from Darwin I had stayed my first night with Jim and Joy Stacey at Katherine Rectory. They had only arrived a few weeks earlier from Nyngan and had told me of Ella – how she had left the Buckeroo homestead and was now in Nyngan. When she heard that I would be travelling back from Dubbo, she invited me to stay with her. We spoke of the old times and she gave me news of past members of the West Bogan congregation. She also gave me news of the Meer Khan family of whom I wrote in Chapter 6 and all of whom had now left Gongolgon. Betty, she told me, was living in Girilambone, Doris in Coolabah, both small railway townships I would be passing through on my way home. Betty, she said, was now Mrs Donnelly and was on the phone. So I rang her.

'Is that Mrs Donnelly?' I asked, and when the voice answered 'Yes' I asked, 'Do you remember Brother Peter?'

'Why yes,' she replied. 'We were only talking about him last week. Do you know where he is now?'

I called on her next morning. She was absolutely delighted and said I must also call on her sister Doris and, if I could manage it, on Thelma in Dubbo and Alma in Sydney.

The visit to Doris was equally happy. She had not made as good a marriage as Betty, in fact she had made a very poor one. She had married a man ten years older than herself who was now retired and who had not worked for years. The house was clean but impoverished and it was clear that they were very, very poor. She had, however, one surprising possession, a diamond ring valued at 450 dollars, presented to her the April before by the jewellers of New South Wales. She was the 'Jewellers' 1979 Best Mother of the Year'. How it was that she had become it was quite a story.

Ten years before, a barmaid had arrived at the Coolabah Hotel. She was unmarried but had a few-months-old baby named Leroy whom Doris helped to look after. A month or so later she told Doris she had to go to Dubbo about a Paternity Order. Would Doris mind Leroy till she returned? She expected to be away two days. Doris agreed, but when after three days she had still not returned, Doris went to the hotel. 'Oh,' said the manager, 'you won't see her again. She was a bad lot. She's gone off with the barman.'

In January 1979 the Sydney jewellers announced the conditions for their 'Best Mother of the Year' award. Leroy wrote in reply:

My mother is the best mother in the world. My mother took me in when I was a baby and no one else would.
She looked after me and fed me and went without things for herself for me. My mother is Tops'.

And so Dot had become the Jewellers' 'Best Mother of the Year'.

I may add that when Doris took in Leroy, she had five children of her own, the youngest aged seven, and, apart from State help and help from her family, they had nothing to live on. 'She went without things for me. My mother is tops'.

In 40 years not only had the lives of individuals changed, the character of the bush had changed also. What had happened to Charlton had happened to all the big stations. As leases expired they had been carved up into smaller properties. In addition, a quick-growing wheat needing little rain had been developed, and several property-owners were trying their luck and sowing up to a hundred acres of wheat, maybe more. Again, the motor bike had largely replaced the horse for mustering. Dogs were still required but they were carried pillion in crates. For mustering cattle in large scrub areas, some breeders were hiring helicopters and pilots. They were expensive, but did the job, I was told, much more thoroughly.

Again, of the smaller properties, i.e. under 20,000 acres, some had disappeared, bought up by more successful neighbours; others had developed. Lemon Grove in the Marra Creek district for example, under old Mr Thornton's sons had become a stud, and for the annual sale of rams, fashion models from Sydney had been brought up to attract the ladies!

But what hadn't changed was the good-neighbourliness and the hospitality.

At the end of my stay in Brewarrina I was allowed to take a few days off in the parish car to visit my old haunts of Cumborah, Lightning Ridge and Angledool. They were now outside the parish, but for me they held many memories. Cumborah was little different, though the Springvale homestead had become Pine-Opal Lodge to cater for the increasing number of tourists. I spent my first night there (June 28th) after celebrating Holy Communion, with the Rector of Walgett's permission, in St Peter's Church.

Next day I found Lightning Ridge changed out of recognition. The source of the only 'black' opal in Australia, it was now a major tourist attraction. Externally, the old weatherboard hotel was the same; internally, it was transformed and became, after dark, a nightclub. Six or seven old Sydney trams, collectors' pieces, had been brought on trucks to Lightning Ridge and furnished to provide a motel. Visiting a working opal mine was one of many attractions.

Les Semance, a married Church Army officer from Walgett, acted as my guide. St George's church was being modernised and repainted, and Les was taking services in a hall. It was uphill work.

I continued my journey to Angledool, where I stayed with Rory and Jane Treweeke. The old Angledool station had covered more than 400,000 acres. What was left of it was now owned by Rory's father, who lived in Queensland, and

Rory was managing it on his behalf. Rory and Jane had been married while undergraduates at Adelaide University by Barry Marshall, its Chaplain and an ex-Bush Brother. They were a charming and enterprising couple with four young and lively children, In addition there was Jack, an old bushman in his eighties living with them as one of the family. What was he doing there? Rory explained. Jack, he told me, had started working for his father more than 70 years before. The time came when he could no longer look after himself and he would never have been happy in an old people's home, so they had adopted him.

He loved whisky – it was one of his troubles – and after dinner he prepared to go to bed. 'Just a tiny drop,' he pleaded.

'All right, Jack,' was the reply, 'but it will only be a small one.'

And with the 'small one' he tottered happily off.

On my last Sunday, July 1st, after taking an 8 a.m. Celebration in Brewarrina and another at 11.30 a.m. at Weilmoringle, 70 miles out, we held there a combined meeting of the Parochial Church Council and I presented my report:

> During my five-week stay, I held Holy Communion at 8 a.m. in Brewarrina each Sunday and a similar service in Goodooga on my third Sunday; also two Celebrations in Weilmoringle. I gave religious instruction five times in Brewarrina School, four times in Goodooga School and twice in the Aborigine School at Weilmoringle. I visited Church families assiduously and everywhere was warmly welcomed.
>
> There is no doubt that bush people want a Rector in Brewarrina and I myself am convinced the necessary money would be forthcoming providing the right priest is appointed. Without the appointment of such a priest, it is inevitable that the Church's work and witness will go back and back.

I said my farewell to Brewarrina the following morning and left by the railway road-coach for Dubbo. I again stayed with Bishop John Hudson in Brotherhood House that night, and caught a train to Bathurst next day, where I reported to Bishop Leslie. The following day, July 4th, I caught a morning train to Sydney.

What happened in Brewarrina? The Bishop appointed Fr Bill Scattergood, the unmarried Rector of Nyngan, for a 12 month trial period, but it was not a success. Within a matter of months he had antagonised three-quarters of the congregation – why, I do not know – and poor Brewarrina parish was back to square one, with the manager of Charlton, the hard-working and much-appreciated Mervyn Wearne, supplying what services he could.

But before closing about Brewarrina, I must mention one further link-up with Bush Brother days. It was with Rosie O'Sullivan, and I met her again on my farewell visit to the hospital. Her mother, 40 years earlier, had been postmistress in Gongolgon, and on one occasion, described in Chapter 6, Rosie had vacated her bed that I might sleep in it. In 1979 Rosie was a patient in Brewarrina hospital when I visited it for the last time, and – wait for it! – an M.B.E! Why was she given it?

Some 20 years earlier, when Rosie had succeeded her mother as postmistress, the West had suffered first a long drought and then even more disastrous flooding. The Bogan had burst its banks at Gongolgon and all but one of those living there had been rescued by boats. Rosie was that exception. She refused to go. Her place, she insisted, was at the switchboard. And so at the switchboard she remained, day and night, and I picture her perched on her stool with the waters swirling beneath her till they finally subsided. She had a small, frail body but a very large heart. She served as postmistress in Gongolgon for more than 30 years.

I spent from July 4th–10th in Sydney, staying in the YMCA and usually lunching at McDonald's. I made a few reunions, among them; with Mary Morrison, née Cork, from Brewarrina, whom I prepared for confirmation; with May Fuller, née Shave, once a Sunday school teacher and now the Verger at St Thomas' Church, North Shore; and with ex-Bush Brother Fred Dryden, now married to Gwen. Another ex-Bush Brother, Sid Ashfold, now married to Grace, has corresponded with me for many years and keeps me informed on Australian matters.

I did the rounds, visiting St Andrew's Cathedral, the Aborigine Museum, the new Opera House – what an amazing place – the Zoo, and Manley Beach, were I went rock-climbing with four delightful children, Rachel, Amanda, Rebecca and Emma Charters.

I enjoyed it all, but I had been a long time away and was not really sorry to catch an Ansett flight to Adelaide and Darwin on the 10th. The Bishop being away, Andy Hawes met me at the airport and took me to Bishop's Lodge, and I spent the Wednesday with him. The following day I caught the 6.40 p.m. Quantas flight from Darwin, which delivered me safely at Heathrow at 7 a.m. next morning! Explanation? We had gained 24 hours in flying westwards.

Back in Sevenoaks, I quickly picked up the threads of my ministry, telling the congregation at St John's and audiences at meetings elsewhere of my adventures. I still have the scripts of these addresses, copies of much contemporary correspondence, and all my diaries from 1953 onwards. Thus I am able to record events, even conversations reasonably accurately. I am happy to be by nature a hoarder. Marjorie is by nature a chucker-out; it is the one big matter upon which we constantly differ!

23

The Through Faith Mission

This deserves a chapter to itself, albeit a short one. What locally came to be called 'The Real Life Mission' was a project of the combined Mission Committee of the Sevenoaks and District Council of Churches and of the Sevenoaks and Shoreham Deanery Synods. This committee had long believed that an evangelistic effort in Sevenoaks was overdue and in 1982 had written to York to enquire if there was any possibility of David Watson being able and willing to lead it. When David, alas, became terminally ill we had to think again, and when we heard that Hildenborough Hall, the residential centre of the Tom Rees Mission on the Otford Hills, were planning a mission to Sevenoaks to be led by the Revd Daniel Cozens, Rees Missioner in the Diocese of Ely, we decided to join forces.

I was a member of the Organising Committee which recommended this and it was decided that the following should be the objectives of the Mission:

To communicate the Gospel of our Lord Jesus Christ to everyone in the Sevenoaks District.

To encourage the Christian growth of those who respond, through the fellowship of the Church.

To strengthen the ongoing evangelism of the Church.

To deepen the faith of those taking part.

To bring Churches together through serving and glorifying God.

A strength in fulfilling them was that from the start Daniel and his team emphasised that they were coming to help the local churches in this task – not to do the work for them.

Combined prayer meetings for the Mission began in 1984 and team-training in 1985. Five thousand copies of a colourful leaflet were distributed quarterly by the participating churches, and preparations for the Mission were well covered by the local Press. Daniel Cozens, his colleague Peter Adams, and the Mission team-trainer, Graham Jefferson, all helped in the pre-Mission preparation. The Revd John Tattersall, minister of the Vine Baptist Church, was chairman, and a tower of strength.

It had been agreed that the Mission should open on Saturday, June 8th 1986 and close on Saturday the 21st; that the opening events should be a Procession of Witness through the Sevenoaks High Street on the Saturday morning and a Commissioning Service in St John's in the evening; that the first week should be devoted to 'Meeting the Missioners' – the missioners being not only Daniel, Peter and Graham but also a small army of men and women recruited from previous missions; and that each night of the second week – the *big* week – should focus on a large rally in the Stag Theatre to which well-known people would bear testimony and at which Daniel would speak. The Stag Theatre could seat 400, but should this be insufficient the meeting was to be relayed to the St Nicholas' church hall. The 'Through Faith Mission' team would then return home and it would be over to the local churches.

Finance was a matter for prayer and the final figures were remarkable. Receipts totalled £10, 878 and expenses £9,157, allowing £1,721 to be divided between 'Through Faith Mission' trusts and Sevenoaks Combined Youth Fellowships, who were holding their own crusade a fortnight later. Local churches donated £4,701. Personal donations amounted to £4,429.

Looking back, certain memories stand out. First the Open Air Procession on June 7th for which I was made responsible and which the Town Church, a breakaway from the Baptist

Evangelical Church in Biggin Hill, organised. They had had much experience of open-air witness and were terrific. When I had applied for police permission for the procession they had asked me what numbers we expected. I hoped, but it was only a hope, around 200. In the event more than 400 gathered in St Nicholas' Church that morning. It was to be a happy procession led by the band of St Nicholas' Church Companions, and as we assembled in St Nicholas' Church songs and choruses were practised. Around 20 churches were taking part. Each had prepared a banner and these were distributed at equal intervals throughout the procession. No attempt was made to gather participants under their own church banner.

At 10.30 a.m. the procession moved off. Sevenoaks is a very staid town and it is safe to say that in its long history it had never seen anything like it. Leaflets were distributed by painted clowns from the Town Church, who also rattled collecting tins and handed out balloons printed with the Real Life logo to the children. Traffic going northwards was diverted and southbound traffic was halted. One might have expected the halted drivers to be annoyed. They were not. They enjoyed the fun. To quote from the official report: 'The sight of this long line of Christians from many churches walking together in glorious sunshine, singing and praising, gladdened the hearts of many'. At the Vine Gardens we gathered together, a short prayer was said, and notices were given out.

A second memory is of a Healing Service put on at short notice in St John's Church at 8 p.m. the following day, Sunday June 9th. St John's was packed, and when the laying-on of hands began, given at three different stations in the sanctuary, almost everyone present, so it seemed to me, went forward when directed by stewards. At 10 p.m. people were still coming forward and I slipped away home. Quiet music and singing were maintained throughout. Just to be present, healed.

Other memories were the 'Meet the Missioners' meetings, one in particular held in the Clergy House in Quaker Hall

Lane. The missioners on this occasion were Alf and Syb Ramsay, an elderly working-class couple who had come down from Newcastle to help bear witness. They had come at their own expense and had given up a week of their fortnight's holiday to be present. They told their story of what Jesus had come to mean to them simply, and when a curate present tried to engage them in a theological discussion they wisely refused to be drawn. I was reminded of the story from St John, Chapter 9, of the man born blind whom Jesus healed and of when the Pharisees questioned him. Jesus, said the Pharisees, was a sinner, for he healed on the Sabbath. The man is recorded as replying, 'Whether he is a sinner or no I know not. One thing I know, that whereas I was blind, now I see'. The couple from Newcastle were equally guileless, and one's heart went out to them.

My main memories, however, are of the rallies in the second week in the Stag Theatre. Each evening, after music and singing, a special guest was interviewed by Max Sinclair of Hildenborough Hall, after which Daniel Cozens took the floor with a mission appeal. Among the special guests I remember were Gerald Williams, BBC sports commentator, Baroness Cox, Member of the House of Lords, and Vijay Menon, an ex-Hindu who was delightfully frank. As with the others, Max asked him how he had come to accept Christ. He also questioned him concerning his wife: had she become a Christian also? She had, he replied, but he never forced it upon her. She came of her own free will after many years. And, asked Max, had it made any difference? 'Oh yes,' replied Vijay, 'a great deal of difference. When she was a Hindu she did whatever I said. Now she is a Christian she does what she likes!' However, he still thought her being a Christian was a very good thing.

Each night after his address Daniel made his appeal: 'Would those who wish to dedicate, or rededicate, their lives to Christ come forward.' And we 'counsellors' had been carefully schooled as to what we were to do. We had each been asked to bring a non-church friend with us. If they wished to go forward, we were to go forward with them.

290

There was never, alas, a very good response, perhaps 50 on the first night and each night fewer. Hundreds had been expected and prepared for. The climax was to have been when Daniel spoke about the Cross. That night there were less than a dozen. What was the reason? The real reason lay with us would-be counsellors. I for one had not had the guts to invite non-church neighbours and accompany them.

Each morning, team and counsellors met in the Baptist Hall for prayer-breakfasts and planning. On the morning after the Appeal of the Cross failure, for that was what it was, we were all dejected. Daniel was magnificent. Inwardly, he must have been more discouraged than us all but he never showed it. We had, he said, done our best – he had, we hadn't – seeds had been planted. Results were in God's hands. 'Seeds grow secretly, we know not how'. We left encouraged.

The Mission Team departed and the Organising Committee disbanded, leaving me, as regards the Through Faith Mission, out on a limb. I would have liked to have given my name in as ready to assist Daniel in future missions – I had in the past helped Brother Kenneth, SSF – but felt too old. I therefore opted to be a Mission Prayer Partner, and am still one today, my prayers enlighted by the Mission prayer leaflets regularly sent me.

In addition to parochial missions, Daniel's team have recently embarked on 'Walks of a Thousand Men', the first along the Pennine Way in 1991, and the second, in 1993, through the highways and byways of Cornwall. In all 750 men aided by 180 women took some part in the 1993 Mission, all clad in yellow jumpers bearing the logo 'March of One Thousand Men'. From time to time they had organised meetings, but mostly it was just 'talking the gospel', and the impact was considerable. They focused on pubs – 'where local people meet' and in general found a ready audience. Over a thousand pubs were visited.

Now, with the support of the Archbishop of Armagh, the Most Revd Dr RHA Eames, they are planning a 'Walk' in

Northern Ireland. Is this the way forward in this Decade of Evangelism?

The latest news is that on March 20th, 1994 at Choral Evensong in Canterbury Cathedral, Archbishop George Carey installed Daniel as a 'Six Preacher' for the next five years. It will provide him with opportunities for evangelism in the Diocese of Canterbury. Incidentally, when Archbishop Cranmer founded the Six Preachers in 1636, Statute XXI instituting them enacted that 'a stable be assigned by the same for the horses of the Preachers and a loft of hay'.

I cannot imagine Daniel claiming this right, but I count it a privilege to be among his Prayer Partners.

24

Member of the Society of Retreat Conductors

Soon after Marjorie and I returned from Zimbabwe in 1952 and renewed our friendship with Brother Kenneth, SSF, we became Companions of the Society of St Francis. The chief obligations of a Companion are to pray for the Society and to aim at simplicity of life, but a further recommendation is attendance at a retreat, annually if possible.

Stacklands, the retreat centre of the Society of Retreat Conductors, is a purpose-built building in over 80 acres of garden and woodlands only a few miles from Sevenoaks. Attending a retreat there in 1980, I was moved to offer myself to the SRC for training. Resident at Stacklands was Michael Robson, its Warden/Secretary and Fr Donald Nicholson, Superior of the Society. Donald was a contemporary of mine at St Chad's College, Durham, in 1931 and he readily accepted me for training. In 1981 I became a member and conductor in the Society.

The SRC was founded over 50 years ago to be a centre of Ignatian spirituality in the Church of England. Its two founders are buried at Stacklands – one, Fr Herbert Mather, in a small cemetery in the garden, the other, Major Frank Bowker beneath a large crucifix a hundred yards away and due west of the main building. I visit the crucifix as often as I visit Stacklands and stand silently before it to offer a prayer as the emotive inscription beneath requests:

293

HERE ARTHUR FRANK BOWKER GENTLEMAN OF WROTHAM
ARTILLERYMAN ENGINEER PILGRIM AND CHRISTIAN
BEING COME HOME AT LENGTH IN KENTISH SOIL
UNDER THE STANDARD OF HIS KING BESIDE THE HOUSE
HE PLANNED TO SHELTER THOSE WHO TRAVEL BY HIS ROAD
RETURNS TO STORE ALL HIS EQUIPMENT AND BEGS OF YOU
THE FAVOUR OF A PRAYER — 12 JUNE 1950

In 1981 retreats, whether Anglican or Roman Catholic, were invariably preached retreats, normally at Stacklands either from Friday evening until after tea on Sunday or mid-week from Tuesday evening until after breakfast on the Friday. The programme for a typical weekend retreat is:

Friday   – Supper 7.00; first address 8.15
Saturday   – Breakfast 9.00; second address 9.45
              Eucharist noon; Lunch 1.00; Tea 4.30
              Third address 5.00; Supper 7.00; fourth
              address 8.00

Sunday   – Breakfast 9.00; fifth address 9.45
              Eucharist noon; Lunch 1.00; sixth address 3.30
              Tea and depart 4.30.

Strict silence would be kept from after the first Address on the Friday until after the closing Address on the Sunday, but quiet music was often played during lunch and supper. I invariably played a tape from Taisé and never gave more than five addresses.

During the nineteen eighties, however, a new style of Ignatian retreat developed: the individually directed retreat – for short the IDR. This was in fact a return to St Ignatius' own method. Ignatius never ever 'preached' a retreat. His training of those wishing to join his Order – The Order of Jesus, whose members are known as Jesuits – was always one-to-one for 40 days.

In 1983 I attended the first IDR at Stacklands, an eight-day retreat conducted by three Jesuit Fathers. In an IDR, the retreatant meets his or her director each day for about

294

30 minutes and is usually given a short passage of scripture to meditate upon during the day – no other reading is allowed. Retreatants are instructed to write down their reflections - what the Holy Spirit says to them – and next day read them to their director. The director goes over these reflections one by one and then selects another passage from scripture for the retreatant to mull over until they meet the following day. Complete silence is observed throughout. Services, meals and relaxations help to fill the day.

There were 13 – an unusually large number – on the retreat I attended. Ideally, no director has more than five retreatants to advise and at our first meeting directors were allocated. I was allocated to the eldest of the priests, Fr Anthony Nye, S J. He was a dear.

At Stacklands a grace is provided for lunch and supper. Some are rather formal, and after a few days Fr Nye, who was in charge and always said grace, decided to make up his own. On a day in which our thoughts were on John the Baptist he began the lunch grace with a reference to him:

> O God, we thank you for feeding St John the Baptist with locusts and wild honey in the wilderness. We thank you... [he paused] We thank you ... we thank you for feeding us very much better at Stacklands!

The retreat had a profound affect on me. One Bible passage given me to read concerned Judas Iscariot. I had always felt a certain sympathy for Judas because, following a suggestion made by Dorothy Sayers in *The Man Born to be King*, I accepted that Judas thought he was right in betraying Jesus because Jesus – called to suffer and to die that we might live – was, Judas thought, about to betray this calling by inciting the nation to take up arms against the Romans. Our Lord's cleansing of the Temple (*Mark 11: 15–17*) was in Judas' mind the final proof. It was something he believed he must at any cost forestall. Hence his bargain with the chief priests (*Mark 14: 10–11*) and his kiss in the Garden of Gethsemane when the temple guard came to arrest his Master (*Mark 14: 44–45*). Poor deluded Judas was trying to say, 'I am still your friend, Jesus. It is for your own good that I am doing this.'

During this retreat I became conscious of why in the past I had felt such sympathy with Judas. Like him, I had often in the past acted as though I knew better than Jesus: could you really, in this day and age, take all he said literally? Since then my desideratum has been to make my own the Mind of Christ. How confidently St Paul declares in *I Corinthians, 2: 16* 'But we have the mind of Christ!' What a different world it would be if we had!

I have never contemplated directing an IDR myself – I know I lack the necessary skills – and for beginners I still believe that the preached retreat is the best way forward.

The SRC is at the moment a divided society as a result of the ordination of women to the priesthood in the Church of England. In June 1993 the Society held an Ignatian Act of Corporate Discernment at Stacklands. It lasted from Sunday evening, June 20th, until after supper on the 21st, and, as in a retreat, strict silence was observed. I was among the 16 attending. On the Sunday the proposed procedure was explained and we met three times on the Monday. At the first meeting we were each asked to say what we thought would be good about allowing women to exercise a priestly ministry at Stacklands. Some found this hard to answer! At the second meeting we were each asked to say what we considered wrong about it, and at the final meeting we were each asked to give our final position. Meanwhile, we sought the Spirit's guidance. The matter is still unresolved.

Both retreats open to everyone, and retreats for special groups of people, are conducted by members of the Society at Stacklands. On the 1994 programme conductors sympathetic to the sacramental ministry of woman priests are starred. It reveals three SRC conductors as sympathetic and ten to the contrary. In addition Stacklands plays host to many parish and diocesan groups bringing their own conductors with them. All such conductors are welcome.

The future policy of the Society is mostly concerned with

296

membership. Under its present constitution, membership is restricted to Anglican priests. Many members of the Society believe that this is too narrow and there is a move to change the constitution to allow membership to non-Anglicans also, and to men and women.

For myself, the choice which I believe faces all Anglicans at this time as regards the ordination of women to the priesthood is a choice between tradition and Jesus.

What, in today's circumstances do we believe Jesus, again incarnate, would do? In Galilee he followed the teaching of the scribes and elders as normal practice: 'The scribes and Pharisees sit on Moses' seat, so practise and observe whatever they tell you' (*Matthew 23: 2*). But he did not follow their teaching when it offended the law of Moses (*Mark 7: 9–13*) nor even the law of Moses itself when it offended natural truth. (*Matthew 19: 8–9*). He also said to the apostles: 'I have many things to say to you but you cannot bear them now. When the Spirit of truth comes, he will guide you into all truth' (*John 16: 12–13*). I firmly believe that one of the things the Spirit is saying to his Church today is that women should be ordained to the priesthood and that Christ's blessing is upon them.

I also believe that it is the special vocation of the Church of England to be all-embracing – to show to the world that the one thing that Christ asks of his followers is that they should put him first and believe in him. I love God, I love Christ, and, despite all its failings, I love the Church of England and the Anglican Communion.

25

Sermons and Addresses

In Chapter 24 I gave a short account of the Society of Retreat Conductors and of how I became a member. In this chapter I give the text of five sermons preached during my ministry and two favourite retreat addresses. I have given them because they describe certain happenings in my 'story' not given elsewhere and because they help to show how over the years I have grown in the understanding and in the love of God.

I have arranged the sermons and addresses as follows:

1. The Prayer Book Collect for Christmas Day
2. In Bow Brickhill Church
3. Why Jesus Had to Die for Us (retreat address)
4. Christ's Detergents
5. The Eternal God (retreat address)
6. The Power of Intercession
7. Diamond Jubilee Sermon

I give a brief introduction to each.

1. *The Prayer Book Collect for Christmas Day*

First preached in St John's Church, Sevenoaks, on Sunday, January 14th, 1979 (Epiphany II)

Invocation

Sadly, we never seem to appreciate anything properly until we lose it.... The Prayer Book Collect for Christmas Day is an example. When we had it regularly for Christmas Day and the Sunday following, I thought little of it.

> Grant [it runs] that we, being regenerate and made thy children by adoption and grace, may daily be renewed by thy Holy Spirit.

I used to ask myself 'What has daily being renewed by the Holy Spirit to do with Christmas?' And I still have to confess that, as far as I can see, very little.

And yet now that we no longer so pray on Christmas Day in the *Alternative Service Book*, I miss it and am sorry. For not only at Christmas but always we need continual renewal by God's Holy Spirit just to survive. And this renewal of our lives for the most part goes on quite unnoticed. The renewal of our bodies certainly does.

This body I now inhabit contains, doctors tell us, not a single particle of my original body, the body I received at birth. Every bone in my body, each piece of tissue, every drop of blood, they tell us, is renewed many times in a person's life, and our blood, they tell us, comes from the marrow in our bones, and that blood, I think I am right in saying, only lasts nine months when we are young and less as we grow older, and unless it is continually renewed, we die. 'Grant, O Lord that it may be daily renewed by thy Holy Spirit.'

'And grant, O Lord, that our spirits may likewise be

299

renewed by thy Spirit', for again, unless they are, we die.
Not, mind you, at once. It is a gradual process, sometimes
a very gradual process, just as pernicious anaemia can be.
But unless the decline in our souls is reversed, unless they
are constantly renewed, they too die. Like water to a plant,
so is renewal to our souls, and renewal comes, as does
water, through many channels:

Sunday is a channel – if used for worship. Prayer is a
channel; Bible reading is a channel. The sacraments are
channels, especially the Body and Blood of Christ which,
says the Prayer Book 'are verily and indeed taken and
received by the faithful in the Lord's Supper'. A truly
wonderful channel of God's grace, which, devoutly received,
really changes us. Thank God for Holy Communion.

And thank God, too, for what Oliver Cromwell called 'God's
daily assurances' – those little day-by-day happenings which
cause us to lift up our hearts to God in love and gratitude
because in some very precious and personal way they assure
us of his presence, his control and his graciousness. When we
live close to him they come constantly, often quite
gratuitously.

I would close by telling you about one such 'reassurance'
I received and have never forgotten nor ceased to give
thanks to God for, which came on this very Sunday exactly
five years ago.

Maybe you remember it – it was a truly dreadful Sunday.
We awoke to find the whole countryside completely covered
in snow. Some three inches had fallen during the night; no
snowploughs or gritting lorries had been out and even the
main roads were like skating-rinks.

I returned from taking the 11.15 a.m. Celebration at St
John's to learn that my brother-in-law's aunt was dying in
a nursing home in Beckingham. I didn't have to go but I
thought that I should, so I scrambled down some lunch and
left.

The roads were deserted but not as bad as I expected, and
Polhill, which I thought might be my undoing, was successfully

climbed. I reached the nursing home just before 1.30 p.m. and the nurse-on-duty told me: 'Your brother-in-law's aunt is just the same but she could go at any time.' She showed me to her.

She opened the door of the sickbay and we stopped involuntarily. 'She's bad,' I exclaimed.

'She is dead' said the nurse. 'She must have died as you rang the doorbell.'

So I said the commendatory prayer, kissed her with the kiss of peace and made the sign of the Cross on her forehead.

'I didn't know you used the sign of the Cross in the Church of England,' the nurse remarked – which was, I thought, to say the least, surprising. Then we went to her office and she began phoning round for a doctor. None seemed available.

While she was phoning we talked. She had only been at the home six months, she told me. Her marriage had broken down. She was sad about it. She was a Catholic – she didn't believe in divorce. She had one little boy of six ... that was why she was working.

A workman came in. Water from melting ice, he said, was leaking through the roof in one of the wards and running down the electric light flex. It was dangerous. He was trying to fix it.

Her little boy came running in – a jolly little lad in gumboots, loving the snow. His mother sent him to find someone.

She continued to try to get through on the phone – the line was bad – and in between we talked spasmodically, effortlessly; I might have known her all her life. And all the while, I watched her – she was young and had a lovely face, and suddenly I said to myself: 'She's good; she's brave; she's kind; she's not at all embittered.' and I felt all at once: *How good people are, and how wonderful God is. He ever giveth us the victory.*

'I must be going along,' I said. 'It will be dark soon.' And she helped me on with my coat and showed me to the door. And I drove home rejoicing.

A brief encounter! Yet I was – and still am – uplifted by the memory of it. The infection of a good courage? Perhaps. I don't know. But it helps, I think, to show how in most ordinary ways God can renew us. And how, just by being true to ourselves and to him, we can help others.

I began this morning with the Prayer Book Collect for Christmas Day. I will close with a Collect for Epiphany II:

> Almighty God, by whose grace alone we are accepted and called to your service, strengthen us – daily renew us – by your Holy Spirit and make us worthy of our calling.

2. *In Bow's Brickhill Church*

I preached the original version of this sermon on Sunday, May 5th 1968 (Easter III) in St Peter's Church, Stoke Goldington. I have used this sermon many times since and the version given below is that used in the Church of St Edmund, King and Martyr, West Kingsdown, at its Parish Communion on Sunday, October 13th 1991.

Invocation

Words from Revelation 21: 5 – part of St John the Divine's vision of worship in heaven:
'He that sat upon the throne said, "Behold, I make all things new." '
and words from St John's Gospel 10: 9:
'Jesus said: "I am the door." '

Our theme this Sunday is 'The Christian Hope' and it is about that hope that I wish to speak this morning. The Christian hope is that this life is not the only life; that this world is not the only world. That beyond this life with all its pains and frustrations, all its temptations and disappointments, there is a better life; and that beyond this world, this world which we can see and which is always growing old and passing away, there is another better and eternal world, the world of God and the holy angels.

And I want to tell you this morning how that hope became real to me in a surprising manner in an empty church some 20 years ago when I was Rector of four small parishes on the Buckinghamshire–Northants border.

They had lovely names – Stoke Goldington, Ravenstone, Weston Underwood and Gayhurst – and were about five miles from Newport Pagnell and ten miles from Bletchley,

303

now part of the new city of Milton Keynes. And in those days as one approached Bletchley from Newport Pagnell along a narrow winding road and just before one reached a canal bridge, one could see on the left, about two miles off, the tower of a church standing among trees on a limestone ridge. It looked attractive and I often thought as I drove along that road that I would like to have a closer look at it.

One afternoon the opportunity came, I had driven my wife to a Mothers' Union meeting in a small, close-by village and had the afternoon to spare.

It was a lovely afternoon in April. One approached the church through some woods. The churchyard was a joy, beautifully kept and gay with daffodils. And the view was breathtaking.

I approached the church. One never knows about country churches these days. When they are isolated, as this one was, one often finds them locked. I feared this one might be, but no, it was open and had recently been decorated and was perfectly lovely. I had brought a book with me and, after looking round the church and saying a prayer, I settled down to read.

But suddenly I was disturbed. A swallow had somehow got itself trapped in the church and, startled by my presence, started fluttering about. The windows in the church were all of clear glass and, to my distress, the swallow kept dashing itself against them.

Concentration was impossible, so I went to the porch, opened both it and the wire-caged door beyond and for some time tried to persuade the swallow to fly through. But it would not. The trouble was that the doorway was low and in a shadow. Looking through the sunless porch, one could see the waving trees and the sunlit flowers. But the swallow would not fly low enough to see them. It haunted the roof timbers and the bright light of the windows and, alas, continued to dash itself against them. There was no escape that way. All were closed. But the swallow did not understand.

I returned to my seat in the north aisle opposite the porch

and, picking up my book, continued to read fitfully – one eye on the print, one eye on the swallow. Suddenly the swallow, flying low along the central aisle, saw the sunlight beyond the further porch door, swerved to the left and was free. I waited a moment, then closed the wire-netted door and returned to my seat.

'I am the door [says our Lord in St John]. I am the door. By me, if any man enter in, he shall be saved and shall go in and out and find pasture.'

That door in Bow Brickhill Church seems to me a kind of picture of the Christian life; and that swallow, dashing about here, there and everywhere, dashing itself again and again against the glass windows and getting nowhere, seems to me a picture of today's restless, worldly, unsatisfied humanity, wanting freedom, wanting life, and trying this, that and everything to get what it wants, except – except the one way through which life and freedom comes, through Christ and His Church. But mention 'Church' to them! You know what they say: 'The Church? The Christian Church? You're joking! In any case, who goes to church nowadays? Who believes in the Church nowadays?' The last thing they see any need to have contact with in their search for life is the Church. Yet for the worldling, as for that swallow trapped in Bow Brickhill Church, life, freedom, music, dancing, lies through the Church's seemingly unattractive doorway.

It is, is it not, the paradox of Christian living that it seems on the surface so dull and restrictive: doing what you're told, denying yourself, thinking of others, keeping commandments. What a load of rubbish, think the worldly. This life doesn't go on for ever. Get all you can for yourself while you can. Gather ye rosebuds while you may. And yet it is only in and through costly self-surrender that light and love and laughter burn in the human heart. 'Solid joys and lasting treasure none but Zion's children know.'

A further point. Have you ever happened to notice that when after the Confession in the *Alternative Service Book* the priest pronounces the Absolution, he makes a significant change from the *Book of Common Prayer* when reciting the final sentence?

When in the *Alternative Service Book* the priest pronounces the Absolution he says:

> Almighty God ... pardon and deliver you from all your
> sins and *keep* you in everlasting life.

In contrast, when he says the Absolution in the *Book of Common Prayer* he says:

> Almighty God ... pardon and deliver you from all your
> sins and *bring* you to everlasting life.

'Bringing', as in the *Book of Common Prayer,* suggests something entirely new. 'Keeping', as in the *Alternative Service Book,* suggests something which to some extent we are enjoying already.

Both phrases have, of course, truth in them. In a sense, the life the departed live with God now in Paradise *is* refreshingly new. The words of our text:

'Behold,' says he who sits upon the Throne, 'I make all things new.'

'Now we see,' says St Paul, 'as through a glass darkly but then face to face.'

Yes, it is a new kind of life, a new vision of God, which we enjoy after we have passed through the tunnel of death.

That on the one hand, but on the other hand, that new life the departed enjoy in the Nearer Presence of God is not entirely different from our life here on earth. We do get occasional foretastes of it here and now on earth. Here at Holy Communion, for example, not every time, but sometimes we do get a glimpse of what full communion, utter oneness with God, might mean. Time stands still, we lose consciousness of kneeling at a rail; we are caught up into heaven; we kneel in the presence of God and all his holy angels. 'Bring us'; 'Keep us'. There is truth in both.

And now we are back once more in Bow Brickhill Church.

The swallow has flown through the doorway, all is peace and quiet, and a feeling of joy fills me. 'It is wonderful,' I say to myself, 'to be here alone – but not alone because God and all his saints and all who have worshipped here in the past are with me. And how wonderfully light and airy it all is.'

And so for a moment it seemed to me – light and airy – until I looked through the porch, and there beyond the porch was real light and the outside world I knew: a world of light and movement, of trees swaying in the breeze, of daffodils nodding in the sun; birds singing. And I said to myself: 'As that is to this, so is the real world, the world of God and his saints and angels, the world that lies beyond the valley of death, to this transient world in which nothing abides and all grows old.' And I thought with joy of that lovely text of St Paul which he quotes from Isaiah:

> Eye has not seen, nor have ears heard, neither has it
> entered the heart of man, the good things which God has
> prepared for them that unfeignedly love him.

I shall not quickly forget that afternoon I spent in All Saints' Church, Bow Brickhill.

To God all praise and glory.

Note

In the sermon as originally preached I called the bird trapped in Bow Brickhill Church a starling. I have since come to believe it was more likely a swallow.

3. *Why Jesus Had to Die for Us*

Based on a Retreat Address given at Stacklands

If anyone sins, we have an advocate with the Father, Jesus
Christ the righteous; and he is the propitiation for our sins

I John 2:1

Reading Psalm 50: 16–21

Why had Jesus to die for us? I would begin by setting out
the answer most frequently given, an answer I remember
hearing when in my teens in a sermon in Holy Trinity
Church, Hounslow. The preacher began by stressing that
basically sin was disobedience and an insult to God, and he
referred to the first sin mentioned in the Bible – the sin of
Adam and Eve in the Garden of Eden (*Genesis 3*). Sin, he
said rightly, made God angry and death was its just
punishment (*Romans 6: 23*). Then came Jesus, conceived
by the Spirit, born of the Virgin Mary – Jesus, the friend of
sinners. And Jesus, said the preacher, took our sins upon
himself and paid the ransom required to placate God's
anger and so by his death destroyed death and opened for
us the gates of heaven.

This, we can grant, is in accordance with scripture. When
it became clear to Jesus that his enemies were determined to
kill him, the wonderful Chapter 53 of Isaiah became, I
believe, his comfort. God, he perceived, was laying on him
man's iniquities, and by his stripes mankind was to be
healed (*Isaiah 53: 5*). 'The son of man,' he told James and
John, 'came not to be ministered unto, but to minister, and
to give his life a ransom for many' (*Mark 10: 45*).

But there is a fatal flaw in such an answer. As expressed
above, it postulates, sets before us, two Persons in opposition

of whom that can never be true. It postulates an angry Father demanding vengeance and a loving Son taking the sinner's side. It puts in opposition Father and Son; and that is in flat contradiction to the whole body of the Church's teaching on the Incarnation and to the whole body of our Lord's teaching concerning his relationship with his Father.

'I and the Father are one,' said Jesus to the Jews in Jerusalem (*John 10: 30*).

'He who has seen me has seen the Father,' said Jesus to Philip in the Upper Room (*John 14: 9*).

We can therefore be sure that if in any circumstance the Father is angry, the Son is angry: and if in any given circumstance the Son is loving, so is the Father. And we may ask: who suffered most on Calvary, Father or Son?

To see someone one loves suffering is often harder than to suffer oneself. What parents worthy of the name would not prefer to suffer themselves rather than see their child suffer? And the Father saw it all and heard it all on Calvary. He saw his Son being jeered at, mocked, spat upon, as he hung in obedience on the Cross. He heard him cry with a loud voice in the hour of darkness:

'*Eloi, Eloi, lama sabachthani* – My God, my God, why has thou forsaken me?' (Mark 15: 34)

And this was his beloved Son!

No, Jesus and the Father are one. 'Such as the Father is, such is the Son and such is the Holy Ghost' (*The Athanasius Creed*). And so this angry Father demanding vengeance and loving Son paying the price, as usually presented, just won't do; yet, deep down, there is a truth in it – the truth that God hates sin and cannot ignore it. Yet hatred of sin and love for the sinner can go hand in hand and, because they can, Jesus's love for the sinner is equalled by the Father's love, and the Father's wrath against sin is matched by our Lord's.

Of the latter, St John the Divine reminds us when he describes the kings of the earth and the great and the rich and the strong as hiding in caves and among the rocks of the mountains and calling on them to shelter them from God's anger:

> Fall on us and hide us from the face of him who is seated on the throne, and from the wrath of the Lamb; for the great day of their wrath has come, and who can stand before it?'
>
> *Revelation 6: 15–17*

'Such as the Father is, such is the Son and such is the Holy Ghost'. Like Father, like Son.

The scribes and the Pharisees had also good reason to fear the 'wrath of the Lamb' when he attacked their sinfulness:

> But woe to you, scribes and Pharisees, hypocrites! because you shut the kingdom of heaven against men; for you neither enter yourselves or allow those would enter to go in.
>
> Woe to you, scribes and Pharisees, hypocrites! for you traverse sea and land to make a single proselyte, and when he becomes a proselyte, you make him twice as much a child of hell as yourselves.
>
> *Matthew 23: 13,15*

'Woe to you!' – the 'wrath of the Lamb!' God hates pride, hypocrisy, bigotry, greed. God hates sin.

And this theme of God's hatred of sin runs throughout the Bible. The prophets are unanimous in their condemnation of the sins of Israel, their rulers and their people. And the recurring complaint of the psalmists is that God does not punish sin as he should and that, in consequence, the ungodly take his name in vain.

Let us return to our reading. Having attacked the sins of Israel, the writer of Psalm 50 makes God declare:

> These things hast thou done and I held my tongue, and thou thoughtest wickedly that I am even such a one as thyself; but I will reprove thee and set before thee the things that thou has done.
>
> *Psalm 50: 21*

But he hasn't! says the psalmist, and because he hasn't, the ungodly think he doesn't mind, and God's own good name suffers.

And common experience tells us that this *is* what happens when evil is allowed to go unrepudiated and unchecked. Supposing a boy starts bringing home all manner of things he quite obviously cannot have come by honestly, and supposing his parents do nothing about it? Supposing his parents even commend him – 'That'll be useful, Son' What do the neighbours say? 'His parents? They are as bad as he is!' And they are.

As Leonard Hodgson says about 'Rewards and Punishment' in his book *And Was Made Man*: 'If a member of a football team is deliberately guilty of "dirty" play, it is the team which is held responsible. The good name of the team depends on its disowning the act of the individual player.' If they do not, they are as bad as he is. If not sacked, he must be at least suspended or fined.

The ungodly, say prophet and psalmist alike, must be reproved, and they are in no doubt as to the form God's reproof must take – punishment.

And punishment, let us agree, is the normal means parents use, it is the normal means used in the courts of law. But, while vindicating honour, punishment is rarely remedial and it can have the very opposite effect – it can harden and alienate; 80 per cent of released prisoners, I am told, return again.

But, I would claim, punishment is not the only way of vindicating honour. There is another way: God's way in Jesus Christ.

The newsagent in Sevenoaks from whom I used to collect my papers also sold sweets. One morning, while I was waiting to be served, a well-dressed woman, very distressed, and holding a box of chocolates in her hand, was speaking to the man in charge. 'My little girl,' she said, 'brought these chocolates home yesterday. I knew she couldn't have bought them and so I questioned her. Eventually she confessed. I

311

am so ashamed, I don't know why she did it. I've brought the chocolates back.'

That mother repudiated sin in the other and better way. She had shown her small daughter how wrong what she had done was. She had shown her the deep distress it had caused her parents. And she had made reparation. That is the other way, the better way, of vindicating honour.

> 'The Son of man came,' says our Lord, 'not to be served but to serve and to give his life a ransom for many' (*see supra*)

> 'In this is love,' says St John, 'not that we loved God but that God loved us and sent His Son to be the propitiation for our sins'
>
> (*I John 4: 10*)

> He died that we might be forgiven,
>   He died to make us good;
> That we might go at last to heaven,
>   Saved by his precious blood.
>
> *Mrs Alexander*

I would ask you in conclusion to reflect upon God's overwhelming, almost incredible love revealed to us in Jesus Christ.

In the century before Christ, Israel and the world had got into such a state that the time had come for God to fulfil his eternal plan and to repudiate once and for all sin and wickedness. Ungodliness was multiplying and even the godly were beginning to doubt: was God really on the side of righteousness? And God could have expressed his abhorrence of evil in the way that John the Baptist – all Israel – expected.

But who of us are perfect? Are any of us sinless? By punishing, God could have alienated himself from all his children. By punishing, he could have destroyed us – but he didn't! He took the punishment himself. He so loved us, so desired to win us back, that he chose the other way – the way of suffering love – by which to vindicate his honour and redeem us. He sent His Son. And, in the person of Christ, he himself mounted the Cross of Calvary, to show to us and to all mankind just what sin does.

> He was wounded for our transgressions, he was bruised for our iniquities; upon him was the chastisement that made us whole, and with his stripes we are healed
>
> *(Isaiah 53: 5)*

God came. God suffered. God showed.

Who, looking at the Cross, can say: 'Sin doesn't matter?'. Sin crucified Christ. Not spectacular sin, ordinary sin, the sins we are all guilty of: the greed and jealousy embodied in Caiaphas and Annas; the love of money and pride embodied in Judas; the cowardice embodied in Pilate; the timidity embodied in the disciples in the courtyard: 'Who do you want me to release to you?' asked Pilate to the crowd in the courtyard, 'Barrabas, or Jesus who is called the Christ?' But the priests stirred up the mob to shout 'Barrabas!' Christ's followers said nothing.

Sin crucified Christ. And no one looking at the Cross can say, 'God doesn't care; God is indifferent to good and evil'. God cares so much about sin that in Christ he died to remove it.

When I was a Bush Brother in Australia, I used to visit and teach in the small bush schools. One Holy Week I was teaching about Good Friday and about Christ hanging on the Cross for us. And to conclude I pinned up a picture of the scene on Calvary. There was a moment's silence and then a small boy blurted out: 'Please, sir, he didn't have to stay there. He could have come down.' Yes, he didn't have to endure it all. He could have escaped from his enemies. He could have avoided being nailed to the Cross. But he knew that only by enduring to the very end, until he could cry triumphantly: 'It is finished', could he win forgiveness for us. 'By his stripes we are healed.'

> Love so amazing, so divine,
> Demands my soul, my life, my all.

Jesus our Lord, we thee adore. O help us to love thee more and more.

4. *Christ's Detergents*

This is my most-used sermon at Parish Communion Services. I first preached it at the Stoke Goldington Group Service on September 6th in 1970 and I preached it for the twentieth time when officiating at the Parish Communion in Horton Kirby Church in this deanery in 1994. I still believe that it has a message for Christians everywhere.

Invocation

'Lord God, Lamb of God, you take away the sin of the world, have mercy upon us.'

It is about those words I wish to speak this morning. They come, as you know, from the ancient Christian canticle, *The Gloria in Excelsis* which we sang at the beginning of the service. And later on we shall sing them again just before we make our Communion:

> Lamb of God, you take away the sins of the world, have mercy on us.
> Lamb of God, you take away the sins of the world, have mercy on us.
> Lamb of God, you take away the sins of the world, grant us peace.

What I want you to notice about them is that they are not in the past tense but in the present – not 'you took' but 'you take'.

Although Jesus took away once and for all the guilt of sin on the Cross, his work still goes on; he is still taking away sins from the world, and I want to suggest this morning one way in which he is still doing it – through us – if we are willing.

Have you ever tried washing greasy plates without soap and in cold water? I remember once trying to do so in a

314

stream when camping. It is very difficult. And even if we have unlimited supplies of hot water, we don't really get rid of the grease – we simply wash it down the drain. But if we use a modern detergent – Fairy Liquid, shall we say? – the result is miraculous: the grease just disappears and the water, to all intents and purposes, remains the same; as far as one can see, it isn't changed. Amazing!

Now our Lord often taught his disciples the kind of people they were meant to be, for example, they were to be like light: 'Ye are the light of the world ... a city set on a hill cannot be hid.' Just as light disperses darkness, so are we his followers to disperse it. There are many dark corners in the world today. The stories in the gutter press, the political intriguing, the dirty tricks campaigns in high places; the evil in all our hearts which appalls yet fascinates. Why do people *want* to read these horror stories? Why is violence to some so attractive? 'Jesus bids us shine'. Through his light shining in us, we are to help him to dispel darkness in the world he loves.

And again, we are to be like salt. 'Have salt', says Jesus, 'one with another.' Just as salt rightly added brings out the flavour of what it is added to, so we are to bring out the savour of life, to reflect the joy of God in all he has made. And, like salt, we are to preserve and purify – to preserve and purify society.

Now there were no detergents as we know them today in our Lord's day - their only cleasing aid was 'fuller's soap' – but had modern detergents existed then, I can well imagine Jesus telling his disciples they must be like them – that, just as Fairy Liquid absorbs grease but remains itself greaseless, so must we absorb evil but be quite unaffected by it. And, as always, he himself set the example.

'They that passed by, railed on him'. They had no pity. You remember the dreadful jeering crowds on Calvary? They saw Jesus hanging in agony on the cross and jeered: 'Ah you who would destroy the temple and rebuild it in three days! If you are the Christ, save yourself and come down from the cross and we will see and believe.' They saw him hanging on the cross and jeered.

So also the chief priests: 'Let the Christ, the King of Israel, come down from the cross that we may see and believe.' So likewise the Pharisees; so likewise the unrepentent thief.

And it would have been quite in keeping with fallen human nature – though not with his own – if he had returned railing for railing. Dare I suggest what we might have said, how we might have reacted, if we had hung there?

'You brutes, you beasts,' we might have replied. 'I taught in your synagogues. I healed your sick. I never spared myself. I gave myself to you, body and soul. And is this how you treat me? Animals are kinder. And that's what you are – animals, beasts, pigs'.

That's how *we* might have replied. But if we had, would it have stopped the railing? You know it wouldn't. There would have been a slanging match.

'If he hits you, son, you hit him back!' That is the advice we sometimes give our children; and, I grant you, sometimes it is the lesser of two evils; sometimes aggression has to be dealt with or it multiplies. It may sometimes be necessary but, if it is, it is a necessary evil. It never does away with sin.

And even if, suffering wrong, we contain ourselves, we do not answer back, but we let the wrong we have suffered affect us, the devil has triumphed. Suppose, for example, the devil gets hold of someone we know and trust; and we discover that, behind our back, she is spreading lies about us; and suppose we don't hit back – 'Truth will triumph' – but we say to ourselves: 'Right. I have learned my lesson. Henceforth I keep myself to myself. Henceforward I trust no one' – still the devil has won. We may not be evil but we are less good than once we were. The devil has given us a chip on our shoulder.

And our Lord's enemies would have won if our Lord had

been embittered by the treatment given him. But no! Despite everything, he continued loving. He replied, you remember, 'Father, forgive them. They know not what they do.'

He absorbed the poison and refused to let it embitter him. He remained true to himself. And so in him the poison stopped. He had cancelled it.

Let me close with a story. It concerns a missionary – I think in Papua – 50 years ago. One day he received a message at his mission house: would he go to a chief some 20 miles away, who was dying? He was somewhat mystified by the message because, to the best of his knowledge, the chief had never shown any interest in Christianity. Nonetheless he went; and he found on arrival the chief on his bed and, indeed, dying, and almost the first words the chief said to him were: 'I want to be a Christian.'

'Why,' asked the missionary, 'now, after all these years, do you wish to be a Christian?'

'It is a long story,' said the chief. 'It happened long, long years ago when I was at a mission school. The missionary was a little man. I was a great hulking fellow. One day he said to me something I didn't like, and I went up and slapped his face. Then I drew back, frightened, but the missionary only smiled. "Well, son," he said. "If that helps you to feel better, hit this one too!" And he turned the other side of his face to me! And he never took it out on me afterwards. He was just as kind and fair to me as ever.' There was a pause. And then the chief said a second time 'I wish to die a Christian.'

'When he was reviled,' says St Peter, 'he reviled not again. When he suffered he threatened not.'

'You are to be like detergents.' I can imagine Jesus saying. 'To absorb evil as I absorbed it and to remain the same.' But it isn't easy. We can only do it with his help, and to get his help we need to soak ourselves in prayer. And we are not very good at it – and nor are those in authority, those who rule. With them, as with us, it is all too often 'an eye for an eye; a tooth for a tooth.' And so we pray:

O Lamb of God, your way alone takes away sin from the world.
Help us to be like you. O Lamb of God, have mercy on us.

5. *The Eternal God*

This again, is the substance of a retreat address. I include it because to think of God simply in terms of a 'heavenly Father', as some sort of supernatural celestial man, is to rob him of awe, mystery and wonder, and ourselves of those 'deepest, tenderest fears' which lead to cleansing and worship.

Invocation

Our text is:

> The eternal God is thy refuge, and underneath are the everlasting arms
>
> (*Deuteronomy 33: 27*)

We go on this morning to something very difficult: to think, as far as human minds *can* think, of God as he is in himself, and, as part of that, of the relationship of time with eternity. And the relationship of time with eternity is a very confusing subject, but without some understanding of it in relation to God and ourselves we can run into all sorts of trouble. For example, as often as we say the Apostles' Creed, we declare: 'I believe in God, the Father almighty, creator of heaven and earth.' And for the Christian, the fact that the world did not, could not, make itself, is one piece of evidence for the existence of God – that Supreme Being whom man from his first emergence has sought to know, placate and worship.

If a person says he or she does not believe in any such Supreme Being we can always reply: 'Well, what about creation? The world didn't, couldn't, make itself. We didn't make it. If God didn't make it, who did?'

And if they reply with, they think, the thousand dollar question: 'If God made the world, who made God?' Our answer is simple: 'No one! For God by definition is eternal, outside of space and time.'

But unless we know what we mean by saying 'God is eternal; outside of space and time' our answer means nothing.

Can we begin, then, with some consideration of what we mean by 'time'. When we think of 'time' we usually think of it, I suggest, as either past, present or future. And we think of time as a kind of stream flowing everlastingly from the past, through the present into the future. 'Time like an everflowing stream, bears all its sons away.'

But what *is* this 'present' phase in time as we know it? Has the 'present' as we know and define it, any real existence? Some people claim that it hasn't.

We can, of course, distinguish the 'present' from the 'past' and 'future' in those categories of time that we ourselves have invented. We can speak, for example, of 'the present decade' or 'the present year' or 'the present month' or 'day' or 'hour', the period of time embraced growing less and less, and we can continue *ad infinitum* the process, moving from hour to minute, from minute to second, from second to split second, the past and future growing ever closer together until what we call 'the present' is reduced eventually to that 'tiny, tiny point of time in man's consciousness which divides what has passed through it from what it thinks as coming into it'. The 'present' as a 'period of time' virtually disappears.

The older of you may remember those amusing Shell Petrol posters which 40 or 50 years ago enlivened the roadside hoardings – a workman in a cloth cap with a spotted red kerchief round his neck trying to look in three directions at once; and underneath, the caption: 'That's Shell; that was!'

It expressed vividly how man as a creature of time sees time – always in procession; either as the future drawing ever nearer and nearer to the present: 1991 becoming 1992; 1992 becoming 1993 and so on. Or, as the present (1993) receding further and further into the past; before 1992, 1991, before 1991, 1990, and so on. And we claim, especially as

320

we grow older, how time flies!

That is how we see time. But is it how God sees it? Because the Christian claims that God is 'eternal', the Christian claims that God sees time differently.

By nature I read very slowly. I chew over every sentence, every word, I read – is it true? Is it in accordance with fact, with reality? What is the writer's background? Motive? I can take weeks, months, years sometimes, reading a single book. So when in my last parish in North Bucks I discovered that there was in Northampton, nine miles away, a course starting to enable those attending to read faster, I decided to attend, and still possess a *Faster Reading Manual*. It did me little good. I did not work hard enough. But the lecturer tried hard and used, throughout the course, various devices. One device used constantly was a screen on which the page of a book was projected in semi-darkness. Then a spotlight was switched on and one was able to make out the type on the screen as the spotlight moved along, illuminating it. At the opening session it moved quite slowly. One could follow easily. But as session succeeded session, the spotlight moved quicker and quicker until in the end it was really racing along the line.

That was one device, but there was another. The lecturer reminded us that when we first began to read, we looked at every letter we were reading, we spelt out every letter: C-A-T – cat. But then, he pointed out, as we improved, we no longer spelt out every letter, we took in the whole word at a glance – cat. And most adults, he said when in a hurry, scanning over a script, take in five or six words at a glance. The real way to faster reading was gradually to increase the number of words we could take in at a single glance.

So back we went once more to the dimly lighted screen and the projected page, But this time, instead of the lit-up section being just three or four words moving along, it became five or six words, which we were told to take in at a single glance. Then six or seven words were illuminated, then half a line; finally, a whole line flashed on-off, on-off, to be taken in at a glance. And then we had comprehension exercises to test our progress.

Now think of history as it spans the centuries. We, willy-nilly, look at each period consecutively: the coming of the Danes, the Norman Conquest, the Plantagenets, The Tudors, Queen Victoria, the First World War, the Second World War, and so to the present day. Because we are creatures of time, we see time as ever-flowing, running along as the illuminated script ran along in the first device on the lecture screen.

But God is not in time, not in any exclusive sense. In his eternity, he is outside of time. You remember the story of the Burning Bush? Moses enquired of his Name when sent by God to bring the Israelites out of Egypt. 'When I appear before Pharaoh, Whom shall I say has sent me?' And God replies: 'Say I AM has sent you. I AM who I AM' (*Exodus 3:14*).

And so, because HE IS and because he is outside of time, God sees the whole process of time, not as we do, as a moving spectacle, but as a single concrete whole, just as the spotlight in the second device in the lecture hall illuminated a whole line as a single unit.

'I am the Alpha and the Omega' says the Lord God, 'who is and who was and who is to come, the Almighty' (*Revelation 1: 8*).

The whole of history from beginning to end is at every moment present to him: primal chaos, prehistoric man, neolithic man, modern man, all that lies ahead to the end of time, he sees it, not as we see it, as year succeeding year – he sees it as a single whole. All the highlights of history: Abraham offering Isaac on Mount Moriah, Jesus dying on Calvary, Harold dying at Hastings, the *Titanic* sinking in the Atlantic, man walking on the Moon – all are eternally present to him.

And not only the big events, the little events equally: myself being born, coming from my mother's womb. 'Joy that a man is born into the world'; and all the events of my life – myself kneeling in Wells Cathedral being ordained; myself a Bush Brother in Australia; myself being married in India; myself sitting here speaking to you; myself dying, which for me, because I live in the time-stream, hasn't

322

happened yet, but which for the Eternal because he lives outside the time-stream has. All are present to him because with him are neither past nor future – just one eternal present held in the embrace of his everlasting arms. 'I AM who I AM'.

And fools, blind guides, so tied and bound in the chains of time and space that that they cannot even in thought get beyond its categories, ask, as if it is a clever question: 'And who made him?' – he, the Beginning and the End, who is by definition Uncreate and Eternal!

The simple answer to those who ask such questions is: 'Your god is too small. You are denying not the true God but a man-made, space-time god of your own imagining.

As Christians, we declare our faith not in any man-made, space-time god, but in the true God, the God and Father of Jesus Christ.

And this [comments John] is life eternal, that they might know thee the only true God and Jesus Christ, whom thou hast sent.' (*John 17: 3*)

'My heart is athirst for God, even for the living God. When shall I come to appear before the presence of God.' (*Psalm 42:2*).

To ponder:

Ponder the transcendence and eternity of God.

> Ask yourself: 'Is my God the eternal God or a man-made, space-time god of my own imagining?

6. *The Power of Intercessory Prayer*

The *Church Times* on August 27th 1993 reviewed a book *God in Us – the case for Christian Humanism* by Antony Freeman, the Bishop of Chichester's Adviser for Continuing Ministerial Education. In his book Antony Freeman said he did not believe in an 'all-powerful interventionist God'.

The next issue of the *Church Times* printed a letter from the Revd Harold Helsop in which he declared that 'virtually no one in the average Church of England congregation genuinely believes in such a God'.

Jesus did and I do, and I believe that 90 per cent of Christians in Great Britain do, and I state my reasons in the sermon which follows.

I give it as preached in the Church of St Edmund, King and Martyr, West Kingsdown, at their Parish Communion on Sunday, August 11th 1991 (Pentecost 12) on the Gospel for the Day, St John 17: 20–end.

Invocation

Our gospel this morning was our Lord's 'high-priestly' prayer for his Church, prayed in the Upper Room on the eve of his betrayal; and in praying it he was doing nothing new. Throughout his ministry he was always praying for those about him, and such prayer, intercessory prayer, is the commonest and most basic prayer of all, whether we are praying in public or privately. It is about the importance of such prayer that I wish to speak this morning.

It is so important that, as you know, in public worship special places are provided for it: in Morning and Evening Prayer in the prayers that follow the third collect – the 'second prayers'; and in this service when, after the Creed, we pray 'for the Church and for the world' and thank God for his goodness. And not only on these special occasions, throughout public worship we are interceding: in collects and canticles; in hymns and psalms.

And in private prayer, 'asking' prayer is the commonest prayer of all. Probably the first prayer most of us here were taught was the familiar prayer:

'God bless Daddy; God bless Mummy and make me a good boy – or girl.' And when persons say, as they quite frequently do, 'I don't go to church but I always say my prayers, you can be fairly sure that they are speaking of the asking, the 'God bless Daddy' type of prayer.

Prayer is a 'many-splendoured thing'. Asking prayer is not the only kind of prayer but it is the commonest and, you remember, when the disciples came to Jesus and said to him, 'Lord, teach us to pray as John also taught his disciples', Jesus said, 'When you pray ...' and taught them the Lord's Prayer. And the Lord's Prayer – have you realised? – is after its opening salutation *all* intercession – but intercession at its highest: 'Your Name be hallowed – Your will be done – Give us our daily bread – Forgive us our sins – Lead us not into temptation...' After the opening Salutation, all intercession.

Tennyson writes: 'More things are wrought by prayer than this world dreams of' and, because I believe that, I am not happy with those who urge us to pray, to open our hearts to God, to intercede with him – but urge us to do so on purely subjective grounds, 'because,' they say, 'interceding is so good for us'.

Now it is quite true that we are made and changed by the prayers we pray. No one can pray sincerely for others, even an enemy, and not come to love that person; in the same way the more we give ourselves to a person, the more we come to love that person; the more we give ourselves to a cause, the more we come to love that cause.

But never, never, let us imagine that that is the be-all and end-all of our intercessions. 'More things are wrought by prayer than this world dreams of' – and I would claim that our intercessions in addition to what they do to ourselves

325

are mighty in the world, mighty in breaking down strongholds and mighty in working miracles and enabling God's will to be done on earth.

And I would suggest to you: is it not true that those who doubt or deny this power of intercession, do so mostly in the belief that everything in life is fixed, that the 'laws of nature' cannot be changed and that they prevent God intervening in response to our prayers? – which is, surely, a quite ridiculous belief.

What of the so-called 'miracles of science'? How is is that scientists are able to work the wonders that they do? Isn't it only because of the fixity of these so-called 'laws of nature'? Because 'I, the Lord, change not', because God doesn't change his 'laws', scientists are able to work wonders, to achieve ever more and more – and sometimes, I suspect, to achieve more than God wills them to achieve. In some spheres, I suspect, we have attained to greater knowledge than is good for us.

But let that pass. My main point is: is it not ridiculous to imagine that scientists are cleverer than God? That they with their partial knowledge of nature's laws can use their partial knowledge to attain their ends and that God with his full knowledge cannot do the same?

There is a delightful centuries-old prayer I pray constantly. I love it. It runs:

> O God of unchangeable power and eternal light, look
> favourably on thy whole church, that wonderful and sacred
> mystery and, *by the tranquil operation of thy perpetual
> providence, carry out the work of man's salvation.*

In that 'tranquil operation' of God's perpetual providence, I believe intercession has a special part to play.

But, in any case, belief in the complete fixity of nature is largely old hat nowadays. Scientists today are much humbler, far less dogmatic than their predecessors, and a growing number of them believe that there is deep down in nature an element of chance – of contingency – and that all is not as fixed as once they thought it was; nature, like God, is full of suprises. And if that is so, I like to think that in that 'law-free' freedom of creation God has preordained a special place for man's intercessions; and that, just as at Nazareth, on his return visit there, Jesus was prevented from doing all the mighty works he wished to do because of unbelief, so too in the world today, if we fail to intercede as God wishes, God's hand is shortened; that like Jesus at Nazareth he is prevented from doing all he would like. I believe that he needs our prayers just as he needs our hands, our eyes, our feet, to do his work in the world today.

It is not just 'Lord, hear our prayer', it is also 'Lord *use* our prayer – to your glory'.

I do not think that we can ever overestimate the value to us and to God of 'asking' prayer.

Will you stand, please

> Help us, Lord, to pray better and
> to love you more
> Lord, *use* our prayers and let our
> cries come unto you. Amen.

7. My Diamond Jubilee Sermon

Preached in St Martin's Church, Eynsford, on Friday, June 11th 1993 on the occasion of the 60th anniversary of my Ordination to the Priesthood. My three sons came from Beverley Minster, Nottingham and Kettering to be present; two Archdeacons represented the diocese.

In the script I have condensed the account of my collecting Melox Marvels from J & T Trower's cellar in 1926 as I have already described it in Chapter 2.

Invocation

The Mashona tribes in Zimbabwe have a very pleasant custom. If you offer them a gift, no matter how small it is in size, they always receive it with both hands. To receive it with one hand would, they think, suggest it was of little value, and that would be insulting to the giver.

My subject this evening is God's gifts to us, gifts so valuable that we hold out both hands to receive them, for without his gifts we are nothing. And so our Collect this evening prays that God will not leave us destitute of his gifts. It is the Collect for St Barnabas in the *Book of Common Prayer*:

> O Lord God Almighty, who didst endue thy holy apostle
> Barnabas with singular gifts of the Holy Ghost: Leave us
> not, we beseech thee, destitute of thy manifold gifts, nor
> yet of grace to use them alway to thy honour and glory.

A very lovely Collect and one especially dear to me in the early days of my ministry, for I felt then, as to some extent I still do today, destitute of many of the gifts which normally go with ministry.

Take singing, for example. I cannot sing. I am the despair of all my organists. It amazes me, David, how when the organist gives you a note you can pitch that note perfectly. That is and always has been something quite beyond me. I like singing, but if ever I am standing in a pew with Marjorie and I start to sing out loud, Marjorie always says 'Shsh! Shsh!'

And not only Marjorie. I took many services at St Mary's, Kippington, 18 years ago during its last interregnum. St Mary's has a mike in the prayer desk and, after taking my second service there, when I was standing at the back after seeing the people out, one of the churchwardens politely and very diffidently said to me: 'You know, Mr Lovejoy, we wouldn't really mind if you switched off the mike in the prayer desk during the singing.'

Or again, another normal pastoral gift I have never had: the gift of preaching. Never, in 60 years, have I found preaching easy, and even today I have to write out word for word and memorise every sermon I feel called upon to deliver. And while it can be effective, it can be terribly wearing – and on one occasion led to a near disaster.

Early in my ministry I was with the Bush Brotherhood of the Good Shepherd in New South Wales. Once when driving along in the bush I ran my car straight into a bore-drain. Bore-drains are shallow trenches from artesian bores which run for miles across the Australian bush, providing water for livestock. They are visible for miles for eyes which see. How, then, did it happen? I was driving along with the sermon I was preparing to preach on the seat beside me. I was reading and rereading it, trying to memorise it, not looking where I was going. Suddenly the bore-drain loomed ahead and I was in it. There had not been rain for two years when it happened, and when I walked to a homestead a few miles away saying I was bogged, they couldn't believe me!

Again, a priest and pastor must be able to communicate,

to 'talk the gospel'. In my early days in the ministry I was so uncertain of myself I just couldn't; and if any question of faith arose in a conversation, I hastily changed the subject.

If, then, in those days I was so uncertain of myself, why did I apply for ordination and why did the SPG, the Society for the Propagation of the Gospel, accept me for training?

I had been quite certain once; 18 months earlier, when an apprentice with J & T Trower of Colchester, I had been descending the steps into the cellar to fetch some dog biscuits when God had suddenly said to me: 'I want you.' God wanted me! 'This, Lord,' I had said to him, 'is most inconvenient. The lady is waiting for her Melox Marvels.' Nevertheless, there and then I had given myself to him.

But if I was so certain then, what in the next 18 months had unsettled me? What had unsettled me was a book which my elder brother in all good faith had lent me when he heard I was thinking of ordination. The book, *Reality* by a Dr Streeter, sought to reconcile science and religion, and in this was quite helpful; but what had confounded me was the writer's attitude to scripture. I had at the time no knowledge of the Bible at all, apart from the simple Bible stories I had been taught in Sunday school, and I took every word of the Bible as literally true. Canon Streeter in this book *Reality* seemed to have no such belief at all. It knocked me for six. I began to wonder even whether I could believe in God.

And then, when I was all at sixes and sevens, the SPG wrote and asked me to appear before their selection committee. I well remember the interview. Some half-dozen learned members of the Society sat behind a table and fired questions at me. The climax came when the Chairman put me, as it were, on the spot:

If, he said, the Society furnished the funds for my training, those funds would be provided by many poor people. If the funds were found, would I undertake at the end to offer myself for ordination?

It was an undertaking I knew I couldn't give, and I said so. I said words to the effect that that was in God's hands, not mine. To my relief one of the Board took my side: 'Quite

330

right, quite right,' he boomed. 'That was a question no one could be sure of answering.' My heart went out to him.

Ten days later I heard that SPG had accepted me for training, just as eight years later they also accepted Marjorie – which is why I have asked that the offering this evening be given to USPG – SPG's successor. It is only by God's grace mediated through SPG that Marjorie and I are now here together to give thanks to God

And we *do* give thanks to God. We have both of us so much to be thankful for.

And first I would say thank you to God for bodily health and safety throughout my life. Until recently, I have never had to take a thought for my body when planning for the future, always it has been a most faithful servant. And though I tend to be accident-prone – as car-insurers have found to their cost, although they have been most understanding – I have never seriously injured either others or myself; for which I am grateful.

And then a big 'Thank you, Lord' for Marjorie herself. When I prepared to propose to her, as with my sermons, I wrote out carefully what I wanted to say to her – I even put in the pauses. Then I got out my cycle and pedalled to the Community House in Delhi, where she was living. I knocked at the door and enquired of the Head of the Community, was Miss Kellaway at home and could I see her? Being shown to her room, without more ado I fired my proposal point-blank at her. She was astounded. We had never before spoken two words alone together. No wonder she was amazed! But what a blessing she has been to me and to many! And what a blessing our three sons have been – again, to us and to many. And again, thank you, Lord.

And yet again, what a blessing our friends have been to us. I thank God daily for the wonderful friends he has given me throughout my ministry. I think especially of Maxwell Fisher, Vicar of Holy Trinity, Yeovil, where I served my title – he was wonderfully kind and understanding – and of Elfric Matimba, my African colleague in Zimbabwe; both are now dead.

May I say a word about Elfric? I once asked him how old he was. He had no idea when or where he was born, but he remembered, he said the Matabele Uprising of 1889. He was, he said, a boy at the time, but he remembered his parents saying: 'We must fly to the caves. The whites are coming to kill us.'

'What,' I asked him 'did you wear then?'

'My parents,' he answered, 'wore skins. We children wore nothing.'

But such is 'the communion of saints', the fellowship of all who believe, that I felt more at one with him than with many of my European farmers; and he taught me more than I can say. Thank you, Lord.

And 'Thank you, Lord' for the joy you have given me in yourself, in all your creation and in all your creatures. Thank you also that you have given me a sense of fun. My laugh, like my cough, is, if I may say so, famous.

One year in Zimbabwe my family and I took a holiday in the Inyanga Mountains and spent a night *en route* in the Penhalonga Mission, then run by the Mirfield Fathers. After returning to Hartley, a parishioner said to me, 'While you were away, Mr Lovejoy, were you ever in Penhalonga?' I said I was. 'I thought you must have been,' said my questioner. 'Last month my wife and I were in the hills overlooking Penhalonga' – Penhalonga was in the valley about two miles away – 'and suddenly a laugh re-echoed round the valley. "That laugh", my wife said to me, "must be Mr Lovejoy's!"'

Finally and above all I thank God for his greatest gift – his gift of love, love for himself – 'My God, how wonderful thou art' – and love for all his creation.

> For the beauty of the earth,
> For the beauty of the skies,
> For the love which from our birth
> Over and around us lies,
> Lord of all, to thee we raise
> this our thankful hymn of praise.

Thank you, Lord, for all your mercies. Thank you, all of you, for coming here this evening. And especially, thank you, David, and all of you from the United Benefice, for making Marjorie and me so welcome from the very start.

> For these and all your mercies, and for the mercy of forgiveness, Father, we thank you. *Amen.*

26

Two Further Locums in Zimbabwe

This story of my life would not be complete without a brief mention of two further locums I undertook in Zimbabwe, the first in 1982 and the second in 1987.

After Tony Grain met me at the Diocesan Synod in Salisbury on September 1st 1972 and entertained me so well, we lost touch. But in July 1982 I received a letter from him. He was now, he wrote, in charge of St Mary's, Cranborne, a sub-district of the Cathedral Parish in Harare. He would be on holiday from September 16th to November 10th. Could I stand in for him?'

I travelled by Zambia Airlines and arrived in Harare early on September 17th.

A diocesan link between Rochester and Harare had just been proposed, and when Canon Don Ruddle, Vicar of East Malling, its Secretary, heard that I was planning to spend ten weeks in Zimbabwe, he invited me to go on the diocese's behalf to help inaugurate the link. The Sevenoaks Council of Churches were also seeking an overseas link and they in their turn invited me to sound out a possible link between Sevenoaks and Gweru.

My commission to commend a Rochester–Harare diocesan link took me near and far, chiefly by buses as I had no parish car. Many showed interest, and by the time I left, four parishes and five mission districts had expressed a desire to be linked. Others were nibbling, and the link was firmly established.

In my addresses I did my best to describe both the Rochester diocese and its cathedral. One set of statistics always evoked questions. The total population of the diocese was, I said, just under one and a quarter million, which meant, on the national average, that about 60,000 babies were being born each year in the diocese, 40 per cent of whose parents claimed to be C of E. Yet in 1980 only 2,383 of the estimated 24,000 babies born were confirmed of whom more than 40 per cent had lapsed within five years.

'We are doing better than that here,' was the usual response.

To which I would reply, 'You see, then, the value of a link? We have things to learn from you, no less than you have things to learn from us.'

My most cheering visit was to the half-built church of St Francis, Glenora, in a Harare suburb. The steel framework had been erected and roofed and a concrete floor laid some years earlier, and then they had run out of funds. It was a windy day, and before I arrived tarpaulins had been tied up to protect the altar but were quite ineffective. No candles could be lit and the celebant had to keep his hands over the ciborium to prevent the wafers being blown away. There were no chairs or hassocks and the congregation sat on newspapers. When they went to stand for the gospel, many newspapers blew away.

The collections at all Confirmations in the Rochester diocese that year were being given for the completion of six unfinished churches in the Harare diocese, and before I left Glenora I was able to tell the churchwardens and congregation that theirs was one of the churches selected and that funds to enable them to complete their church would shortly be arriving from England.

My chief responsiblity in the diocese was, however, the pastoral care of St Mary's, Cranborne. Before Independence, Cranborne had been a white artisan district in the cathedral parish, and the home of the RAF. At the end of the Second World War, the RAF had returned to England

and the Rhodesian Armed Forces had taken over the aerodrome and the Nissen hut, which they had converted to be their chapel. This converted hut was the St Mary's, Cranborne, in which I was to minister. The three OHP (Sisters of the Order of the Holy Paraclete of Whitby) in St Mary's House with whom I was staying – Sister Muriel, Sister Margaret Shirley and Sister Mary Margaret – were paid by the cathedral and spent part of their time as diocesan religious instruction directors and part as pastoral assistants in Cranborne.

Zimbabwe's independence was having a transforming effect on Cranborne. Half the white population had already left – chiefly to the Republic of South Africa, to Australia or Great Britain – and most of the rest were in process of leaving. Into their houses were coming the newly created black middle class: clerks, teachers, businessmen, artisans – and church finance was plummeting. The whites they were replacing had been for the most part 'established' – they had paid for their houses, their cars, their televisions, and so forth. They had money to spare to support their church. The newcomers hadn't. They were still struggling to pay for their houses, their cars, the new living standards to which they aspired. And some had never learnt to give. But the church and the OHP Sisters struggled on.

There were two Sunday morning services at St Mary's: a Parish Communion in English, for which I was responsible, and a 9.30 a.m. Shona Mass, taken by the Revd Captain Cuthbert Mavudzi, the Government-paid Chaplain to the Army, who took the Shona service for black Christians in the Army and for their families and friends. At 8 a.m. there would be perhaps 20 whites and 10 blacks. I imagine the 9.30 a.m. service was crowded.

I should perhaps explain that one outcome of independence was the removal of any stigma attached to 'black'. 'Black is beautiful'. In Rhodesia it paid to be white; in Zimbabwe the shoe was on the other foot.

Rodney Tait and Nancy Sams, both now in England, were churchwardens and put themselves out to make me feel welcome and to give me all the help they could. Their lists of people to visit was invaluable. Rodney was the headmaster of a flourishing Government junior school and the driving force behind plans to build a new St Mary's Church on the plot already containing St Mary's House.

On January 23rd 1983 I had a long letter from Sister Muriel, OHP, full of thrilling news. The steel framework of the new church was, she said, now in place and roofed. Moreover, the cathedral parish had provided R$ 15,000 to enable the project to be completed. It was completed and in use six months later.

On Tuesday, October 19th 1982 I was able to borrow a car to revisit St Mark's, Mhondoro. I travelled via Beatrice and the Beatrice–Hartley Road, arriving at the St Mark's turn-off at noon. A soldier on duty stopped me when near St Mark's and enquired my business. 'To see St Mark's,' I replied.

'Why do you want to see St Mark's?'

'To see what it is like.'

This he seemed to find funny, but he let me pass.

In the afternoon Fr Amos Matonda showed me round. I was pleased with all that I saw. In 1972 he had been both Priest-in-Charge and Headmaster. Now a layman, Mr Matthias Chimedza, was in charge of the school. The school was full and both staff and pupils happy. Among the latter were young 'freedom-fighters' who because of the guerilla war had missed out on their schooling. I spoke to the school captain, 21 years old and in Standard 7. Another scholar had been a guerilla captain and another a major in the hostilities. I tried to question the school captain about conditions among the freedom fighters during the fighting but he wisely refused to be drawn. 'We must forget the past,' he replied. 'We must look to the future.' And one saluted the foundations of a new beginning.

In 1991 Matthias was made headmaster of Daramombe Junior School – a much-deserved promotion – and now Fr Amos is once again saddled with dual responsibility at St Mark's.

My commission to test out the possibility of a link between Sevenoaks and Gweru I was only able to fulfil during my last weekend in Zimbabwe. Fr Cuthbert Mavudzi had kindly offered to take both the English and Chishona Sunday morning services at St Mary's and I left Harare bus station for Gweru at 6 a.m. on Saturday November 6th. A friend in Sevenoaks, Mr Henry Bouche, had given me an introduction to Peter and Jean Lock, who were running Coolmoreen Farm, seven miles from Gweru, and I arrived there by taxi from Gweru in the early afternoon.

When Peter and Jean had taken over Coolmoreen Farm it was run-down and almost derelict but in a few years they had turned it into a profit-making poultry and dairy farm, training pupil-farmers who settled all over Zimbabwe. In addition Peter and Jean were keen Moral Re-Armament evangelists. They made Colmoreen Farm an MRA Residential Centre and their residential courses changed dramatically the lives of many black and white Zimbabweans. I spoke to some of them.

On the same afternoon as I arrived, I arranged to visit the Bishop of the Lundi, the Rt Revd Jonathan Siyachitema, in Gweru, to speak at a Rotarian lunch being held in Gweru on the Monday and to address and show slides at a public meeting in the evening. I also arranged to visit Fr Junius Gwekewere next day.

Marjorie and I had given a bed to Junius at 73 Dartford Road, Sevenoaks, some years earlier when Junius was a curate at St Peter and St Paul's, Charlton, Dover. USPG had recommended him, and Fr Michael Shields had invited him to preach in St John's, which he did most impressively. He was now Priest-in-Charge of St Martins's, Amaveni, Kwe-Kwe, and when I phoned him up he asked me to preach for him on the following morning. Kwe-Kwe was 38 miles north of Gweru on the road back to Harare but Junius promised to arrange transport.

This visit to Kwe Kwe I well remember. I had been given to understand that the service would start at 8.30 a.m.

However, when I arrived at 8 a.m., I was offered tea and Junius seemed in no hurry. His wife joined us and over tea we talked. Much was being said at the time about the Mashona–Matabele rivalry. 'It's all the fault of the politicians,' said Victoria. 'If they would only leave us alone we should be happy'. And she went on: 'I should know. Junius is a Mashona and I a Matabele.' I asked her how she came to marry Junius. 'Lots of Mashona boys take Matabele brides,' she replied. 'Matabele fathers are not as greedy as Mashona. They do not ask so much *lobolo*.'

'Yes, Mashona fathers ask too much. Matabele brides are cheaper!' Junius added.

A little later Junius looked at his watch and said he must be off. 'I have to give a sick communion,' he said. 'Go across, if you like, to the church. You will find them singing.' And so they were. The actual service must have started at about 10 a.m. and finished around 11.30 a.m.. But did they leave? They stayed on talking among themselves for another hour. 'You whites have the watches but no time. We blacks may have no watches but we always have the time!' is a popular saying.

Alas, when at last I got away. I had missed the native bus which was to take me to Gweru via St Patrick's Mission, and when the bus I caught, the last that day, arrived at the St Patrick's turn-off, I could not visit St Patrick's as intended. Had I stopped I would have been marooned there that night and unable to fulfil my Gweru engagements next morning.

I remember the bus well. It was a single-decker and both old and dirty. Two of its tyres were worn down to the canvas! Inside was a notice *Sitting room: 24 only; Standing room 40.* Luckily, it was half-empty and it carried me safely to Gweru.

Next morning I spoke briefly at the Rotarian lunch but they showed little interest and only nine attended the public meeting called at short notice at 8 p.m. that evening, to which Gweru Councillors had been personally invited. The only link the Councillors were interested in was commercial: what industries had Sevenoaks? Could they be persuaded to

Come to Gweru? Sevenoaks's one large employer was Marley Tiles and they were already established in Bulawayo. So I had nothing to offer.

I returned to Harare empty handed on the Tuesday and next day, November 10th, flew back to Heathrow.

* * *

The second of my further two locums in Zimbabwe was in 1988. Since my visit in 1982 I had kept in touch. I received the *Cranborne Messenger* monthly through the kindness of Ernest Holwill, reviews of the Zimbabwe press from the Britain–Zimbabwe Society, and many letters from friends. I prided myself upon being something of an 'authority' on Zimbabwe. But Zimbabwe was changing rapidly and by 1987 I felt that if I was to keep myself up-to-date I must make a further visit. Accordingly in January 1988 I wrote to Bishop Peter Hatendi offering help. He made mention of my offer in a diocesan circular but gave a far from flattering picture of me. 'The Reverend Lovejoy,' he wrote, 'is advancing in age and should not travel or sleep rough during his stay in this country. Although he is looking for a vacant ecclesiastical division with a residence, he could not be housed in the church houses at say, Mutoredzana, Mhondoro, or Chivu, because the basics for living aren't there, such as piped water, toilet, kitchen utensils, electricity....'

Not surprisingly, there was no response. I then wrote round to clergy friends offering my help for Sunday duty while in Zimbabwe and got booked up for three Sundays.

Then came the breakthrough. Olive Granger, Secretary of the Transvaal, Zimbabwe and Botswana Association (TZABA), was in Harare visiting Canon John Adams, her widowed son-in-law and Rector of St Mary's, Highlands. 'His diabetes has got out of control,' she wrote 'and he wishes to return to the Winchester Hospital in England where his diabetes had been first diagnosed. Would you be prepared to live in the Rectory and take charge of St Mary's, Highlands, in his absence?' I gratefully agreed.

340

I left Gatwick by Air Zimbabwe on Thursday, April 14th and arrived in Harare inauspiciously at 6.05 a.m. on April 15th. 'Inauspiciously' because I had been lying all night stretched out flat on an 'economy' seat and my back had set. I could hardly move but just managed to stagger down the gangway to where Sister Mary Margaret, OHP, was waiting to greet me. She whisked me off to her doctor's; he quickly released my back, and I was able to proceed as planned to Frank and Betty Forbes at Waterfalls Rectory, where I was to spend the weekend. It proved full and interesting. On the Saturday Frank took me to see two old friends, Fr Julius and Flora Murumbedzi. Some six months earlier Julius had lain unconscious in hospital for more than a fortnight as a result of an horrific car accident and his life had been despaired of. Now he was well on the way to recovery. I had sent him a second-hand typewriter from England. He showed me it and took me to see St Michael's Church and Hall, in which Synod is sometimes held. The dress rehearsal for a wedding was taking place in the church but all that I saw of it was the prospective bride and bridegroom practising dancing together up the aisle to the music of a band!

I preached at the 7.15 a.m. Parish Communion at Waterfalls next morning, the small church being packed to capacity, and in the afternoon Frank and Betty took me to visit the Falls from which the district gets its name. There, beneath the Falls' at the water's edge, a breakaway sect of the Apostolic Church was standing giving thanks for the gift of running water. Like the Rechabites of old (see Jeremiah 35) they had opted out of contemporary society and lived by weaving and basketwork. They refuse to send their children to school and hence are in trouble with the Government but are, by all accounts, peace-loving, honest and God-fearing.

On the Monday morning I joined Fr John Adams at the Highlands Rectory. St Mary's was a large and lively parish. It held a Sung Eucharist on alternative Sundays at a daughter-church, St Andrew's, Arcturus, ten miles distant, and had many weekday services. Twice a month it held a corporate Communion service at Nazareth House, a large Roman Catholic home for the elderly, half a mile from St Mary's, and once a month the same at Blue Kerry, a local retirement village.

The regular Sunday services at St Mary's were at 7 a.m., 8.30 a.m., and 6.30 p.m. in English, and a Shona Mass or Shona Evensong at 3.30 p.m. Congregations at the English-speaking services were 95 per cent white for, unlike at Cranborne and Waterfalls, there had been no large sell-out of houses to Black Zimbabweans. St Mary's still remained a pre-independence white parish. A study group met at Charles Gaunt's house at 7.45 p.m. on Wednesdays. On the three Wednesdays when I was present they listened to tapes by David Pawson, a Baptist minister, on 'Judgement', 'Hell' and 'Heaven', and lively discussions followed, the majority siding with me against David Pawson!

On Saturday, April 23rd, the Diocesan Synod met in Harare. There were sessions at 9 a.m., 2 p.m. and 4 p.m. I attended as an observer and renewed acquaintance with many clergy friends. It met again on the Sunday morning but I was booked that morning to take the Parish Communion at St Mary's, Cranborne. The new church there, begun in January 1983, had been consecrated by the Bishop amidst great rejoicing the following August. It could seat a hundred. But when Sister Margaret Shirley, OHP, collected me at 7.30 a.m. on April the 24th she confessed that it was already too small and that they were considering an extension. The service began at 8 a.m. and the church was full. I spoke in English but all else was in Shona. There was hardly a white face to be seen. Some infants were present with their parents, but their elder brothers and sisters were outside attending Bible classes in the shelter of the trees. After I had given the Blessing they filed into church and I blessed them at the Communion rail. Then they joined their parents and we sang the final hymn. It was standing-room only. Afterwards Ernest and Bubbles Holwill kindly invited me to breakfast.

On the first Monday in May, a Bank Holiday in Zimbabwe,

I visited the Borradaile Trust, a delightful village for the elderly to which Phyl Matthews had retired. Nearby was a former Native Purchase Area called, I think, Jombo Tombo, where Fr Noel Bororowe had bought a small plot on retirement. He and Victoria were as happy there as Phyl was at Borradaile. Both made me most welcome.

I was not only renewing old friendships (I had known Phyl and Noel in Rusape days) I was also making new ones. I made frequent visits to the city centre and to the cathedral and on one occasion, having attended a mid-day Communion, I stayed to watch the daily food distribution. Each day a hundred or more hungry men, women and children, whose names were recorded, were fed in the cathedral cloisters. They each received a bowl of vegetable soup and a bread roll, the bread being donated by a Harare restaurateur who had become a born-again Christian. 'Give your bread to the hungry', he had read in the Bible, and this was his way of responding. He had provided rolls free for the past four months.

Helping in the distribution were two Franciscan friars in their brown habits. As a Franciscan Companion and Chaplain to the Companions in Kent, I was naturally interested, and learnt that they came from Westwood Friary on the outskirts of Harare.

On May 12th I paid Westwood a visit. The friary consisted of several makeshift buildings erected on the site by the diocese in 1974 to serve as a hostel for its ordination candidates attending courses at the university. It proved too far from the city for the purpose, became a diocesan hostel and was eventually closed. Empty, it was badly vandalised.

In 1986 the Society of St Francis had been invited to work in Harare and had sent out a Brother Geoffrey and a Brother Roger. The diocese offered them Westwood as their centre. They enlisted volunteers to help them make it habitable, and by the time of my visit in addition to Geoffrey and Roger, two new novices, Simon Peter and Mackintosh, and five postulants were living and working there. Three high-density suburbs, Warren Park, Kambuzuma and Waruka had grown up around Westwood. To these Africans and to others in need in the city, the friars ministered.

Since then, its African members have formed their own religious order, the Community of the Divine Compassion, working under the wing of the SSF in Penhalonga outside Mutare (Umtali), and Bulawayo. Westwood has been handed back to the diocese. Fr Geoffrey is at Penhalonga.

On May 15th, the Sunday after my visit to Westwood, a priest on the cathedral staff took services for me at Highlands and I fulfilled a long-standing engagement at St Paul's Church, Marlborough. Its Rector, Andrew Thomson, an old friend, was taking the Sunday off and I was deputising. I celebrated and preached at the 7 a.m. Holy Communion, went to the adjoining Rectory for breakfast and then preached again at the 9 a.m. Eucharist, at which a retired priest, Fr Donald Gibb, celebrated. All went well with the sermon but a few minutes later, standing in my stall during the singing of the Creed, I suddenly began going hot and cold all over. The last thing I remember was saying to myself, 'I must sit down', and then all went blank. When I came round I was lying on the floor of the passageway leading to the Rectory, a crowd was around me and I was vomiting like a dog. Immediately, I felt well again but could get no one to believe me. 'It was a triple heart attack,' I was told, 'combined with an apoplectic fit.' This was nonsense but despite my protests I was rushed off to nearby St Anne's Hospital, where I spent the rest of Sunday and the whole of Monday and Tuesday. As I knew quite well, there was nothing at all wrong with me. These 'turns' had happened before and have happened since. It is just God's way of saying to me, 'Geoffrey, you are trying to do too much. You must have a rest.' As for my heart, our local GP at my last annual check-up was amazed. 'Many a man of 40,' he said 'would envy a heart like yours.'

I was discharged from St Anne's on the Wednesday but, alas, it was not the end of my misfortunes that week. On

344

the Friday afternoon I was driving along the fast lane of the three-lane Samora Machel Avenue when I saw the turn-off I wanted on the right. I braked and was promptly bumped from behind. The parish car was not extensively damaged – I was able to drive away in it. But the car which bumped me was a write-off. (It was one of those 'ultra-safe' Swedish cars which crumple on contact.) It was my fault in that I braked too quickly but it was equally the fault of the driver of the car behind in that she was travelling too closely behind me. I explained this to the police when they charged me with 'careless driving', and eight days later they dropped the charge, but the accident cast a shadow over my last eight days in Zimbabwe.

They were fulfilling ones. Though I had spent many years in Rhodesia/Zimbabwe I had never seen the Victoria Falls. I wished to see them and realised that in all probability it was now or never. I also wished both to revisit St Mark's and to fulfil an engagement I had missed while in hospital. By the kindness of friends all three wishes were granted.

My visit to the Victoria Falls exceeded all expectation. I left Harare by plane on Tuesday, May 24th, spent the night in the four-star Makesa Sun Hotel, and returned to Harare on the Wednesday afternoon, the inclusive cost being only £76. There is everything for the tourist at the Falls: superb hotels, cruises on the Zambezi, visits to a crocodile farm and a game reserve, white-water rafting, air flights, night-life and so forth, but the Falls themselves have been quite unexploited. Apart from the gravelled paths, they appear to the traveller today just as they must have appeared to Livingstone in 1855 when he wrote in his diary: 'On sights as beautiful as this, Angels in their flight must have gazed.'

At the Falls the mighty Zambezi, over a mile wide, drops precipitately into a narrow gorge 400 feet below. Their local name is 'The smoke that Thunders'. (From the air the *smoke*, i.e spray, is visible ten miles away.) I still see in my dreams that colossal, overwhelming, mass of water pouring ceaselessly over the precipice, falling, falling; and hear its thunder.

The day after my return a parishioner, Mrs Gerrity Webster, kindly drove me to see St Mark's. All was well there, the one big change being quite independent of the Mission: the Government had built a concrete dam across the Umfuli River just below St Mark's, and the Umfuli, instead of being nearly empty, was full. Mrs Webster was enchanted: 'You could do boating, sailing. You could have a lido.'

My third wish fulfilled was my broken engagement of May 16th. It was to visit Mark and Catharine Collier on Cold Comfort Farm, just beyond Westwood on the outskirts of Harare, and it was Fr John Adams who took me. He had returned from England completely cured on Friday, May 27th, the day before I was due to fly back to England, and had asked me if I had done all that I wished. When I replied that I had, except for visiting the Colliers, and he heard that my flight book-in was not till 7.30 p.m., he said at once, 'I will take you tomorrow morning.'

I had first met Mark and Catharine ten years earlier. They had come from South Africa and were running a residential prayer centre at Crockham Hill outside Sevenoaks. In 1984 they were called to take on something very different: the management of the Cold Comfort Farm Trust, a large government-funded experimental farm, with agricultural, horticultural, poultry, carpentry, weaving and metalwork departments and a school with 350 children drawn from the adjacent townships. Under Mark the annual sales of less than £15,625 in 1984 had risen to £106,250 in 1987 and the Trust was fast becoming independent of Government aid. Two more departments were added in 1987: cement block-making and wire-mesh welding. But when John Adams and I visited the farm on my last Saturday, Mark's pride and joy was a newly established water-conservation programme.

The farm had been taking vegetables daily to hotels and hospitals in Harare and had, in consequence, started a pig unit fed by the hotel and hospital 'swill'. The sties needed washing out daily and were water-expensive. The answer was the water-conservation scheme. The water from their borehole is first pumped into a large reservoir standing on a ridge overlooking the farm. The first use of the reservoir is as a swimming-pool for staff and schoolchildren. Then, twice a day, water from it is taken and piped by force of gravity to wash out the pigsties beneath. The resulting solid manure is spread on the fields and its liquid faction gravity-fed into a treated ripening-tank. Five days later the algae-rich water is gravity-fed into six large earthen ponds each stocked with 8,000 tilapia fish. Finally, twice annually the fish are harvested and the water pumped on to the fields as a nitrate-enriched fertiliser. Nothing is wasted.

Orange trees have been planted around the pig unit and I am told that the latest development, started in 1993, is growing grapes and exporting raisins to Europe!

I left Harare for England at 10.15 p.m. and arrived at Gatwick at 7 a.m. (BST) the following morning.

What impressions did I take back with me? Chiefly, I think the vitality of the country. It was still suffering from the ill effects of the War of Independence. Crime on a level unknown before stalked the streets of the cities. Security was the watchword. Fr John had handed me an immense bunch of keys when he left. Not only the front and back doors of the Rectory, every room had to be locked in my absence.

Also ancestor-worship had increased. During the war the Mashona and Matabele forces invoked not the white man's God, but the ancestral spirits. Moreover, few if any boy or girl freedom-fighters living unsegregated in the bush had retained their virginity. The freedom war, as all wars, had encouraged promiscuity. Aids today is rampant.

But, set against these ill effects, are tremendous grounds for hope. The Programme of National Reconciliation launched at independence has received nothing like the attention it should. The three forces fighting in the long freedom war, those of ZANU, ZAPU and the Government, were mutually opposed, yet in the Victory Day Celebrations all marched together. Imagine the British Army, the IRA and the RUC all marching together in Northern Ireland! And there were no trials following independence, no hunting down of war criminals. Ian Smith retained his seat in parliament and Robert Mugabe on becoming Prime Minister invited Ken Flowers to become the head of the Central Intelligence Organisation – and did this in full knowledge that Ken Flowers, as head of the CIO for Ian Smith, was said to have tried three times to assasinate him. Again, spirit-worship may be on the increase but the Christian churches are also very much alive. They are proclaiming Jesus Christ as the only Saviour, waging war on Aids, and caring for the outcast and needy.

The people of Zimbabwe, black and white, are far from perfect but they are, in general, kind, forgiving and godly.

And they are not easily defeated. There is a story of a small African boy taking a religious knowledge test and faced with the question 'What is the sin of adultery?' He hadn't a clue. What could it be? He thought hard. Then he wrote: 'It is the sin of pretending you are more grown-up than you really are!' I can picture his small determined face. *I mustn't let this beat me.*

Zimbabwe is a lovely country, rich in natural resources; and I believe that in the application and inventiveness of that African boy lies Zimbabwe's hope for the future.

It is now March 1995 and the latest news from Zimbabwe is (i) that Mark and Catharine Collier have left Cold Comfort Farm and have returned to England. (ii) that what may well prove to be the largest platinum mine in the world is now being developed near Chegutu (Hartley), (iii) that Zimbabwe is now the fourth largest supplier of cut flowers to Europe, and (iv) that the population growth and the consequent high youth-unemployment is still, together with inflation of 20 per cent p.a., her chief problem.

27

In the Departure Lounge

The opening gambit of our purchase of 73 Dartford Road, Sevenoaks, in 1976 was made while I was away in India. The closing stage of our obtaining our present home, 61 Old Mill Close, Eynsford, began while Marjorie and I were on holiday with Antony and his family in Porlock, Devon.

I was 80, I had kept the Golden Jubilee of my priesthood five years earlier, and I was still working as hard as ever. Marjorie and I wanted a quieter time and we knew it would never be possible in St John the Baptist's parish. Marjorie's two sisters had, however, moved to Sevenoaks and we had many friendships at St John's we wanted to maintain; so, while wishing to move, we did not want to move too far, and as soon as I returned from Zimbabwe at the end of May 1988 we began house-hunting in earnest.

Our choice fell on where we are living now, a small terrace house, then two years old, built on a new development on the outskirts of Eynsford and seven miles from Sevenoaks. It was new, and spotless, and had a lovely view along the Darent Valley from the sitting-room French window. At first sight I fell in love with it. The problem was the price. It was offered at £110,000 freehold and 73 Dartford Road was not expected to realise more than £90,000. I had no spare cash, but owned with my brother a small house in Hounslow. Originally it had belonged to my mother, and we became joint owners on my father's death. Jim, although not wishing to sell, generously agreed to do so for our sake, and Roper, Son and Chapman, the estate agents managing it for us, offered to buy it for £45,000 net.

Selling 73 Dartford Road proved much more difficult. Our hopes were raised by a telephone call to Porlock the day before our return, and though this particular hope, like so many others, came to nothing, soon afterwards a master at Sevenoaks School made a cash offer of £85,000 and contracts were exchanged.

We moved on Friday, October 14th. Peter, Christopher and Antony all came down to help us move. Although they were at first critical of our choice: 'You will have no friends in Eynsford', we quickly made friends and continue to be thankful that God guided us here. Hardly a day passes but we exclaim, looking out from our sitting-room window, how lucky we are to be able to sit and watch squirrels, magpies, thrushes, starlings, robins and an occasional duck pecking around in our pocket-handkerchief garden, and to be able to gaze across the fields which line the Darent Valley to Farningham Church and distant hills. We are also grateful to the neighbours and church people of St Martins who welcomed us warmly.

St Martin's, Eynsford, standing in the centre of the village opposite a ford across the Darent, dates from the eleventh century, and is entered through a striking Norman arch enriched with two orders of chevron moulding. Its bell-tower has a ring of eight bells which echo across the valley morning and evening every Sunday. It has a fine Norman font, and its Early English piscina in the south wall of the chancel is unusual. It has two bowls, one fluted, one plain, so that the holy water used in the cleansing of the chalice can drain into the churchyard separately from the unblessed water used for the ablution of the priest's hands. I am reminded of a *Church Times* cartoon of a High Church vicar who, showing his friend round his new vestry, pointed proudly to three taps running into his washbasin. 'They are,' he explains, 'hot, cold and holy.' How God must laugh! (Or weep?)

In addition to his care of the parish of Eynsford, its Rector has also the care of the parish of St Botolph's, Lullingstone, one and a half miles to the south, and the care of the parish of St Peter and St Paul, Farningham, one and a half miles to the north. Both are interesting.

St Botolph's, 'the church on the lawn', was originally Norman but was restored six centuries ago at the time of Edward III in the Decorated style. It stands in the grounds of Lullingstone Castle (hence the 'church on the lawn') and possesses a beautiful Tudor chapel containing the tomb of Sir George Hart and his wife Elizabeth. Their descendant, Guy Hart-Dyke, now lives with his wife in the Castle – actually a red-brick part-Tudor, part Queen Anne, mansion. Guy's mother, Zoe, Lady Hart-Dyke, created a silkworm farm in the grounds in 1936 and Lullingstone silk was used in the coronation robe of King George VI and in our present Queen's wedding veil. In the porch of St Botolph's there is a notice:

11 a.m. Service every Sunday
The 1662 Prayer Book and the Authorised Version of
the Bible are used at all Services

and St Botolph's is a useful escape-route for all those in the three parishes who dislike the *Alternative Service Book* and wish to continue to worship in the traditional words. It means that the ASB can be used without interruption on all Sunday mornings in Eynsford and Farningham.

The parish church of St Peter and St Paul, Farningham, like St Martin's, is built in flint, which is abundant in the area. The chancel is the oldest part of the church and is of the Early English period. On its north wall is a monument to Antony Roper, who left a charity to the village and was the son-in-law and betrayer of Sir Thomas More, the 'man of all seasons' beheaded by Henry VIII.

When Marjorie and I arrived in Eynsford in 1988, Denis Sweetman had been its Rector since 1971, but three months later, on Christmas Day, he made a shock announcement – he was retiring on January 31st. For the following six months I was almost as busy as ever, but on September 11th the Revd David Springthorpe was inducted as Rector of the United Benefice and I was able to relax.

David came with his wife, Jo, and two daughters Jane aged 11 and Rebecca aged 8, from the nearby parish of Ash with Ridley. On September 10th I was booked to take the morning Eucharist in Ash, and Marjorie and I attended David's Farewell Service there on Sunday, September 3rd to see how things were done. The church was packed and the closing organ voluntary was perhaps unique. As David processed down the aisle the organist struck up *For he's a Jolly Good Fellow* and we all joined in.

He was much, much, more. Quiet and a little shy, at Ash he had worked with a team of volunteers in redecorating the interior of St Peter and St Paul and in relaying the surface of the church car park. In the United Benefice he soon turned his attention to the long-overdue redecoration of the interior of St Martin's. He enlisted the help of his churchwarden, Michael Caswell, a chartered building surveyor, as foreman and together they enlisted, in all, some fifty helpers: furniture-removers, painters and decorators, cleaners, tea ladies, and the like. David himself led the second group, wielding a nifty paintbrush.

They attacked the work in five stages:

The first (May 1990) the porches
The second (August 1990) the vestry
The third (November 1990) the south transept
The fourth (April/May 1991) the chancel and apse
The fifth (September 1991) the nave

Every Saturday night while the work was in progress, volunteers made the church available for Sunday worship. The hire of the scaffolding and purchase of materials were the main expenses and the total cost was under £4,000. A Service of Thanksgiving was held on Sunday,

September 29th when all was finished.

The following year, David led another team of volunteers to redecorate the interior of St Botolph's, Lullingstone, which was equally successful. The interior of St Peter and St Paul, Farningham, needed no attention, having been redecorated by a professional firm a few years earlier.

David had also on arrival, a large team to help him in more traditional ways: the Venerable Edward Francis, Archdeacon of Bromley, who lived in Farningham, the Revd Michael Johnson, a schoolmaster in Swanley, and myself as priests; the Revd Hazel Salmon as a deacon; George Macknelly, Peter Davis and Alan Gillott as lay readers; and organists, choristers, bell-ringers, flower-arrangers, tea ladies, and the like. He started Sunday schools and crèches, which were greatly needed; Alan Gillot and Hazel Salmon began Bible study groups; and church life flourished.

The latest news of Eynsford is that David has now left us. In March 1994 there was serious trouble in a London parish in the diocese and the Bishop appealed to David to become its Vicar and help bring peace. The United Benefice of Eynsford, Farningham and Lullingstone was once again vacant. I am now frail and unreliable, so I deemed it best this time not to take any services. However on October 13th we in Eynsford, Farningham and Lullingstone received a new Rector and once again all is well.

Richard Freeman, our new Rector, is very different from David but just as likeable.

Earlier on March 21st 1992 there came an interruption in the quiet tempo of our life. Going up to bed in the dark at 10.45 p.m. to avoid waking Marjorie, I lost my way on the top landing. Where was the bathroom? Where was my study? I took a step backwards and fell the whole length of the staircase on my back, finishing by knocking my head against the wall at the bottom. Marjorie phoned the doctor on call. He came in 20 minutes and 15 minutes later the ambulance arrived to take me to St Mary's Hospital, Sidcup, where I was kept waiting four hours on a stretcher. It was Saturday night, the hospital was short-staffed, and drunks from the pubs kept being carried in, bruised and bleeding, some accompanied by their equally drunken comrades, I was in no pain and watched with interest, and at 4.30 a.m. an X-ray showed that I had a broken collar-bone. After strapping me up the sister sent me home with instructions to report again on the Monday.

That morning our own doctor, Dr Perry, ordered the ambulance and I was told at the hospital that I was making satisfactory progress. I reported again a week later and on April 13th, Monday in Holy Week, I was well enough to celebrate Holy Communion at 7 p.m. at St Mary's, Horton Kirby, a nearby parish.

St Mary's Hospital discharged me on April 27th and gave me permission to drive again. My fractured collar-bone proved however, the least of my woes. Eight months later my back and neck were still affected and rheumatism had begun to affect my bones and muscles. For the first time I began to feel my age. But perhaps this would have happened anyhow, for Marjorie is also feeling hers and we commiserate and laugh together.

Some years ago a *Brains Trust* on television asked: 'What in the panel's opinion is old?'

There were numerous suggestions:

'Old is ten years older than you are yourself.'
'Old is when your address-book begins to look like a country churchyard – full of RIPs'
'Old is when you have joined the "My dear, you are wonderful; how do you do it"? category.'

And you may have heard the story of the vicar who tried to remonstrate gently with a very old parishioner. 'My dear,' he is reported to have said, 'should you not be thinking less about food, more about the hereafter?'

'Vicar,' she is said to have replied, 'I think about the hereafter constantly. I go upstairs for something and no sooner am I upstairs than I say to myself "But what am I here after?" '

Alas, by 1994 Marjorie and I had reached that stage. I more than Marjorie. We were constantly knocking things over, losing our belongings, forgetting names and numbers: 'What day is it?' – we were having to consult the daily paper to discover! We now travel as little as possible and I no longer take services.

The Diamond Jubilee of my ordination to the priesthood in 1994 was on Friday, June 13th, and the Thanksgiving Eucharist in St Martin's at 8 p.m. that evening was my swansong. On reflection, I had decided that, as at my Golden Jubilee at St John's ten years earlier, I would preach the sermon myself. I recalled a eulogium given by a friend of one of my fellow-priests on a similar occasion. He was heard to remark afterwards, 'Yes, it was a lovely sermon but, you know, who *was* the priest the preacher was talking about? – it wasn't me!' My address at least was 'me' and you will have read its script in Chapter 25.

St Martin's Church was full, and it warmed one's heart to see so many well-wishers gathered together and to have so many of one's family present. Peter from Nottingham, Christopher from Beverley, Antony from Kettering. David as Rector presided and took the first part of the service. I celebrated. There were 106 communicants and the collection for the USPG amounted to £232. Afterwards, at the reception in the Olive Seal Hall, Marjorie was presented with a magnificent bouquet of flowers.

I had promised myself a six-month 'Sabbatical' afterwards, but the six months have expired and now it is permanent. I get so worked up over the smallest thing and I have become so unreliable that it would be folly to resume. 'They also serve who only stand and wait'; and I find much joy in intercession.

Old age and death have been compared to a departure lounge

in a busy airport, crowded with passengers of all ages, some reconciled to delay, some fearful, some expectant. The first are seasoned travellers. They wait patiently for the 'Boarding' call just as they have waited patiently for it in the past. 'Why worry? Sooner or later the call will come.'

Others are first-time air-travellers and nervous. This is their first flight. 'What is it going to be like?' They have read the 'First Time you Fly' brochure cover-to-cover, but it hasn't helped much. 'Will we be airsick?'

And, thirdly, there are the expectant ones, young couples, maybe, or teenage children. They have no fears. For some, travelling by air is second nature and they are excited at the thought of getting home or seeing something fresh. I remember sitting in a plane at Entebbe on my first flight to Zimbabwe. I was somewhat tense. I knew 80 per cent of accidents occurred when a plane was either taking off or landing. Then suddenly some dozen schoolgirls with satchels on their shoulders came bouncing in, laughing and giggling, taking a weekend flight back to their homes in Dar-es-Salaam. I at once felt better.

At eighty-seven I am a little like both the seasoned travellers and the excited schoolgirls. I know that the 'Boarding' call will come in the not-too-distant future. I am content to wait patiently for it. But I am also excited. What will the far country, the land of everlasting life, be like? But I no longer read theological theories about it. What is the point? Soon I shall know. And I have ceased trying to imagine. It is beyond all imagining. How can you describe colour to a man born blind? But I like to reassure myself – if I start to question – by recalling as far as I can remember it, the story with which Dr Paterson Smyth begins his book *The Gospel of the Hereafter*.

A certain doctor, the story goes, was visiting a dying man. The doctor had his dog with him but had left her downstairs while he went upstairs to attend to his patient. The patient was worried about the thought of the future, and as the doctor was preparing to leave asked him, 'Had he any idea what the next life would be like?' The doctor, we are told, was wondering what to say when he heard a scratching at the door and the answer was given him. 'You hear that scratching?' said the doctor. 'It's my dog. I left her downstairs, now she's outside. She has no idea what it is like in here but she knows that I am here, so she wants to come in. I've no idea what heaven is like but I know God is there. Isn't that sufficient?'

When I was Chaplain of the RAF troopship returning to England from India in 1945, a free-church minister organised a daily prayer meeting which I used to attend. Leadership was shared. I am not, generally speaking, in love with extempore prayer – often one listens but one does not pray. But one of the prayer-group's leaders I instantly related to, and it was, I realised on reflection, because all his words were scriptural.

I, too, express myself easier in the words of scripture or of well-known hymns than by groping about for words of my own, and so I would conclude this chapter and my 'story' by quoting the first verse of Hymn 511 in the *English Hymnal*. It sums up what I really feel.

> When all thy mercies, O my God,
> My rising soul surveys,
> Transported with the view, I'm lost
> In wonder, love, and praise.

In the words Dag Hammerskold used when Secretary-General of the United Nations:

> For what has been, thanks.
> For what will be, yes.

POSTCRIPTS

I fall asleep very easily now – especially when I am saying the Morning and Evening Office which I love! I look forward to the time when I shall fall asleep and awake to those good things which God has prepared for those who unfeignedly love him – good things quite beyond our understanding.

(*I Corinthians 2: 9*).

By faith Abraham obeyed the call of God, and set out not knowing where he was going, and came to the promised land. (*Hebrews 11: 8*)
God give me a faith like Abraham's.

> The day Thou gavest, Lord, is ended,
> The darkness falls at Thy behest;
> To Thee our morning hymns ascended,
> Thy praise shall sanctify our rest.

(*Hymns ancient and Modern No.477*)

Comparative Value of the Pound, 1930–1994

The purchasing value of £100 in 1928 had become:-

£92.30 in 1930	£1289.80 in 1981
£115.00 in 1940	£1359.50 in 1982
£140.30 in 1950	£1431.80 in 1983
£208.00 in 1960	£1497.40 in 1984
£315.70 in 1970	£1582.60 in 1985
£344.30 in 1971	£1641.40 in 1986
£370.60 in 1972	£1702.10 in 1987
£409.80 in 1973	£1817.40 in 1988
£488.30 in 1974	£1957.40 in 1989
£609.70 in 1975	£2140.30 in 1990
£701.60 in 1976	£2235.90 in 1991
£786.80 in 1977	£2293.50 in 1992
£852.80 in 1978	£2337.10 in 1993
£1000.00 in 1979	£2406.00 in 1994
£1151.10 in 1980	

To find the purchasing value in 1994 of a pound in any previous year divide £2406 by its purchasing value in that year, e.g. a pound given to buy Christmas toys in 1940 would have bought toys to the value of £2406 divided by 115, i.e. £20.95 in 1994 and even more today.

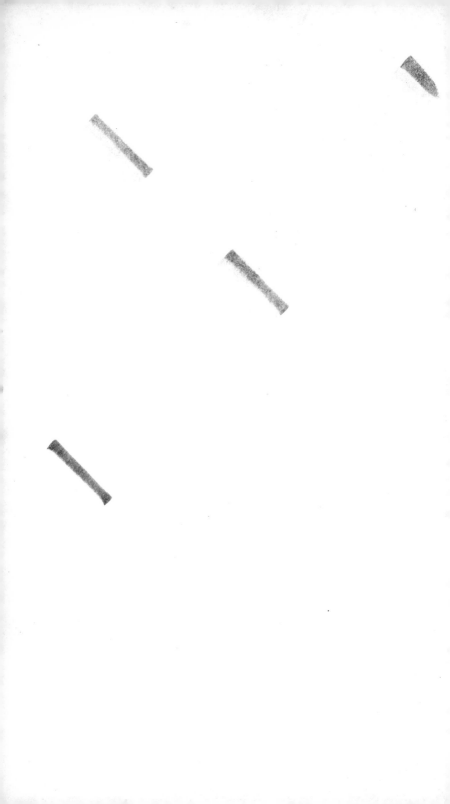